HOW TO BE
GOOD IN A
WORLD
GONE
BAD

HOW TO BE GOOD IN A WORLD GONE BAD

LIVING A LIFE OF CHRISTIAN VIRTUE

JAMES S. SPIEGEL

Kregel
Publications

*How to Be Good in a World Gone Bad: Living a Life of
Christian Virtue*

© 2004 by James S. Spiegel

Published by Kregel Publications, a division of Kregel, Inc., P.O.
Box 2607, Grand Rapids, MI 49501.

Cover design: John M. Lucas

Library of Congress Cataloging-in-Publication Data
Spiegel, James S.
    How to be good in a world gone bad: living a life of Chris-
tian virtue / by James S. Spiegel.
        p.   cm.
Includes bibliographical references.
    1. Virtues. 2. Conduct of life. 3. Character. I. Title.
BV4630.S655   2004
241'.4—dc22   2004019278

ISBN 0-8254-3695-8

Printed in the United States of America

04 05 06 07 08 / 5 4 3 2 1

CONTENTS

PREFACE

The subject of my previous book was the vice of hypocrisy. *How to Be Good in a World Gone Bad* dwells mainly on the positive end of the moral spectrum. If my previous book was calculated to convict, this book aims to inspire. Its purpose, quite simply, is to help the reader live a better life. Thus, *How to Be Good in a World Gone Bad* seeks not just to analyze the virtues but also to illustrate them with concrete examples that inspire as well as clarify.

This book is a companion to some recent works by writers as varied as Diogenes Allen, Peter Kreeft, Josef Pieper, Timothy Sedgwick, David Wells, and Dallas Willard. Each of them has called Christians to deeper moral commitment by either helping readers to understand how central virtuous living is to the Christian worldview, or by providing practical assistance in growing in virtue. This book aims to achieve both of these ends in some measure.

Broadly speaking, the intended audience for *How to Be Good in a World Gone Bad* is anyone who cares about how life should be lived, which of course should include everyone. More specifically, I'm writing to Christians at various levels of moral seriousness: the devout Christian, because even the most mature among us needs to improve in some ways; and the nominal Christian, because she's probably been influenced by faulty conceptions of what constitutes the good life, and because her tenuous connection to the Christian community likely grows out of suspicion of its morals.

This book should also be of value to those who are not Christians, if only because the discussion will provide a picture of what the Christian moral life is supposed to look like. Whatever the reader's worldview, there is much to be gained here for building a better conception of the good life and how to live it.

The sequential arrangement of chapter topics is not arbitrary. Some of the virtues discussed in the first few chapters (e.g., self-control and humility) are more foundational than others, and some toward the end (e.g., faith and love) are more contingent upon other virtues. Nonetheless, each chapter is fully comprehensible when read in isolation. Readers are encouraged to browse according to their topical interests and read in any order they choose.

A note about gender inclusive language: rather than rely on neutral pronouns throughout—and sacrifice stylistic fluidity as a result—gender-specific pronouns are used in each chapter, masculine and feminine constructions alternating chapter-by-chapter (with only a few exceptions due to context).

Portions of two chapters were drawn from essays of mine previously published elsewhere. Much of chapter two appeared as "The Moral Irony of Humility" in *Logos: A Journal of Catholic Thought and Culture*[1] and some of chapter ten appeared in "Aesthetics and Worship" in *The Southern Baptist Journal of Theology*.[2] I thank the editors and publishers of those journals for their permission to reprint those materials here.

I acknowledge, too, the assistance of many people in the production of this book. My faithful colleagues at Taylor University are a constant inspiration to me, modeling all of the virtues discussed here. My friends at New Life Presbyterian Church in Yorktown, Indiana, provided much useful feedback when this project was in its nascent stages. Jim Weaver has been wonderfully supportive, and I will remain indebted to him for his confidence in my work and his wise editorial counsel. Erin Carter gave me valuable suggestions on earlier drafts of several chapters, as did some of my students. Finally, I thank my wife, Amy, for her enthusiastic support through all phases of this project. It is to her that this book is dedicated.

---

1. James S. Spiegel, "The Moral Irony of Humility," *Logos: A Journal of Catholic Thought and Culture* 6, no. 1 (winter 2003), 131–50.
2. James S. Spiegel, "Aesthetics and Worship," *The Southern Baptist Journal of Theology* 2, no. 4 (winter 1998), 40–56.

INTRODUCTION

Why Virtue?

The virtues are making a comeback. Both among scholars and in the public forum, the last decade or so has seen a steady increase of interest in what it means to be a person of good character. William Bennett's *Book of Virtues,* for example, is a best-seller, and discussion of the virtues is more popular than ever among ethicists. The religious and irreligious alike are calling upon the rich heritage of the virtues that dates back to the ancient Greeks.

The reasons for this renewed interest are likely both cultural and philosophical. The moral decline of Western, and especially American, culture has been well documented. Our society seems to be increasingly violent, compulsive, indulgent, greedy, and rude. Mainstream America exhibits a pervasive nervousness about these trends and a shared concern as to how we might steer our culture onto a better moral path. Philosophically, the Western world has entered a transitional phase known as postmodernism. The rigid rationalism of the modern mind is slowly dying, and with it the principled but impersonal approaches to ethics that focus on duty and utility are losing their power to motivate people.

Enter—or better *reenter*—the virtues. To be virtuous is to be a morally excellent person, to exhibit certain character traits that humans were designed to display. A person of virtuous character is, for instance, patient, generous, kind, sincere, courageous, and self-controlled. These qualities are just the sorts that naturally attract us to people and are those most of us would like to emulate. They are the traits we'd like to see prized in our culture, as they are natural antidotes to the corrosive vices we find on the rise in America today. Moreover, the idea of a virtuous character and how one might display it in various contexts is much more inspiring than talk about abstract moral principles.

The chapters that follow discuss more than twenty different virtues. Most chapters are devoted to a particular virtue, although some discuss two or more virtues, as when several fall into a more general category. In each case the discussion draws from philosophical, literary, and/or theological sources, and most chapters glean from some particularly relevant biblical texts. While *How to Be Good in a World Gone Bad* aims to be theoretically sound, its overarching goal is concrete application, thereby helping the reader better understand the nature of each virtue discussed and how it is nurtured. This book may be conceived, then, as a manual for virtuous living.

The Postmodern Shift

As noted, the reasons for revival of interest in the virtues are cultural and philosophical. The latter relates to postmodernism and has to do with a shift in thought in the Western world, a shift that is taking many different forms. Where the modern mind places ultimate confidence in reason to address our most pressing questions, the postmodern mind is suspicious of reason. Where the modern mind focuses on the individual subject, the postmodern mind emphasizes community. Where the modern mind attempts to approach issues from a broad, universal standpoint, the postmodern mind approaches them from local perspectives. And while the modern mind sees the universe in mechanistic terms, with humans as functional parts within the cosmic machine, the postmodern mind takes a more organic approach, emphasizing human freedom and affirming a more dynamic relation between humans and their environment.

From a Christian perspective, these changes, in many respects, represent good news, but serious problems are inherent in postmodern thought. Many postmodernists, because of their suspicion of reason, have concluded that objective truth is a myth, or at least that knowledge is impossible, whether it regards human nature, the existence of God, or the fundamental nature of the cosmos. For the modernist, reason was our best, and perhaps only, hope for knowledge regarding these issues. The postmodernist claims that since reason is a bust, so is our quest for absolute truth, and all truth claims, then, become relative. From a Christian point of view, such a conclusion is clearly unwarranted. Reason is not our only tool for gaining knowledge, for we also have a special revelation from God—the Bible. A balanced Christian perspective on the postmodern shift will affirm the usefulness of reason as an important supplement to special revelation but will deny the sufficiency of reason alone as an avenue to a complete worldview.

So the modernist is right in believing in objective truth and the possibility of genuine knowledge about God and the world. But he's wrong in thinking that reason is sufficient to get us there. And the postmodernist is correct in denying the sufficiency of reason but mistaken in thinking this implies that all truth is relative. Universal, transcendent truth does, indeed, exist, but we need God's help to guide us in our quest for it. To recognize this is to take a more humble attitude in the search for truth and will breed an irenic spirit in the seeker. Dogmatic rationalism in any subject area is out of place. This postmodern insight, too, should be heartily affirmed by the Christian.

Two major moral traditions arose out of the modern period—utilitarianism and Kantian ethics, both premised on the modernist assumptions noted above. Both of these ethical theories proposed a particular moral principle as the universal standard for goodness, the final rule for judging all actions. For John Stuart Mill and the other utilitarians, the principle of utility was the ultimate principle: one should always try to maximize pleasure for all involved.[1] The great enlightenment thinker, Immanuel Kant, focused on moral duty and offered the "categorical imperative" as the chief principle of ethics; one should only do that which one could will to be a universal law.[2]

Both of these approaches to ethics have been tremendously influential. While their emphases are quite different—one focusing on utility and the other on duty—they do share key modern assumptions. Specifically, both assume that reason is sufficient in ethics, that we need only think through a situation for ourselves to determine the right course of action. Both utilitarians and Kantians approach ethics from a perspective that is at once universalistic and individualistic—universalistic in assuming that a single principle will do for every situation, individualistic in assuming that the individual alone can discover what is morally right in each case.

If, as the postmodernist suggests, reason is an insufficient guide for human conduct, then both utilitarian and Kantian ethics must ultimately fail, for each rests finally on a foundation of reason. The problems with these approaches, however, run even deeper. Neither utilitarians nor Kantians can provide an adequate motive for abiding by their principle, nor for generally being moral. Why

---

1. John Stuart Mill writes, "Actions are right in proportion as they tend to promote happiness, wrong as they tend to produce the reverse of happiness." *Mill's Ethical Writings* (New York: Collier, 1965), 281. Mill equated happiness and unhappiness with pleasure and pain, respectively.

2. In Immanuel Kant's words, "Act only according to that maxim by which you can at the same time will that it should become a universal law." *Foundations of the Metaphysics of Morals,* trans. Lewis White Beck (Indianapolis: Bobbs-Merrill, 1959), 39.

should I be moral? They both answer, "It is the rational thing to do." But why be rational, especially when acting irrationally can give me immediate and extreme gratification? A further problem is that these two theories are impersonal. They tell us only to abide by this or that principle without taking into account the nuances of our personal lives, such as special affections for family members and close friends. Finally, they ignore the whole domain of personal character and the development of traits that define a good human being and find their proper expression within a dynamic community.

A virtue ethics approach overcomes these problems. While it recognizes the failure of the rigid rationalistic methods of Mill and Kant, virtue ethics does not deny objective truth in ethics. It takes a personal, local approach without relativizing values, and it provides a more adequate motivation for moral living. Virtue ethics incorporates, when properly applied, the strengths and insights of a postmodern perspective without following through to its errant conclusions.

Although *How to Be Good in a World Gone Bad* focuses exclusively on the virtues, it does not suggest that considerations of utility and duty are dispensable or that virtue ethics is sufficient by itself. On the contrary, this book contends that a full-bodied Christian ethic incorporates elements of all three of these theoretical approaches. The Western Christian mind today, however, is most in need of regaining a proper appreciation of the virtues to restore a balance that has been lost largely because of the influence of modernist thinking over the last two centuries.

Our Cultural Crisis

The postmodern age is one of suspicion, not just of reason, but of all institutions and practices forged by the modern mind. This state of mind means that postmodern culture tends to be morally relativistic, seeing moral values as merely reflecting the preferences of local cultures or even individual persons. In any case, for the moral relativist there are no standards of conduct that bind everyone. Instead, there are only varying points of view on moral issues, and the individual is at liberty to choose which among those perspectives he prefers.

While this perspective satisfies a natural human desire for freedom and autonomy, it has distressing implications as well. Without a universal moral standard, no behaviors—no matter how atrocious—can be universally condemned as wrong. The youth of America seem to recognize this as well as anyone. A 1997 article by Robert Simon in *The Chronicle of Higher Education* reported that a growing minority of college students, perhaps as many as twenty percent, are unwilling to condemn the Nazi holocaust as absolutely morally wrong.[3] Such a judgment is impossible, they maintain, because no perspective is more authoritative than the next.

Not only is our culture morally relativistic, it increasingly regards universal moral claims as intolerant and oppressive. Those who believe in objective moral truth are often thought of as naïve and intellectually unsophisticated.[4] At worst, they are considered dangerous and worthy of censure. Such a state of affairs in public life constitutes a genuine cultural crisis. If no standard for goodness exists, nor guidelines as to how we should conduct ourselves, then our culture seems doomed to collapse. Indeed, signs of cultural disintegration are all around us.

The story, however, is not over. There is yet time for cultural renewal, and it must begin, of course, with a change in the way we think about values. Moreover, it can easily be argued that the values holding the most promise to redeem culture are biblical ones. The trick, though, is finding ways to make these values compelling to our culture and, as worldviews go, nothing is more persuasive than a life well lived. If this is so, then, as Christians, the primary focus in addressing our cultural moral crisis should be the ordering of our own lives. The contemporary testament to the truth of Christianity is only as strong as the moral character of Christians. This is why we need to focus on the virtues.

The current cultural crisis can be seen as a direct result of the church's failing to do its job of moral renewal within society, a failure that reflects a loss of a biblical moral vision. The church has succumbed to the individualism of the modern mind, prioritizing personal experience, particularly of an emotional nature, over moral goodness. We have not yet fallen so far as to redefine salvation

---

3. Robert L. Simon, "The Paralysis of Absolutophobia," *The Chronicle of Higher Education,* 27 June 1997. Simon, a philosophy professor at Hamilton College, notes that his students "accept the reality of the Holocaust, but they believe themselves unable morally to condemn it, or indeed to make any moral judgments whatsoever: Such students typically comment that they themselves deplore the Holocaust and other great evils, but then they wind up suspending moral judgment" (sec. B, p. 5).

4. It's curious that in the world of philosophical ethics this is not the case. The overwhelming majority of philosophers are moral objectivists, persons who believe in absolute moral truth. I take comfort in this fact, given that philosophers are those who study values most closely and who are the experts, if anyone is, on moral theory.

itself in terms of exhilarating experience, but I fear we are quite on our way. Dallas Willard makes the powerful argument that Christians are called to something in the Christian life, and this something—the kingdom life—is *moral* in nature. The life of discipleship in Christ is an essentially moral project.[5] But this plain biblical fact has been obscured by the modern emphasis on personal experience. The primary *moral* benefits of Christ have been displaced by the secondary *psychological* benefits. God is decreasingly regarded as a moral legislator and judge, and increasingly seen as a cosmic therapist. So we, as a church, desperately need a doctrinal corrective. Yes, Christ addresses our psychological wounds and provides emotional healing, but more fundamental than these benefits are the means for their provision—the forgiveness he provides (our justification) and the moral improvement in which he guides us (our sanctification). To be a disciple is, indeed, therapeutic, but the most basic business of a disciple is moral in nature.

A symptom of this loss of biblical moral vision is the impoverishment of our moral vocabulary. Even those who are both moral objectivists, and who properly emphasize the moral nature of Christian redemption, often (perhaps even typically) fail to understand the Christian moral life in anything but vague or general terms. When asked "How ought we to live?" most Christians would respond by saying that we ought to be "godly," "Christlike," or "righteous." True enough, but what do those terms *mean?* Many would respond that we ought to obey God, or that we ought to act as Jesus would in various life situations, as in the popular slogan "What would Jesus do?" In regard to being godly, though, God's commands tend to be more or less general, which calls for additional wisdom about particulars. The biblical commands also don't usually speak to the matter of personal moral character, the very thing required if one is to enjoy much success in obeying divine commands.

As for the exhortation, "Do what Jesus would do," it begs the question—Just what *would* Jesus do in a given situation? This is the very heart of the issue. The slogan can't be of any help if we don't have a clear idea of what it's telling us. The sad fact about this now ubiquitous "WWJD" slogan is that large numbers of Christians don't know what Jesus *would* do in many circumstances, because we're ignorant about many aspects of his moral character. That is, we often neglect contemplating the specific moral traits that Jesus possessed and that constituted the moral foundation upon which his choices and actions were

---

5.   Dallas Willard, *The Divine Conspiracy: Rediscovering Our Hidden Life in God* (San Francisco: Harper San Francisco, 1998).

consistently based. In the end, the WWJD movement is half right. Jesus Christ is, and always will remain, our moral exemplar. When it comes to the specifics of his moral example, however—the living standard at which we properly aim—we lack understanding. We have virtually lost, in fact, the moral vocabulary necessary to be conversant about Christ as our model. Addressing this loss is, of course, where the virtues come in.

The Definition of Virtue

Before proceeding to a discussion of the virtues themselves, the word *virtue* needs to be defined: What is it and how is it developed? A virtue is a specific moral excellence, a trait that contributes to a good character. The Boy Scouts' pledge declares that "a Scout is trustworthy, loyal, helpful, friendly, courteous, kind, obedient, cheerful, thrifty, brave, clean, and reverent." These qualities, many to be discussed in this book, are all virtues. From a Christian perspective, they are the sorts of traits that define the human character as God intended it. To be virtuous is to live up to the divine standard for human life. Or better, it is to embody that standard, to display it in one's conduct.

Virtues are not acquired spontaneously through a simple act of will. Rather, they are the product of long-term training, developed through practice. They are, as it were, deeply ingrained good habits (just as, on the negative end, vices are bad habits). Aristotle explains:

> Men will be good or bad builders as a result of building well or badly. . . . This, then, is the case with the virtues also; by doing the acts that we do in our transactions with other men we become just or unjust, and by doing the acts that we do in the presence of danger, . . . we become brave or cowardly. . . . Thus, in one word, states of character arise out of like activities.[6]

To gain a quality, one must display it repeatedly until it becomes a habit and eventually settles into a permanent part of one's character. The nurturing of virtue is intentional, and without purpose and planning, moral excellence will never come.

---

6.   Aristotle, *Nicomachean Ethics,* in *Introduction to Aristotle,* ed. Richard McKeon, trans. W. D. Ross (New York: Modern Library, 1992), 352–53.

This Aristotelian model of character formation may be represented as follows:

Virtuous Acts ▶ Virtuous Habits ▶ Virtuous Character

A person's character, good or bad, is the result of the choices he's made, for good or ill, over time. The result is a certain moral disposition, a tendency to act in particular ways in particular situations. Because one's moral disposition tends to be fairly stable, it can often be predicted how a person will respond in a given circumstance. Upon hearing some report of what a friend has done, we might say "Oh, that sounds like something he'd do" or "She'd never do that." We make our judgment based upon our familiarity with our friend's character or moral disposition. The idea behind training in virtue is to slowly alter that disposition for the better, to bend it in a positive direction through purposeful, consistent performance of good actions. By doing so, new habits are created and, over time, these produce a better disposition, a morally good character.

Human society features hundreds of practices, each involving many different skills. And, in the words of Plato, "There is a specific virtue or excellence of everything for which a specific work or function is appointed."[7] Whether a person is a carpenter, dentist, hair stylist, teacher, musician, or computer programmer, that person must possess certain skills that enable him to carry out the tasks necessary to fulfill his professional function. If a carpenter is not good with the drill, or a teacher is a poor communicator, then he'll be a less effective practitioner of his trade. To lack a specific skill compromises one's professional ability. The virtues can be seen as moral skills. They are developed only through repeated practice, and each skill pertains to some special function that a person performs within his community. Thus, to lack a particular moral skill compromises one's merit as a human being. A person might be generous, sincere, courageous, and kind, but if that person lacks self-control or is unjust, then his overall moral quality is diminished.

So to be a person of good character, one must master a variety of skills. This is one reason why it's so difficult to be a good person. One must work hard to develop each moral skill, none of which is easily mastered. It's fortunate, however, that the virtues tend to be unified; growth in some virtues contributes to growth in others. There's another reason why moral development is difficult: It's a matter of doing as much as knowing. Gaining insight and understanding

---

7.   Plato, *Republic*, in *The Collected Dialogues of Plato*, ed. Edith Hamilton and Huntington Cairns, trans. Paul Shorey (Princeton: Princeton University Press, 1961), 603.

about what it means to be virtuous is beneficial but not sufficient to make someone good. To become virtuous, one must, as noted above, *do* virtue. This sounds
paradoxical, of course, for doesn't the *doing* of virtue show that one already *is*
virtuous? Not exactly. Anyone can do something virtuous upon occasion, but
only the person of virtuous character does so consistently and as an expression
of a trained disposition. The person of good character is morally mature, that
is, well-developed in virtue. That person's virtuous deeds are not occasional
bursts of goodness, but manifestations of something deep and abiding. And it is
practice that has brought that person from inconsistent acts of virtue to a mature moral character.

From a Christian perspective, mastering skills is not the whole story about
building moral character. The entire process of moral development is governed
by the Holy Spirit who oversees our growth, inspiring and enabling us along the
way. Thus, moral development is a cooperative effort, at which humans must
earnestly work, but for which God deserves all credit for our success. Paul sums
up this point when admonishing the Philippians: "Continue to work out your
salvation with fear and trembling, for it is God who works in you to will and to
act according to his good purpose" (Phil. 2:12–13). Biblically speaking, then,
character formation is a joint venture between human and divine agents. In
recognition of this fact, our venture to grow morally must be guided by prayer
and careful meditation on scriptural moral standards. Hard work, by itself, is
not enough. Nor is a willing heart sufficient to get us there. We must take an
active part in the process of moral development and seek divine blessing as we
do the work, recognizing that any progress we make is a gift from God.

The discussion that follows will assume the necessity of both hard work and
divine grace in moral development. Some chapters might seem to emphasize
one more than the other, but a balanced Christian view of the matter affirms
both. It is God's will for us to be virtuous people. We must try hard, and he must
bless our efforts. Proceeding now to the virtues themselves, the succeeding
chapters offer a more detailed picture of what it means to be a person of good
character.

1

TAMING THE BEAST WITHIN

The Virtue of Self-Control

An appropriate starting place for discussing the virtues is self-control. Being a morally upright person is, after all, mostly a matter of managing one's impulses and desires. Thus, self-control is a prerequisite for most other virtues. Self-control is not just one moral skill among others, but fundamental to the moral life. It's no surprise, then, that Paul lists self-control as a fruit of the Spirit (Gal. 5:23). And a proverb says, "Like a city whose walls are broken down is a man who lacks self-control" (Prov. 25:28). Without this trait, one has no defense against temptation. Among the qualities that constitute a morally mature character, then, none are more crucial than the virtue of self-control.

The Problem of Moral Weakness

"To err is human," an old adage says—and its truth is confirmed every moment of human history. Yet however much we might affirm it in the abstract, we refuse to believe this about ourselves. My previous book analyzed the different ways that people are morally flawed.[1] The most notorious vice, of course, is hypocrisy, and this comes in two basic forms. The first variety is that of the self-deceived hypocrite, the person who believes herself to be doing the right thing because it's in her interest to believe so. Joy Adamson, the author of the book *Born Free,* was a hypocrite of this kind. Although she advocated protection of wild animals, she secretly purchased a genuine leopard-skin coat and hat. The Pharisees, too, tended to be hypocrites of this sort. They had a motivated bias to believe their legalism would get them to heaven. So they saw their moral hair-

---

1. James S. Spiegel, *Hypocrisy: Moral Fraud and Other Vices* (Grand Rapids: Baker, 1999).

splitting as virtuous, even when it implied that one could not heal someone on the Sabbath.[2]

The other form of hypocrisy is defined by a lack of moral seriousness. This kind of hypocrite makes a masquerade of being concerned about virtue and goodness. She praises virtue and, in certain circumstances, acts like a virtuous person. But in actuality, she's a fraud. Moliere's Tartuffe is a vivid example of such a hypocrite, as he made a pretense of religious devotion in order to seduce and swindle others. Similarly, some contemporary American politicians, in spite of their outward appearance of being morally upstanding, are really only concerned about getting reelected. Such people, we must conclude, are not morally serious. They don't really care about virtue at all but are just moral shams, pretending to care about morality for the sake of personal gain.

Researching and writing on this topic was humbling, because I became more aware of the inconsistencies in my own life. Yes, we're all inconsistent in various ways, but to be reminded of this on a regular basis can be discouraging. I did receive encouragement, however, from friends and colleagues who, after hearing of my project, would tell me that they were hypocrites. The irony was that those who did so were among the more virtuous people I know. A further irony is that those who accuse themselves of hypocrisy are not really hypocrites at all, because to be hypocritical one must continue the charade of being more righteous than one really is. Confession of sin and humble recognition of one's moral failures put an end to such pretense and so disqualify a person from being a hypocrite.

So what do we call persons who fail to live according to their convictions but who recognize this failure in themselves? Actually, this is a description of all Christians, isn't it? If we're biblically serious and somewhat mature, we must admit that at times we fail morally. As John says, "If we claim to be without sin, we deceive ourselves and the truth is not in us" (1 John 1:8). Those who fail to live by their convictions are called morally weak. Those who are chronically weak-willed, captured in the Greek word *akrasia,* are sometimes called "incontinent." (The ambiguity of this English term is amusingly appropriate.) Morally weak people know the good but do not do it. This circumstance is a psychological mystery, to be sure. How can a person knowingly do what she believes to be wrong, or refrain from doing what she knows to be right? This paradox led Socrates to conclude that such moral weakness is an illusion and that to know the good is to do it.[3]

---

2. See, for example, John 5:1–18.
3. For example, Socrates says, "To make for what one believes to be evil, instead of making for the good, is not, it seems, in human nature." From Plato, *Protagoras,* in *The Collected Dialogues of Plato,* ed. Edith Hamilton and Huntington Cairns, trans. W. K. Guthrie (Princeton: Princeton University Press, 1961), 349.

Socrates' view would be a tempting one to take, except that it contradicts both common sense and Scripture. The case of Peter's denial of Christ, for instance, clearly illustrates moral weakness. He declared to Jesus that he would not deny him, even if all the other disciples did. He was even more insistent after Jesus assured the disciple that he would deny his Lord not just once but thrice before the rooster crowed. Well, we know the rest of the story.[4] Peter did deny Jesus three times. But when the rooster crowed, Peter recognized his sin, was deeply sorrowful for it, and repented. So Peter is not properly judged a hypocrite. Rather, he was morally weak. Peter's vice can, of course, be more narrowly construed as cowardice but, generally speaking, what he lacked was self-control. When accused of his association with Jesus, he *knew* the right thing to do. And his *desire* to do the right thing is evident in his emphatic declarations of loyalty to Jesus just a few hours earlier. Still, Peter failed. Somehow his knowledge of and desire for the good did not, contrary to Socrates' claim, translate into good action.

Although Peter's famous denial of Christ is particular to Peter, it points to a basic fact about human nature: All of us, like Peter, sometimes do what we know to be wrong and desire not to do. Paul's description of this struggle is poignant:

> We know that the law is spiritual; but I am unspiritual, sold as a slave to sin. I do not understand what I do. For what I want to do I do not do, but what I hate I do. And if I do what I do not want to do, I agree that the law is good. As it is, it is no longer I myself who do it, but it is sin living in me. I know that nothing good lives in me, that is, in my sinful nature. For I have the desire to do what is good, but I cannot carry it out. For what I do is not the good I want to do; no, the evil I do not want to do—this I keep on doing. Now if I do what I do not want to do, it is no longer I who do it, but it is sin living in me that does it. (Romans 7:14–20)

Elsewhere, Paul sums up the fact of moral weakness like this: "Live by the Spirit and you will not gratify the desires of the sinful nature. For the sinful nature desires what is contrary to the Spirit, and the Spirit what is contrary to the sinful nature. They are in conflict with each other, so that you do not do what you want" (Gal. 5:16–17). So Peter's moral weakness was not unique; it is universal. You and I and every other descendent of Adam share this tendency to do wrong, even against our better judgment and will. It's called original sin.

---

4.   See Matthew 26:31–35, 69–75.

Original Sin and the Quest for Virtue

Before embarking on a discussion of Christian character traits, it's essential to first assess the human moral condition (an area of study sometimes called "moral anthropology"). Doing so paints a realistic picture of the nature of our moral struggle. This assessment also helps in regard to the more immediate concern—understanding the difficulty of self-control.

Sin is an unpopular and controversial topic these days, but important nonetheless. From a biblical standpoint, however, there is no controversy; sin is missing the mark or, more specifically, failing to meet God's moral standard. And, from Genesis to Revelation, one would be hard pressed to find a clearer scriptural teaching than this: All human beings have sinned (see, for example, Isa. 53:6; Rom. 3:23; 1 John 1:8). So, too, is the doctrine of original sin well-grounded in Scripture, as classically conceived, teaching that human beings are naturally or innately sinful. As such, we inherited our natural corruption from the sin of Adam, as expressed repeatedly by Paul in Romans 5: "The many died by the trespass of the one man" (v. 15); "by the trespass of the one man, death reigned through that one man" (v. 17); "the result of one trespass was condemnation for all men"(v. 18); "through the disobedience of the one man the many were made sinners" (v. 19).

This moral corruption takes two forms—guilt and pollution. We share Adam's guilt because he was our representative head, and the curse he incurred is passed down to us by virtue of our being his progeny. In a radically individualistic culture such as ours, such collective judgment is a foreign concept. It is, however, no less biblical. The idea has, of course, an upside too, as evident in the Christian doctrine of atonement for sin. As Paul also explains in Romans 5, Christ's righteousness is applied to believers collectively and vicariously: "Through the obedience of the one man, the many will be made righteous" (v. 19).

Our natural pollution is, perhaps, easier to understand. We all have a tendency to rebel against God in thought, word, and deed, as proven in our particular acts of rebellion. But our sin is dispositional, not just occurrent. That is, sin is not something we merely do; it is something we *are*. As described in the Romans 7 and Galatians 5 passages quoted above, we have, in Paul's words, a "sinful nature." Consequently, we have a certain moral blindness and hardness of heart, which explains our inclination to sin and our predisposition to disobey the standards God has set for us.

Such is the biblical diagnosis of the human condition. It is popular today, even in Christian circles, to conceive the basic human problem primarily in psychological terms, such as neediness, emotional pain, or "brokenness" (a common but theologically empty descriptor). But while we are, indeed, needy, pained, and broken, these conditions are the effects of our fundamental disease, not the disease itself. Our basic problem is moral, the symptoms being legion, many of them psychological. But the symptoms are manifestations of the underlying cause. It's obvious, then, that the disease must be treated, not merely its symptoms. Dealing with the psychological problems that plague us is, of course, an important, even indispensable, supplement to moral treatment. But the former is useless without the latter.

The biblical prescription for the human condition is a humbling one. On our own we are powerless to cure ourselves. We deserve God's wrath, and we can't change that fact. That's the bad news. But the good news (or "gospel") is that God took the initiative to cure our sin problem through Christ's atoning work on the cross. There, both aspects of original sin—our guilt and pollution—are addressed. Just as we fell in Adam, we are made alive in Christ when we commit our lives to him. We are no longer guilty before God but fully justified, now objects of his favor, not wrath. Moreover, God gives us a new nature. Although we still struggle with our moral dark side—our sinful nature—we steadily improve morally, becoming more Christlike through the process known as sanctification. This process is where our effort comes in. Serious and sustained work is, in fact, required of us as we cooperate with the Holy Spirit in becoming more virtuous.

These rudiments of Christian theology have been reviewed here for a reason—to paint a complete picture of the human moral condition. Too often, virtue ethicists neglect or underemphasize (as Socrates did) the fact of human fallenness. Consequently, the moral demands on those who wish to grow in virtue are inadequately appreciated, and frustration necessarily results. The aim herein is to be realistic about our sin problem. Only then can we be realistic in our hope for success in dealing with it. Reviewing the doctrine of original sin reminds us why the call to self-control is so challenging. All of us have a beast within us to tame. Yes, Christians are empowered by the Holy Spirit to withstand the onslaughts of our sinful nature, but our sinful tendencies are potent enough to devour us if we do not take great care. As the Lord said to Cain, "If you do not do what is right, sin is crouching at your door; it desires to have you, but you must master it" (Gen. 4:7). Let us heed this warning—an enemy lurks within.

It's easy to see, then, how a weak theology of sin can be an obstacle to moral growth. But other theological mistakes may hamper our quest for virtue. One of these mistakes is the view that faith is merely a cognitive state, that is, the subtle but popular belief that faith in Christ is an essentially mental and purely inward event consisting entirely in beliefs about what Jesus did and who he said he was. "Believe and receive" is a well-known slogan reflecting this myth. Another symptom of this mistake in theology is the readiness of many Christians to declare that another person is a Christian simply because that person claims to believe in Christ. But such an approach to faith is unbiblical. Although mental assent is a significant part of saving faith, it's not the whole story.

One's faith is not only private but public as well, a matter of behavior as much as belief. Genuine saving faith, the Bible teaches, includes a recognition of one's sinful condition, as well as personal repentance, which will necessarily result in good works. This is why James says, "A person is justified by what he does and not by faith alone" (James 2:24). So saving faith is not mere belief but also a disposition to behave in certain ways—to exhibit moral virtue. As Martin Luther says, "Faith is . . . a live, active, busy, powerful force which cannot help but exert itself in good works without ceasing. . . . It is just as impossible to separate good works from faith as it is to separate heat and light from fire."[5]

Another mistake in theology has to do with moral passivity. Many Christians today take a basically passive approach to personal sanctification. We tend to see growth in godliness as something that we simply sit back and trust God to do in us. A symptomatic slogan of this view is "Let go and let God," an approach based in the conviction that advancing in moral maturity does not require concerted, deliberate effort and self-training. It sees spiritual discipline and hard-core preparation for temptation not only as unnecessary but as a lack of faith. Nothing, of course, could be further from the truth. Jesus himself practiced and taught the spiritual disciplines (e.g., prayer, fasting, solitude, submission, frugality, secrecy, sacrifice, etc.) to prepare for temptation. He did not merely "let go and let God." Rather, he voluntarily "let go" of earthly pleasures in methodical, systematic ways long before he had to, so that he would be adequately prepared when the tempter came. Numerous other biblical models of virtue similarly engaged in rigorous means of moral preparation. To do so is necessary because, as Dallas Willard writes, "The harmonization of our total self with God will not be done *for* us. *We* must act."[6] This proactive, nonpassive approach to sanctification will be discussed further in the section below, "Building Self-Control."

---

5. Martin Luther, *Preface to the Epistle of St. Paul to the Romans,* trans. Adolf G. H. Kreis (San Diego: Adolf G. H. Kreis, 1937), 19–20.
6. Dallas Willard, *The Spirit of the Disciplines: Understanding How God Changes Lives* (San Francisco: Harper Collins, 1988), 68.

Still another theological error pervading the church today is the denial of self-denial. Quite simply, many Christians today don't really believe they must deny themselves in order to be a disciple of Christ. They take the following attitude: "Jesus taught us to deny ourselves, but this is limited to those exceptional moments when I'm tempted to sin. Apart from those occasions, I'm entitled to whatever goods and pleasures I want to indulge in. After all, both Jesus and Paul taught us that Pharisaical restrictions on what one may eat or drink are against the spirit of love and service to God and others." Few Christians would explicitly state such a narrow conception of self-denial, but many of us live it. It's true that we're no longer bound by the Mosaic restrictions about what we may eat or drink, and every tangible blessing is to be received as a gift from God. But Jesus and all the apostles demonstrated that the Christian should voluntarily refrain from indulgence in various pleasures. Jesus fasted regularly and assumed his followers did so as well. And Paul declared that he "buffeted" his body not because such a practice would save him but because it prepared him for more righteous living.

Consider Jesus' words in Luke 9:23: "Anyone who would come after me must deny himself and take up his cross." Jesus here asserts that self-denial is an essential part of discipleship. Now ask yourself these questions: "How in the last week have I voluntarily denied myself something I really wanted?" "What is one significant thing I have deprived myself of recently?" If you can't think of an example and you don't make it a practice to deny yourself, then in what sense do you qualify as a disciple of Christ? These questions might seem overly severe or somehow unfair, but is that because of a misconstrued biblical notion of self-denial? Or, as is likely, have we contemporary American Christians been so ensnared by consumerism and our culture's hedonistic assumptions that we're virtually blind to the basic biblical teaching of self-denial?

Building Self-Control

These theological mistakes are most surely at the root of much moral failure within the evangelical church today. Here's why. First, consider the myth that faith is a mere cognitive state. It probably goes without saying that this view reduces the premium on good works and makes personal sanctification a desirable bonus rather than a mandatory and expected part of the Christian life. For if in order to be saved all one needs is a particular set of beliefs—which means that salvation boils down to a certain "state of mind"—then behavior literally does not matter. And even the most persuasive psychological techniques used by Christian pastors, speakers, and authors to motivate us to serve our neighbors and live morally impeccable lives will be useless. The natural result of de-emphasizing personal repentance as a prerequisite for salvation is that some people will claim to be Christians without repenting from their sins. And this is the very nature of hypocrisy (of the "self-deceived" variety).

The practical fallout of the myth of moral passivity is just as severe as the myth itself. By not taking deliberate steps to develop specific virtues such as self-control, we set ourselves up for moral failure (and charges of hypocrisy). Take, for example, the sin of viewing pornography. If, say, a certain man hasn't made a practice of denying himself of pleasure, then how could he ever expect to turn off the computer or look away from a magazine when the moment of pornographic temptation arrives? Often speakers tell young Christians that essentially all they need to do is just trust God or focus on Jesus. But such an approach is analogous to an athletic coach teaching through diagrams and film alone. Can you imagine a basketball coach *just* diagramming plays to the team without making her players do wind sprints and drills? Or limiting practices to the telling of stories about some of the game's great players? That, of course, would be ludicrous, and the team's performance would prove it. In recent decades, though, Christians have been shown diagrams and told stories, and our spiritual coaches (i.e., pastors and other Christian leaders) have neglected the all-important dimension of training. They've thus set us up for frustration because no one can simply manufacture enough will-power to overcome the strongest of temptations. We haven't been told the whole story of Christian sanctification, which demands careful, systematic self-training as preparation for resisting temptation.

If the myth of moral passivity is a contributor to the problem of moral weakness, then our casual ignoring of the importance of self-denial is all the more so. As Americans sharing in the consumer mentality, we've grown accustomed to thoughtless indulgence in whatever pleasure comes our way. This unconscious training in hedonism that we receive from our culture not only weakens us morally, but also blinds us to the fact that many of our choices (such as what to eat, what to watch, and what to buy) are actually *moral* choices. Christians often assume that everyone must have a television, in spite of the mindlessness of so much of the programming, not to mention the materialism, hedonism, sexism and other lies that so many advertisers promote. Too few Christians would consider limiting their purchases of food or clothing for the sake of living more simply or to practice self-control. And too few Christians refuse to take the vegetarian lifestyle seriously in spite of many church fathers—

and other major theologians such as John Wesley—being devout vegetarians. Finally, very few of us regularly practice fasting or even consider it a normal part of the Christian life. But our glibness in all these areas is likely because we really don't believe in self-denial. Is it any wonder, then, that in the few areas where we do agree that self-denial is important—such as in the area of sex outside of marriage—Christians fail at an alarming rate? The explanation is, after all, very simple: We aren't well-practiced at self-denial, so when we're called upon to do it, we often fail. Lack of moral practice leads to moral weakness.

We often fail to deny ourselves in the big areas because, without even thinking, we've indulged ourselves in a thousand smaller, seemingly insignificant areas. As a good friend once said to me, "Today's Christians talk a good spiritual game, but we actually live like materialists." Look at the cars we drive, the food we eat—and *how much* food we eat. It must be wondered if many of us are just closet hedonists (in the sense of being self-indulgent). But that would be inaccurate. We're not in the closet at all! If I'm accustomed to eating that extra dessert, buying the nicer shoes, or watching the sitcom just because it brings me immediate pleasure, then I have made self-indulgence habitual. And once this moral habit is ingrained, immoral indulgences eventually follow. If only my pleasure matters, then why not cheat on a test, lie to my friend, or steal from my employer?

So what can we do about the problem of moral weakness? How can we develop the moral skill of self-control? For starters, we must correct our doctrine and dispel the three theological myths just discussed. Theory determines practice, and the sooner we fix our theory, the better chance we have of improving our practice. From what's been said so far, it's obvious that merely changing what we *believe* about these things is not enough. We must also begin to change our *practice*. Doing so requires difficult, sometimes downright painful labor. We must commit ourselves to building self-control and moral strength, as recommended in this exhortation from Paul:

> Do you not know that in a race all the runners run, but only one gets the prize? Run in such as way as to get the prize. Everyone who competes in the games goes into strict training. They do it to get a crown that will not last; but we do it to get a crown that will last forever. Therefore I do not run like a man running aimlessly; I do not fight like a man beating the air. No, I beat my body and make it my slave so that after I have preached to others, I myself will not be disqualified for the prize. (1 Corinthians 9:24–27)

What does Paul mean here by "strict training"? What can we do to build self-control in a way that is analogous to what athletes do when they train? First and foremost, we must practice the spiritual disciplines. These include some practices that most Christians already engage in—prayer, worship, fellowship, study, meditation, confession, submission, celebration, and service. But all too unfamiliar to modern evangelicals are the disciplines of abstinence that include fasting, solitude, silence, and frugality. The diligent practice of the disciplines not only better acquaints us with Christ but also trains us in self-control. For a full discussion of the spiritual disciplines, the works of Richard Foster and Dallas Willard are highly recommended.[7] Willard's books are especially useful in helping Christians to reorient their thinking about the moral life and to counteract some of the doctrinal poisons that flow out of evangelical pulpits today.

Secondly, we must resolve to become more aware of our indulgences and to strive against the subtle but strong drive for self-satisfaction. To do so takes great discernment and resolve, because we live in a culture that not only blinds us to the viciousness of this trait but actually encourages it. To be specific, we must become more aware of two basic categories of indulgences. One of these is the indulgence of consumption which regards what we eat and drink and purchase. What may appear to be moderation relative to our consuming society may actually be absolute gluttony and greed. In practice, self-control in this area means keeping a proper diet and avoiding frivolous purchases. Over the years, my wife and I have made some major personal changes in these areas. In terms of finances, we're more frugal and much improved in giving to others. Diet-wise, we maintain a form of vegetarianism. While our abstinence from most meats is not solely for the sake of exercising self-control—we do have a moral conviction about cruelty to animals that has led us in this direction—we've found that so disciplining our diet has a beneficial effect on self-control.

The other category of indulgence to which we must attend more closely is that of amusement. I sometimes challenge people to tally up the hours they spend each day on entertainment, whether that takes the form of watching television, playing video games, or surfing the web for fun. Time management is a crucial part of the Christian life, and many of us are squanderers of the precious resource of time. Several years ago I became convicted about the time I was wasting watching television (I was a news and sports junkie). After repeated attempts to curb my tendency to overindulge, I finally cut that eye out of its

---

7.   Richard Foster, *Celebration of Discipline* (New York: Harper and Row, 1978); Willard, *The Spirit of the Disciplines;* and idem, *The Divine Conspiracy: Rediscovering Our Hidden Life in God* (San Francisco: Harper Collins, 1998), chap. 9.

socket. I got rid of my television and have been without it ever since. There's nothing inherently wrong, of course, with viewing television or engaging in most other pleasures available to us today. But the plethora of such luxuries in our culture makes it all the more important that we limit ourselves. Andre Comte-Sponville notes, "Temperance is a virtue for all times but is all the more necessary when times are good."[8] From the standpoint of resources, times have never been better than they are today for Americans. From a moral standpoint, then, the premium on self-control has never been higher.

A third step one can take to develop self-control is to practice voluntary self-denial. Look for small, even trivial ways to deny yourself every day. Then when the moment of temptation arrives, self-denial will be easier. The philosopher William James once recommended, "Do every day or two something for no other reason than that you would rather not do it, so that when the hour of dire need draws nigh, it may find you not unnerved and untrained to stand the test."[9] James was no Christian, but he still saw the practical wisdom in self-discipline. How many of us regularly practice self-denial even in this small way?

Finally, in addition to engaging in the spiritual disciplines, becoming aware of our indulgences, and practicing voluntary self-denial, we must pray specifically for the Holy Spirit's help in these areas. Sanctification is a cooperative venture between the Christian and God. While the believer has a responsibility to play her part in this process, this does *not* de-emphasize that, as Paul says, "It is God who works in you to will and to act according to his good purpose" (Phil. 2:13). Whatever advance we enjoy in the moral life is properly to be regarded as a gift from God.

Conclusion

Scripture teaches that we are saved by grace through faith in Christ. But Scripture also teaches that salvation has on-going practical implications. Oswald Chambers writes, "If we refuse to practice, it is not God's grace that fails when a crisis comes, but our own nature. When the crisis comes, we ask God to help us, but He cannot if we have not made our nature our ally. The practicing is ours, not God's."[10] Evangelicals once took the spiritual disciplines seriously and were strong advocates of self-training. But we've drifted away from these biblical practices, into the precarious tides of American individualism, consumerism,

---

8. Andre Comte-Sponville, *A Small Treatise on the Great Virtues,* trans. Catherine Temerson (New York: Henry Holt, 1996), 42.

9. William James, *The Principles of Psychology* (New York: Dover, 1950), 1:126.

hedonism, and the pattern of thinking more in terms of personal rights and privileges than in terms of moral responsibility and commitment. Symptoms of this shift in thinking are evident even in our songs. An old hymn says, "Take time to be holy," rightly suggesting that sanctification takes time and hard work. A contemporary chorus says, "I choose to be holy," as if sanctification were obtainable instantaneously and without effort.

As Americans, we evangelicals take practice and training seriously in every area of work and recreation, so why do we think that we need no practice in the most important part of life—living in obedience to God? I can only conclude that much of the church today is under a devilish delusion. Just as Peter would have benefited from training himself—he might even have avoided denying his Lord—so we could profit from practicing the spiritual disciplines and training ourselves to be more self-controlled. Look for ways to deny yourself, even when it's not morally required of you. If you won't listen to me, then listen to William James. If you won't listen to him, then take Dallas Willard's word for it. And if you won't take his word for it, then hear the words and follow the examples of Martin Luther, John Wesley, Oswald Chambers, the apostles Paul and James, and Jesus himself, when they exhort us to practice, practice, practice.

10.   Oswald Chambers, *The Psychology of Redemption* (London: Simpkin Marshall, 1947), 26–27.

2

DISPLAYING MORAL IRONY

The Virtue of Humility

The last chapter looked at the foundational virtue of self-control. This chapter examines what might be the essence of Christian virtue: humility. We live in a culture in which this trait is rarely admired, much less recognized as essential for moral living. To the extent that the Christian is called to be humble, then, he is called to live counterculturally. But not only is humility countercultural, it's counter to human nature itself. The Bible's emphasis on humility calls for, in fact, a complete change in the way we normally think about the world and ourselves. Humble behavior is, then, just the opposite of what anyone would expect, and so a matter of irony. In other words, the Christian mandate to live humbly is a call to be morally ironic.

Divine Irony

It's ironic that Odysseus should defeat Polyphemus, that Romeo and Juliet should fall in love, or that mighty Casey should strike out. From Homeric mythology to Shakespearean tragedy to American folk poetry, irony is a standard literary device that pivots upon a tension between what one expects and what actually occurs. When properly used, irony's effect is to enhance the beauty of a story. The Bible is typically regarded as an excellent work (or collection of works) of literary art. It should not surprise us, then, that much irony is to be found in its narrative. Consider Old Testament history. Abraham was promised the impossible, by human standards: An entire nation descended from him through a barren wife. Then once having begotten Isaac, Abraham was commanded by God to kill this child through whom were to come the promised descendants. Isaac's last minute rescue was, of course, at least as much of a surprise as his death sentence.

The story of Isaac's offspring is equally ironic. Jacob received the birthright due his older brother Esau. And the story of Joseph is, perhaps more than any other, dense with ironic twists. He was a righteous man but was waylaid by his brothers, left for dead, then sold into slavery. Not only did he survive this brutal treatment, he rose to prominence within the Egyptian government, again only to suffer for his refusal to sin with Potiphar's wife. He was thrown into prison but again was restored to leadership and eventually reunited with his brothers. But did he meet them with the rebuke they deserved (and that the reader would naturally expect)? No—he met them with tears of rejoicing.

Stories of other key Old Testament figures are also ironic. Moses, a stutterer and murderer, was selected as God's mouthpiece before Pharaoh. David, a mere shepherd boy, slew the giant Goliath and became the greatest of Israel's kings. At the height of his power, however—and, again to everyone's surprise—he succumbed to temptations spawned by his hidden weaknesses of lust and fear.

The history of the entire nation of Israel is, in fact, a study in irony. God favored them, although they were not righteous but were instead a "stiff-necked" people, slow in believing and displaying short memories of God's faithfulness. Led into Canaan, a territory populated by tribes considerably more powerful and plentiful than they, the Israelites were, in spite of the odds, triumphant in battle and conquered the land.

The New Testament features some equally ironic characters. Peter, a crude and impetuous fisherman, is the "rock" upon which the church is built. Initially an unreliable, confused coward, he was transformed into a valiant proclaimer of the gospel, faithful even to martyrdom. Paul, on the other hand, began as a proud persecutor of Christians, later to be changed into an equally zealous defender of the faith, ultimately meeting the same fate as those he had formerly persecuted. Many more cases could be described in detail, but enough has been said to illustrate the scriptural theme of irony. The story of redemption is full of ironic characters and plotting. But the greatest irony of all—in fact of all human history—concerns the central theme of Scripture.

The Irony of Christ

Jesus epitomizes irony in biblical narrative and in a variety of other ways: his nature, biography, ministry, teachings, method, and mission. First, the union of divine and human natures in Jesus is not just unexpected; it defies rational comprehension, as in a single person the infinite and finite are united. Morally, Jesus' divine-human nature runs contrary to our expectations that a holy God should take on human flesh, which is often associated with sinful desires and actions.

Jesus' birth in human form is, of course, the message of Christmas, a celebration that our culture has made routine. But our customs must not blind us to just how bizarre is this blessed truth—that the transcendent God should become one of us. This is irony of the highest order.

Second, consider the life of Christ. Born to a virgin and into an impoverished family, Jesus was raised by common folk in the dirty town of Nazareth, assuming the menial trade of carpentry. These are just the sorts of things one would *not* expect from God incarnate. Wouldn't we expect instead that he would come as king of a great nation or at least as a great high priest?

The ministry of Jesus is also ironic. He shrugged official religious associations more than he assumed them, challenged and angered the experts on Old Testament law, and welcomed and blessed the simple. In addition, he fraternized frequently with social outcasts and moral reprobates—tax collectors and prostitutes. Moreover, he consistently rejected pressure to assume the worldly kingship he deserved as Creator of heaven and earth.

Fourth, his teachings run counter to natural human inclinations. The theme of the beatitudes is that he who suffers, is poorly esteemed, or otherwise laid low is *most* blessed. The mantra that comes repeatedly from the lips of Jesus is that the last shall be first and the first shall be last. This is, indeed, the very essence of the ironic. When it comes to our conduct toward others—that we should turn the other cheek to those who strike us, bless those who persecute us, and pray for our enemies—the irony of Jesus is downright intolerable to some, perhaps most. Even Christians tend to water down these teachings. How many of us *really* put them into practice?

Ironic, too, is the teaching methodology of Christ, for in spite of his perfect understanding and capacity for direct communication of all truths, he taught indirectly, using parables. The most sublime truths are often masked in cryptic phrases and illustrations. Further, he came into the world to reveal himself as the Son of God, but he rarely announced this fact, only on special occasions openly declaring his true identity.

Lastly, and most importantly, consider irony in the ultimate mission of Jesus. The whole gospel plan is breathtakingly ironic, more so than any other truth claim in history. That the holy, almighty God of the universe should take on corruptible human flesh and die a criminal's death would be inconceivable, were it not for the fact that it actually happened. No wonder, as Paul says, the Cross is a stumbling block. As it was for the first century Jews, so it has been for countless others, for the message of the Cross is excruciating in its irony.

There's a point in considering all the irony related to biblical figures and especially to Christ. Simply put, the Christian worldview is hugely ironic, from its historical development and the principal figures involved, to the essence of its message. This, of course, implies that God, as the author of it all, is himself ironic.

Moral Irony as the Essence of Christian Virtue

As has been shown, a variety of examples of divine irony are evident from Scripture. What, though, are the moral aspects of divine irony? As traditionally understood, the biblical moral law is essentially an extension of God's character. Thus, it's often said that God's law is holy because he is holy. Inquiry into biblical moral ideals, then, is a way of studying the nature of God. To learn something of the essence of the former is to gain insight about the latter.

Nowhere in Scripture is the irony of God more obvious than in Scripture's moral instruction. The Christian ethic is, in fact, *essentially* ironic, which will become clear by looking at two important facts. First, humility is at the very heart of the moral life for the Christian. Second, the virtue of humility is ironic.

But just what is humility? There are two basic schools of thought on this issue. Some scholars maintain that to be humble is to assume a *low* regard for oneself. Others maintain that humility means to have a *proper* regard for oneself. Both approaches seem correct from a Christian standpoint: Scripture tells us that the *proper* view of oneself is a *low* view of oneself, and this is true for two main reasons. First, by comparison to our Maker, we are infinitely low. God is unlimited and absolutely perfect in every respect, while we are finite and imperfect. Second, we are sinful creatures who fail morally on a regular basis. We rebel against God in spite of his having given us so much. So our proper self-estimation is that we are *fallen,* meaning that we are morally low and deserving of condemnation. A proper regard for ourselves does not, however, negate the fact that we bear God's image and are still valued immeasurably by him. And that God still loves us in spite of our daily offenses provides yet another irony within the Christian worldview. God's loving us is also the reason why self-hatred is not an option from a biblical standpoint. Although recognizing our fallenness, we ought not regard ourselves as *absolutely* low, but only as immeasurably inferior to God.

Humility as a Christian Virtue

The Bible stresses the importance of a properly low self-regard. We are repeatedly exhorted to be humble. James gives this charge: "Humble yourselves before the Lord, and he will lift you up" (James 4:10). A proverb warns that God "mocks proud mockers but gives grace to the humble" (Prov. 3:34). The Lord declares through Isaiah, "This is the one I esteem: he who is humble and contrite in spirit, and trembles at my word" (Isa. 66:2). And Paul asserts that "God chose the weak things of the world to shame the strong. He chose the lowly things of this world and the despised things—and the things that are not—to nullify the things that are, so that no one may boast before him" (1 Cor. 1:27–29). The theme of divine exaltation of what is lowly pervades Scripture. Over and over again we see humility as a condition for divine favor and such particulars as protection (Job 5:11), guidance (Ps. 25:9), answered prayer (2 Chron. 7:14), spiritual insight (Matt. 11:25), and salvation (Ps. 149:4).

Nowhere in the Bible is the emphasis on humility more pronounced than, as was noted earlier, in the teachings of Jesus. That the last shall be first and vice versa is a consistent theme in his discourses (cf. Matt. 19:30, 20:16, 20:27; Mark 9:35, 10:31, 10:44; and Luke 13:30). "Anyone who will not receive the kingdom of God like a little child," he says, "will never enter it" (Mark 10:15). The beatitudes underscore the blessings to be enjoyed by those who are meek, mournful, needy, and poor in spirit (Matt. 5:3–10). Even the command to love one's neighbor as oneself is essentially a call to humility.

If Christ's teaching stressed humility, his life offers a vivid illustration of moral paradox. Although divine, he describes himself as "gentle and humble in heart" (Matt. 11:29), a truth confirmed in the gospel narratives in dramatic, sometimes disturbing ways. Most significantly, the key New Testament text dealing with the divine incarnation, the Philippians "kenosis" passage, treats the humility of Jesus as his crowning virtue. Paul writes,

> Your attitude should be the same as that of Christ Jesus: Who, being in very nature God, did not consider equality with God something to be grasped, but made himself nothing, taking the very nature of a servant, being made in human likeness. And being found in appearance as a man, he humbled himself and became obedient to death—even death on a cross! Therefore God exalted him to the highest place and gave him the name that is above every name. (Philippians 2:5–9)

Here we find a summary of the principal ways in which Jesus was humbled: his refusal to rely upon his divine attributes, his assumption of human nature, his servanthood, his obedience, and his degrading manner of death. Paul finishes by noting the exaltation of Christ which is as complete as his humility, a reminder of Jesus' words that the last shall be first.

Further biblical recommendations of humility are to be found in the doc-trines of confession, repentance, and faith. To confess one's sin is to accept blame and admit wrongdoing, weakness, and failure—the very antithesis of pride. Hu-mility is thus a prerequisite of repentance and confession of sin. Such passages as 2 Chronicles 7:14 confirm this: "If my people, who are called by my name, will humble themselves and pray and seek my face and turn from their wicked ways, then will I hear from heaven and will forgive their sin and will heal their land." Repentance, the moral response of turning one's back on one's sin, is a humble act, since it not only implies recognition of guilt by the repudiation of one's prior actions but also constitutes re-submission to proper moral author-ity. Finally, faith itself is morally ironic, for it is to trust someone other than oneself. The exercise of faith tacitly admits one's insufficiency and desperate need for help.

From a Christian standpoint, then, to be humble is to assume an inferior position before others. Inwardly, it is to take a low view of oneself or, at least, not to think more highly of oneself than one ought. Outwardly, it is to willingly submit to others or to painful circumstances.

Thomas à Kempis's classic *Of the Imitation of Christ* is fundamentally a medi-tation on humility. He declares that "the chiefest saints before God are the least before themselves, and the more glorious they are, so much within themselves are they humbler."[1] He sees humility as the most basic of Christian virtues and endorses self-abasement, since "there is no worse nor more troublesome enemy to the soul than you are to yourself, if you be not in harmony with the Spirit. It is altogether necessary that you take up a true contempt for yourself, if you desire to prevail against flesh and blood. Because as yet you love yourself too inordinately; therefore you are afraid to resign yourself wholly to the will of others."[2]

Jonathan Edwards identifies "evangelical humiliation" as one of the tell-tale religious affections by which one may discern true Christian spirituality. He defines evangelical humiliation as "a sense that a Christian has of his own utter insufficiency, despicableness, and odiousness, with an answerable frame of heart."[3] By this Edwards intends a disposition to abase oneself and "exalt God alone."[4] True humility is known by certain signs, among which Edwards includes

---

1. Thomas à Kempis, *Of the Imitation of Christ* (Pittsburgh: Whitaker, 1981), 82.
2. Ibid., 121.
3. Jonathan Edwards, *A Treatise Concerning Religious Affections,* in *The Works of Jonathan Edwards* (Edinburgh: Banner of Truth, 1974), 1:294.
4. Ibid.

(1) an inclination to submit to others and a disinclination to assume authority, (2) a disinclination to speak highly of one's own experiences, and (3) an inclination to regard oneself as an unworthy teacher and an inclination to seek instruction oneself.

In much the same vein as Edwards, Andrew Murray defines humility as "the sense of entire nothingness, which comes when we see how truly God is all, and in which we make way for God to be all."[5] Translating this abstract definition into concrete reality, however, is the challenge. Every Christian might affirm humility; few live it. This is because living humbly before God means suffering and submitting to other sinful human beings, even in the unnoticed details, and refusing to draw attention to one's good deeds. As Murray notes, "The insignificances of daily life are the importances and the tests of eternity because they prove what spirit really possesses us. It is in our most unguarded moments that we really show and see what we are. To know the humble man . . . you must follow him in the course of daily life."[6]

Humility as Moral Irony

As has been seen, the Christian account of humility involves a certain view of human moral worth. Most significantly, it assumes that human nature is morally corrupted. It is just because we are fallen that (1) our moral worth is greatly diminished, relative to our original righteousness; (2) we are inclined to put ourselves before others; (3) we tend to exaggerate our present moral worth (whether that involves underestimating our moral faults or discounting them altogether). This is to say that our current natural condition is one of abject pride.[7] In a sense, this aspect of our fallenness is itself ironic—that we should be naturally inclined to exaggerate our moral goodness *as a result of* our moral corruption. So abject pride is itself a form of moral irony, although of a negative sort.

The virtue of humility runs counter to selfishness and pride, our natural tendencies as human beings. The humble person places others before himself and maintains a proper estimate of his own moral worth. These two aspects of the virtue of humility are not unconnected. It is *because* the humble person so clearly sees his own low moral worth that he places others before himself and

---

5.   Andrew Murray, *Humility* (New Kensington, Pa.: Whitaker, 1982), 12.

6.   Ibid., 44.

7.   What I call "abject pride" may be distinguished from a virtuous kind of pride. While the former is opposed to humility, the latter is opposite shame. So the former is a bad trait, while the latter is good.

their needs above his own. Humility is a virtue, then, which turns the natural fallen moral condition of human beings on its head. But it does not eliminate moral paradox. For in exhibiting this virtue, the humble person consequently increases in actual moral worth and is therefore deserving of greater moral credit than he otherwise would be. But—and this is yet another paradox—the humble person refuses to *act* so as to affirm his greater moral worth. To be consistently humble is, in fact, to successfully resist the temptation to dwell on or take credit for one's increasing moral worth.

Two senses of humility can be distinguished: one inward and one outward. Inner humility refers to an attitude possessed by someone who thinks no more highly of himself than he ought. Outer humility consists in the performance of actions that manifest inner humility. The humble person does not aspire to be held in high esteem, nor does he act in a way that reflects this desire. Humility applies both to proper self-estimation and instances of *under*estimation of one-self. Such application is necessary at times if only to ensure that one doesn't think too highly of oneself. An example would be the superstar ballplayer who voluntarily and cheerfully sits on the bench while inferior athletes play. Such cases are the most striking because of the degree of incongruence between what the person deserves and what he receives or wills to receive.

When understood in this light, it should be clear why humility is ironic. It consists in attitudes and behaviors that would not be expected from a person. It is typical for people to desire *at least* their "fair share." We strive for what we deserve and jockey for a little more besides. The humble person, in contrast, does not seek goods or recognition beyond what his talents warrant and seeks no more than, and perhaps *less* than, his just deserts. Thus, the humble person is a perplexing entity whose words and actions, or lack thereof, will sometimes provoke reproofs from those who do not share his perspective—the viciously proud.

Humility and Suffering

The notion that humility plays a central role in Christian ethics has implications regarding the problem of evil. But as these implications are discussed, two things must be kept in mind. First is the ironic biblical principle that humility ultimately results in exaltation. Partly because of this long-term payoff, it may be assumed that humility is a good and desirable thing. Further, the relevant biblical passages reveal that the connection between humility and exaltation is law-like, at least for the redeemed. That is, as far as the Christian is concerned, there seem to be no exceptions to this rule: humility *always* leads to exaltation of some kind.

Second, in addition to the two senses of humility (outward and inward) discussed above, two kinds of humility can be distinguished in regard to imposition: voluntary and involuntary. Voluntary humility is self-imposed, that is, the intentional lowering of oneself; involuntary humility is that which is not willingly undertaken. Examples of voluntary humility are found in those persons who humble themselves, and in which case humility is a moral virtue. Involuntary humility, on the other hand, is not a moral quality, since it is not intentionally undertaken. Examples include any suffering which is not sought out, whether physical, psychological, or emotional.

The problem of evil, as traditionally set forth, recognizes suffering as an evil and therefore as a "philosophical problem" that theists must solve if their worldview is to be considered rational. But the crucial premise of this approach is false; suffering is not essentially evil but is, in fact, a form of divine grace. John Edelman has made this point powerfully: There is a wisdom that can come only through suffering, namely "the recognition of the limits of human power." Such wisdom comes only through experiencing "the pain . . . one feels in running up against those limits."[8] Edelman adds that such wisdom cannot come through self-inflicted or voluntary suffering—or asceticism—for that is to arrange the lesson for oneself. Doing so negates the gaining of the sort of wisdom here being discussed: *understanding the limits of arranging the world for oneself.* So suffering is a kind of divine grace, disguised though it may be. It grants us a certain wisdom, bringing us directly into contact with the truth of our not being in control. This confrontation with lack of control also explains why pain is often the occasion for people coming to faith. When our suffering shows us our impotence, we look elsewhere for omnipotence.

So suffering (when neither self-inflicted nor justly incurred) is a form of involuntary humility. And, for the Christian, humiliation always leads to some form of exaltation. Consequently, if we maintain a biblical perspective, focusing on the example of Christ, we may expect that those who suffer most will also receive the greatest rewards, assuming a proper attitude on the part of those who suffer. As Jesus said, the first will be last and the last will be first. This means that those who suffer most (and thus place "last" in this world in terms of personal comfort and pleasure) are most blessed (for they shall be most com-

---

8.   John Edelman, "Suffering and the Will of God," *Faith and Philosophy* 10, no. 3 (July 1993): 383.

forted and overjoyed in the next world). How ironic, then, that we should resent suffering, since it is ultimately such a blessing. As Thomas à Kempis writes,
"God will have you learn to suffer tribulation without comfort; and that you
subject yourself wholly to Him. . . . No man so feels in his heart the passion of
Christ as he who suffers."[9]

But here we may ask, "If suffering is a blessing, then what's the sense in re-
lieving the distress of those in pain? After all, they'll be exalted in the end." The
answer is simple: We should relieve suffering because we have a biblical mandate to do so. As in the Calvinist response to the query "Why pray or evangelize
when God ordains all things?" the answer does not attempt to resolve the tension at hand so much as to acknowledge it as a tension with which we must live,
for it's a tension inherent in Scripture.

In the Bible, both painful trials and the relief of suffering are seen as divine
gifts.[10] That suffering is a form of grace is ironic. But the greatest irony of all is
that the very means of the world's redemption should be accomplished by the
most terrible suffering of all. The humiliation of Christ provides the most important clue regarding the centrality of the virtue of humility to the moral life.
God chose suffering and death as the antidote for evil. In Christ, God gave the
world "a hair of the dog that bit it." But unlike the early morning sip of whiskey
for a hangover (to which this idiom refers), we have here a genuine cure. The
humility of Christ is not merely a model for the Christian moral life, mirroring
the entire life of our ironic Messiah—it is also the key to salvation, wrought by
the God who deigns to suffer with us.

Fame, Vanity, and the Quest for Humility

It should be obvious that the humble life, and therefore the Christian life, is
diametrically opposed to the desire for fame and recognition. But in our
culture—where celebrities are idolized—even those who regard themselves as
devoutly Christian are sometimes caught in the snare of vanity. In actuality, no
trait could be more anti-Christian. Desire for fame directly opposes the moral
attitude of Christ, who sought only his heavenly Father's recognition and
approval, although this brought him disdain and abuse. But more than this,
vanity reveals a basic distrust in God. Desire for fame is essentially a wish to be
known and remembered. So to direct this desire toward human beings is to

---

9.   Thomas à Kempis, *Of the Imitation of Christ,* 87.
10.   See James 1:2–4 and 1 Peter 1:6–7. These themes are explored in detail in chap-
      ter 13 of this book.

distrust the knowledge and memory of God. Or consider a person who believes that God will remember him and even preserve him into the next world, but still seeks fame. Such vanity betrays a distrust in divine justice, that God will make that person known to others as much as is appropriate.

We all want, of course, to be remembered. This desire might be natural and good in itself, when understood as an aspect of the desire for immortality. Dependence upon the ability of other humans to fulfill this desire is, however, absurdly misplaced. If God will remember you, then why rely on the memories of mere mortals? And, what makes matters worse for the vain person, human memories are fleeting and useless. Marcus Aurelius notes,

> The man whose heart is palpitating for fame after death does not reflect that out of all those who remember him every one will himself soon be dead also. . . . Furthermore, even supposing that those who remember you were never to die at all, nor their memories to die either, yet what is that to you? Clearly, in your grave, nothing; and even in your lifetime, what is the good of praise—unless maybe to subserve some lesser design?[11]

These observations reveal the appropriateness of the term *vanity* to describe the pursuit of fame. All efforts to permanently secure oneself in the memories of other people are destined to fail. Even if one were somehow to succeed in attaining fame, it would profit one nothing. Consider the few artists and politicians whose fame has reached across the millennia from the ancient world. How much does our familiarity with Homer, Cleopatra, or Alexander the Great help them? As Aurelius notes, it's of no use whatsoever. Likewise, whatever fame you or I achieve is ultimately meaningless. All that matters is what God thinks of us, notwithstanding what our culture might tell us.

The humble person is content to be obscure, and the humble Christian sees his obscurity from an eternal perspective. Far from being anxious about the prospect that he will eventually be forgotten as the generations roll, he takes great joy in the fact that God will remember him and, more than this, perpetually preserve his being. Here we see the connection between humility and faith. Christian humility is premised on the recognition that one's earthly condition is not final but is rather a preface to one's ultimate destiny. This is not to say that our earthly life counts for nothing. On the contrary, the life we live now deter-

---

11. Marcus Aurelius, *Meditations,* trans. Maxwell Staniforth (Baltimore: Penguin, 1964), 67.

mines our heavenly condition, as Christ's principle of moral irony makes clear: "The last will be first and the first will be last" (Matt. 20:16). So the only desire for self-exaltation that is not vain is that which aims at heavenly exaltation.

Developing an eternal perspective is, of course, a key to developing humility. The more clearly we see our earthly lives as tenuous and brief, the more emphasis we'll place on what is unshakeable and everlasting. To nurture this attitude we must immerse ourselves in Scripture. We must also actively practice the virtue of humility by following biblical models, such as by voluntarily submitting to others, as Jesus did (see Phil. 2:7–8). And we must consciously welcome difficulties by giving thanks in the midst of our trials, as Paul says (1 Thess. 5:18), and even taking joy in them, as James tells us (James 1:2). The spiritual discipline of submission is essential to Christian spiritual formation and especially effective in cultivating the moral virtue of humility. It is true that few things in the Christian life could be more difficult. But nothing is more Christlike, and nothing is more ironic.

3

WAITING WITHOUT COMPLAINT

The Virtue of Patience

"Patience is a virtue." We're all familiar with that cliché, and many of us know that patience is listed by Paul in Galatians 5:22–23 as among the fruit of the Spirit. So there's no disputing that the Christian ought to be patient. But as with most of the virtues, the biblical writers assume that we know what patience is and don't give an explicit definition. But do we? Could you define patience if you were asked? And, to make things more tricky, could you do so without simply citing examples of patience? Starting with the basic definition of patience as "waiting without complaint,"[1] we will address some key questions. Why is patience a virtue? What are the different varieties of patience? Why is patience so difficult at times? And how is patience developed?

Why Patience Is a Virtue

When defined as "waiting without complaint," patience might seem to be a morally insignificant trait. What's so virtuous about not complaining? In itself, not complaining carries no particular virtue. Suppose a person awaits the arrival of a friend from out of town, and she spends the time happily reading or watching television. We wouldn't say that, simply because she's not complaining, she exhibits patience in this case. Something else must be required to make one's lack of complaint virtuous. That something is *discomfort*. It's because a circumstance is uncomfortable for someone that we find her refusal to complain remarkable and thus regard her as patient.

So to improve the initial definition above, to be patient is *to endure discomfort without complaint.* This calls into play some other virtues, specifically, self-

---

1. I recall reading this definition somewhere, however my efforts to track down the source have been unsuccessful.

control, humility, and generosity. That is, patience is not a fundamental virtue so much as a complex of other virtues. An example from the life of Christ illustrates this. Jesus was very patient with his disciples. They were sometimes thick-headed, lazy, selfish, and slow to believe. Even from a merely human standpoint, we can see how frustrating they must have been. How much more irritating it would be for God Incarnate to interact daily with these men. In spite of Jesus' miracles and words of wisdom, they were focused upon themselves and wavered in their belief about who he really was. To say that was uncomfortable for Jesus would be an understatement. Yet do we find him railing at his disciples over their foolishness and stupidity? Or making fun of them when they make mistakes? Occasionally he does remark that his disciples are slow to believe, or he asks rhetorically how long they will fail to have faith in him, but these are always appropriate reminders about just what was at stake for them. These were fitting and useful rebukes, not petty venting.

Notice that Jesus' refusal to complain about his irritating disciples can be described as an exercise of self-control. Surely he would have been justified in blistering them with insults. It's worth noting that his omniscience guaranteed that every possible joke and embarrassing remark was at his disposal on any particular occasion. This makes his self-control even more admirable. Also, his refusal to complain involves humility, the conscious decision to lower himself by not exercising his right, as the holy man he was, to judge and dismiss his friends because of their faults. We might even say this is a form of mercy. Finally, Jesus' refusal to complain about his disciples is generous. In spite of their vice and thick-headedness, he remained no less committed to them and served them increasingly as their failures became more outstanding.

While the patience of Christ is exceptional in many respects, the basic features of this virtue are surely the same wherever it appears. Patience involves such things as self-control, humility, and generosity, all of which are themselves virtues. So one might say that patience is a virtue because it's an exercise of several other virtues.

The Varieties of Patience

What are the different contexts in which patience is demonstrated? One way to distinguish types of patience is based upon the nature of the discomfort involved. The following threefold distinction can be made: first is the patience needed when facing a nuisance of some kind. A person or a set of circumstances really irritates you, and you'd love to complain about it, but you hold your tongue, knowing that such a grievance would be petty or simply compound the problem. That person at the office who is so insufferably annoying doesn't, after all, mean to pester you. And what good will it do to moan about those potholes on your street? So you quietly endure these things. Did you know you were being virtuous in doing so?

A second type of patience is called for when facing boredom. Those who fall into a rut at work or at home often experience discomfort over the uneventful routine. To those who don't struggle with boredom, it might seem absurd to suggest it can be a serious trial. But those who endure the plague of drab routine without complaint exhibit the virtue of patience.

A third type of patience is the most serious and significant. It is the patience required when one suffers in some way, either physically or psychologically. If you're struggling with some disease or mental illness, then patience is required of you. Or if you must assist someone else who suffers, a family member or friend, then you are called upon to be patient. Whether you bear the burden of affliction directly or indirectly, your challenge is to endure that discomfort. This doesn't mean you shouldn't cry out in your distress. Scripture, in fact, advises us to do just that, so it's appropriate because the degree of discomfort in some situations warrants complaint. But this raises some important questions: What is a complaint? And which complaints are worthy?

To complain is to make known one's irritation or frustration about some matter. This doesn't necessarily imply that one says anything out loud. Usually we complain by speaking directly about the circumstance that bothers us. But we also complain in nonverbal ways, with a sigh, a huff, a shake of the head, or a roll of the eyes. Many of us are quite expert at communicating our irritation in subtle ways to those closest to us, through means that most people wouldn't recognize as complaining. But our target complainee (the person we complain to) gets the message, and that's all that matters.

Which complaints, then, are worthy? Certainly it's legitimate to raise objections about conditions that are clearly unjust or impractical and need to be changed. But grumbling over things that are merely annoying or against one's personal wishes is petty. And complaining about things that cannot be changed doesn't qualify as a legitimate protest. So a worthy complaint is one that is neither petty nor pointless.

Complaint to God is inappropriate only when its cause is insignificant. Major physical and psychological afflictions are significant, so one's patiently enduring them may actually involve complaint. Thus, complaining to God in prayer in such cases is not vicious but virtuous. It is a useful complaint to someone who is sovereign and therefore in control of whatever concerns us. The Psalms feature several examples of godly complaints, such as the following:

> Why, O LORD, do you stand far off?
>   Why do you hide yourself in times of trouble?
> —Psalm 10:1

> Why do you hide your face
>   and forget our misery and oppression?
> —Psalm 44:24

> I pour out my complaint before him;
>   before him I tell my trouble.
> —Psalm 142:2

And in one of the darkest of biblical passages, the psalmist declares,

> From my youth I have been afflicted and close to death;
>   I have suffered your terrors and am in despair.
> Your wrath has swept over me;
>   your terrors have destroyed me. . . .
> You have taken my companions and loved ones from me;
>   the darkness is my closest friend.
> —Psalm 88:15–18

This is, indeed, a complaint, but the severity of the suffering calls for it. Most importantly, God is the recipient of the complaint. So this is actually an act of faith on the part of the psalmist, affirming divine sovereignty even over his terrible pain.

This point suggests yet another way to categorize patience, one premised upon the biblical idea that God continually sustains the whole universe. God governs every occurrence in nature, so even "natural" events, as it turns out, have a personal explanation—namely God himself. This means that all patience or impatience is ultimately patience or impatience with *someone.*

Therefore, two categories of patience can be distinguish based upon the person (or persons) with whom we must be patient. Sometimes patience is human-directed. Waiting your turn in line or in traffic certainly demands patience. Waiting for a teenager to mature can require an extraordinary amount of patience. In any case, whether a stranger is in your way, your coworker is pestering you, or your teenager is going through a period of acute self-righteousness, you must endure discomfort because of other people.

But even more challenging at times is the patience that is God-directed. In every Christian's life there comes a time when one must wait upon God. Sometimes we must wait for a need to be met, such as finding a job. Other times we must wait for the satisfaction of a significant desire, like finding a spouse or conceiving a child. At other times we wait for God to fulfill a promise, to comfort during a trial, or to give us assurance of our forgiveness for some sin. In these cases, we must be patient with God.

Why Patience Is So Difficult

From a personal standpoint, I don't know which is more difficult—exercising patience with God or other human beings. Both can be tremendous challenges, and none of us have perfected the art of being patient with each other or with God. I, in fact, become impatient with myself (a potential third category worth considering) because I struggle in being patient with other people and with God.

But patience is difficult in both cases. First, why is patience with other people so difficult? A natural response is, "All human beings are sinners and therefore selfish and annoying." But a psychological explanation also helps to explain why patience is so challenging. It concerns what philosophers call the "egocentric predicament," which is the natural human condition of being immediately aware only of one's own thoughts and feelings. When standing in line or waiting in traffic, for example, all the people who are waiting are equally as worthy to get what they wait for or to arrive at their destinations. I know, however, only my *own* thoughts and am intimately aware of only my *own* needs, which naturally incline me to put myself first. The result is frustration that I'm not first, and this strongly tempts me to be impatient.

A second reason why patience is such a challenge is that none of us struggle with precisely the same temptations as do other people. Nor are our particular strengths and weaknesses the same as those of others. One person is even-tempered and can't understand why her friend flies off the handle at times. But the person with the bad temper cannot understand how her even-keeled friend can be habitually late to meetings. And both of them get annoyed at a third friend's tendency to overeat. This is, of course, another aspect of the egocentric predicament. None of these friends knows what it's like to have the others' peculiar weaknesses. Nor does each comprehend how much effort the others are exerting in order to be as moral as they are, for it's not immediately apparent how hard the others work to control themselves. The result, again, is the temptation to become impatient with them.

Why is patience toward God so difficult? The explanation boils down to, again, our tendency to see things only from our own point of view. Further reasons, though, compound the difficulty of waiting upon God. For one thing, patience with God involves faith, and to exercise faith is to surrender final control of one's life. To lack faith is to give in to one's desire for control. So our patience with God will only be as strong as our ability to overcome this desire and surrender every aspect of our lives.

Patience with God is a challenge, too, because sometimes it's not at all clear whether it *is* God we're waiting for or whether we should even wait on him at all. The unemployed person may wonder, "Have I waited too long rather than taking more action?" The person desiring a spouse might second-guess herself, "Have I taken the right social steps?" And the childless couple might wonder, "Should we pursue clinical help in order to conceive?" Sometimes it's simply unclear whether God wants us to wait or take another course of action.

Finally, and most difficult of all, there's no guarantee that God will, indeed, act to satisfy our desires. Most situations that demand patience aren't in regard to specific promises of God. Although he has told us he will meet all our needs, he hasn't guaranteed that all of our desires, even significant ones, will be satisfied. Here, someone might note the biblical promise that if you "delight yourself in the LORD . . . he will give you the desires of your heart" (Ps. 37:4). This, however, is not a promise that all of our present desires will be fulfilled the way we want them to be. Sometimes they are, but often God keeps this promise by adjusting our desires to bring them into line with his will. If this is disappointing, keep in mind that even if God does change our desires, they are still our sincere desires!

How Patience Is Developed

It's been said that nothing teaches like experience. To some degree this is true of the virtues. Pain and suffering teach us endurance and empathy. The experience of mercy and forgiveness inclines us to be more merciful and forgiving. We gain moral maturity each day precisely because each day brings some difficulty that we must overcome. Like it or not, we persevere, and we are morally the better for it. This is why James tells us to "consider it pure joy . . .

whenever you face trials of many kinds, because you know that the testing of your faith develops perseverance. Perseverance must finish its work so that you may be mature and complete, not lacking anything" (James 1:2–4). The Stoic philosopher Seneca echoed this theme, noting the moral value of adversity:

> Pampered bodies grow sluggish through sloth; not work but movement and their own weight exhausts them. Prosperity unbruised cannot endure a single blow, but a man who has been at a constant feud with misfortunes acquires skin calloused by suffering; he yields to no evil and even if he stumbles carries the fight on upon his knee.[2]

Misfortunes are designed to build virtue in us, and among the virtues gained through difficulty is patience. That family member or work associate who annoys you is God's gift to you to build your patience. If you're stuck with a job you don't like, and you can't find any other work, then God is building your patience. Each nuisance, long wait, and affliction, every mosquito bite, traffic jam, and body ache in the life of the Christian raises her threshold of tolerance ever so much. Even tedious sermons and difficult reading (perhaps including what you are enduring right now!) can make you a more patient person.

So through the daily grind, the Christian grows morally, improving in virtue through various experiences that she might not even consider morally relevant, much less significant. But we who affirm the sovereignty of God shouldn't be surprised by this moral growth through even incidentals, for we believe God is always at work in the details, moving always to bring us into closer conformity to his image (cf. Rom. 8:28). That's not to suggest, however, that we can't slow the process of growth by our response to our daily difficulties. Indeed, a bitter or resentful spirit can stunt moral growth. So we must be attentive and pray for the proper attitude toward all our trials, whether petty or profound, and the Holy Spirit will maximize the positive effect of those occasions on our moral-spiritual growth.

---

2.   Seneca, *The Stoic Philosophy of Seneca*, trans. Moses Hadas (New York: W. W. Norton, 1958), 30–31. Seneca adds that the morally mature person regards all adversity as exercise. As in athletics, "Without an antagonist prowess fades away. Its true proportions and capacities come to light only when action proves its endurance." Thus, he counsels, "You must not shrink from hardship and difficulty or complain of fate; [you] should take whatever befalls in good part and turn it to advantage. The thing that matters is not what you bear but how you bear it" (30).

In addition to life experience and the sort of unplanned training that daily living provides in our sanctification, we can do things to accelerate the process of growth in patience (and in virtue generally). We can take steps of moral self-help. One of these is behavior therapy, a practice once popular among Christians but today virtually forgotten. It involves the intentional affliction of oneself with an annoying or tedious task expressly for the purpose of developing patience. I learned of several such exercises in a book from the 1930s called *Strength of Will and How to Develop It*.[3] The author, E. Boyd Barrett, prescribes such tasks as the following:

- Scatter fifty coins on the floor. Then quietly and slowly pick them up and place them in a pile. The author suggests doing this once per day for several days, increasing the number of coins as you go.
- Take a book of at least 150 pages and turn the pages one by one quietly and slowly, making a pencil mark on each page as you go.
- Beginning with the number one, count out loud slowly and distinctly for ten minutes.

Sound ridiculously pointless? That's the point. Such activities test your patience and, thus, build it. Just as weightlifting and jogging accomplish nothing external to one's own body but help the body itself, these exercises accomplish nothing outside one's mind, but help the mind itself. They are forms of mental discipline. If you are seeking exercises of practical value, consider building patience through activities such as meditation, study, and prayer. As you study and meditate on Scripture, you not only store valuable knowledge, you practice patience. Prayer, too, which the Bible says avails much for the righteous, requires and builds patience. So such spiritual disciplines as meditation, study, and prayer also double as behavior therapy.

Cognitive therapy is another important aspect of moral development. As a person matures in virtue, she must have a clear moral ideal at which to aim. Here, the Christian enjoys the ultimate advantage, as we have the example of God Incarnate, the living blueprint of virtue displayed before us in the pages of Scripture. As noted before, many aspects of the life and experience of Jesus provide a profile in patience.

Recalling the varieties of patience noted earlier lends a better understanding of the patience of Jesus. First, he endured nuisance and annoyance from his

---

3. E. Boyd Barrett, *Strength of Will and How to Develop It* (New York: Richard R. Smith, 1931), 122–26.

disciples. No doubt Jesus' patience with them was partly attributable to his empathetic understanding of their weaknesses. In *To Kill a Mockingbird*, Atticus Finch remarks, "You never really know a man until you stand in his shoes and walk around in them."[4] Jesus did know everyone perfectly, completely understanding each person's perspective. Knowing what it was like to be the disciples, as Jesus did, would certainly contribute to his remarkable patience. The lesson for us is that we should strive to imagine what it's like to be certain people, what it's like to walk around in their shoes.[5] This will make us more patient.

Secondly, Jesus withstood boredom. Although this is somewhat speculative, I think it's fair to assume that it was tiresome for Jesus to work as a carpenter for many years before beginning his formal messianic ministry. For over a decade the Son of God pounded nails into wood. Think about that if you feel overqualified for your job. The waiting might have been the hardest part, knowing his own mission as the Messiah but not being able to declare his identity openly for so many years.

Thirdly, and more obviously, Jesus exhibited patience through severe affliction. He suffered intensely during the passion, which we appropriately focus upon because it purchased our redemption. Countless other less dramatic and yet severe frustrations surely dogged him. Jesus knew, for example, that given his messianic mission, he couldn't get married and have children. But this doesn't mean he didn't desire these things. Perhaps Jesus was romantically attracted to some women but refused to act on his feelings. As Scripture says, he suffered as all men suffer, and unfulfilled romantic affection is certainly a form of suffering. It would be but one more painful resisting of temptation that Jesus faced in a lifetime of trials.

Finally, Jesus exhibited patience with his heavenly Father as he waited for and worked toward the completion of his mission. Note that, like the psalmist, Jesus cried out in agony, offering his righteous complaints and pleas to God, even quoting Scripture in the process. This was not impatience but a heading off of the temptation to be impatient by taking his complaint directly to God the Father.

---

4.   Harper Lee, *To Kill a Mockingbird* (New York: Harper and Row, 1960), 294.
5.   This point reveals the moral significance of art. By reading a book or watching a film one may better imagine what it's like to be a certain person or to face a particular problem. This helps to build one's patience, empathy, and compassion for people like those depicted in the artwork.

Conclusion

So patience *is* a virtue, a difficult but important one for the Christian. While every day our patience is tested and, we can hope, increased, we must be mindful of the process of sanctification and how God is at work in our difficulties, even in tiny annoyances, to make us more like Jesus. But as Peter says, we must "prepare [our] minds for action" (1 Peter 1:13). We must be intentional about increasing our patience, perhaps even by using mental exercises, but definitely by practicing the spiritual disciplines. Let us focus ever more clearly on the example of Christ in order to imitate him in all things, large and small.

4

BEING FORTHRIGHT

The Virtue of Sincerity

Most of us have concluded a letter with the phrase "Sincerely yours." How often, though, have we thought about the literal meaning of this salutation? When we write these words, do we typically intend to make the guarantee they imply—that our intentions are true and honest? And do we live our lives in such a way that we could append the words *sincerely yours* to all our actions? One who does so would be a forthright person. As with many of the virtues, the moral goodness of sincerity is assumed, rather than argued for, by the biblical writers. In Paul's second letter to the Corinthians, for example, he identifies sincerity as a godly trait. Jesus' description of Nathanael as "a true Israelite, in whom there is nothing false," too, seems to be praise of that disciple's sincerity (John 1:47). And, negatively, Jesus often scolds the Pharisees for their lack of sincerity, such as in the gospel of Matthew, where he says,

> Woe to you, teachers of the law and Pharisees, you hypocrites! You clean the outside of the cup and dish, but inside they are full of greed and self-indulgence. . . . First clean the inside of the cup and dish, and then the outside also will be clean. Woe to you, teachers of the law and Pharisees, you hypocrites! You are like whitewashed tombs, which look beautiful on the outside but on the inside are full of . . . everything unclean. In the same way, on the outside you appear to people as righteous but on the inside you are full of hypocrisy and wickedness. (23:25–28)

What Paul and Nathanael possessed and the hypocritical Pharisees and teachers of the law lacked was honesty of purpose, a forthrightness about their real intentions. Sincerity, then, may be seen as a form of truthfulness. It is not, however, a mere truthfulness of speech. Rather, sincerity encompasses one's total being, one's thoughts, words, and actions.

Authenticity and Bad Faith

In understanding the virtue of sincerity, it will be helpful to contrast it with the vices opposing it. If a sincere person is forthright and honest about his true intentions, then a person may fail to be sincere in two ways. One may simply hide his true intentions from others, in which case that person is deceitful. Or a person may hide his intentions from himself, in which case he practices self-deception. The former vice is probably the more common of the two, encompassing all cases of lying or otherwise hiding the truth from others. It's also the easier to comprehend from a psychological standpoint. Self-deception, however, is in some respects a mystery. How can a person hide—or even attempt to hide—from himself something that he knows to be true? Is this even intelligible? While some moral psychologists and philosophers believe this to be impossible, most regard self-deception as a real phenomenon. People do, at times, deceive themselves. How is this possible?

On one view, self-deception is due to psychological compartmentalization. Freudian psychologists advocate this approach, which says that the self-deceived person's ego refuses to acknowledge something about which his id or superego is aware. One aspect of an alcoholic's psyche might clearly recognize his problem, while another aspect ignores it. One mental compartment of the alcoholic denies what the other knows to be true. Such is the Freudian account of self-deception.[1]

Another approach sees self-deception as resulting from motivated irrationality. A person may be so biased against a particular belief that she minimizes all evidence in its favor and amplifies the little evidence against it. The mother whose son is repeatedly arrested for drug dealing might yet deny that her son is an addict. Her strong desire for his innocence biases her against the plain fact of his guilt. She downplays the testimonies of police and witnesses, and she overemphasizes the significance of her son's decent grades in school and his insistence that he's innocent. Consequently, she irrationally persists in a false belief about her son and is self-deceived.[2]

A third view regards self-deception as existential disavowal, the refusal to own

---

1. For example, see Amelie O. Rorty, "Self-Deception, *Akrasia,* and Irrationality," *Social Science Information* 19, no. 6 (1980): 905–22; and David Pears, *Motivated Irrationality* (Oxford: Oxford University Press, 1984), chap. 5.
2. See, for example, Alfred Mele, "Real Self-Deception," *Behavioral and Brain Sciences* 20 (1997): 91–102; and James Peterman, "Self-Deception and the Problem of Avoidance," *Southern Journal of Philosophy* 21 (1983): 565–73.

up to one's choices after the fact. The existentialist philosopher Jean-Paul Sartre termed this characteristic "bad faith" and illustrated it as follows. Suppose a woman is on a date with someone in whom she has no romantic interest. He takes her to an elegant restaurant, and at some point during the evening he takes her hand. Not wanting to spoil the dining experience or create an awkward moment, she chooses not to withdraw her hand, although she recognizes that by keeping her hand in his, she falsely communicates romantic feelings for him. So she forces herself to think about other things, such as the delightful atmosphere. In this way she refuses to own up to her real convictions. She disavows her action (or nonaction) by ignoring it. This constitutes her self-deception.[3]

While the first model of self-deception is somewhat speculative and problematic from a psychological standpoint, the latter two likely describe real cases of this phenomenon.[4] People do deceive themselves through motivated irrationality and bad faith. We all are biased in our assessments of situations, other people, and especially ourselves. For the most part, we're inclined to believe the best about ourselves and are endlessly self-forgiving. We're much quicker, though, to condemn others and refuse to sympathize. From a Christian perspective, the explanation for these biases is that each of us has a sinful nature that inclines us toward selfishness. So it seems that the key to avoiding motivated irrationality and bad faith must begin with our basic orientation toward our own moral condition.

Sartre maintained that the opposite of bad faith is authenticity, the characteristic of operating according to one's conscious choices and taking responsibility for one's life situation, regardless of its problems. From a Christian standpoint, such authenticity is most crucial in respect to our moral condition. To be specific, we must be authentic in the sense of *owning our sin*. A biblical perspective recognizes that we have all fallen with Adam, and this basic moral corruption is a real aspect of our nature. Moreover, the various vices that manifest our fallenness are not mere psychological illnesses or the result of our mistreatment by others. They are our responsibility.

Human beings are experts at bad faith, going to great lengths to avoid ad-

---

3. Jean-Paul Sartre, *Being and Nothingness*, trans. Hazel E. Barnes (New York: Washington Square Press, 1966), 96–98.

4. Among the difficulties with Freudian compartmentalism is its failure to adequately account for the unity of the self. For a fuller critical discussion of this account of self-deception, see my book, *Hypocrisy: Moral Fraud and Other Vices* (Grand Rapids: Baker, 1999), chap. 3.

mitting our guilt. Sometimes we blame others, acknowledging that someone is responsible for wrongdoing in a situation but placing the fault on someone else. As children, we avoided trouble by simply pointing at a playmate or sibling when an adult discovered the mess we made or the window we'd broken. As adults, we do the moral equivalent of this but in more sophisticated ways. When I lose my temper, for instance, I might claim that someone provoked me, or when I cheat on my taxes, that the government doesn't deserve my money. Recently, I heard of a Christian minister who'd become involved in an adulterous affair and blamed God for not taking away his feelings of affection for his mistress. Such is an extreme, although tragically real, example of bad faith by blame.

When blame is not an option, we may deflect responsibility through rationalization, explaining away some sin by the circumstances surrounding our action. We've all been guilty of saying, "If you were in my position you would've done the same thing," even when the thing we did was obviously wrong. What makes rationalization so handy, and so tempting, is that it's easy to identify causes for our actions, and causes can be very easily manipulated into excuses. It's true that we're all influenced by various factors in every action we perform, but these factors do not always excuse. It's also true that when placed in the same position, most people might have "done the same thing," but that doesn't exonerate a person's behavior. It perhaps helps to explain a vicious action, but it doesn't remove guilt. A person might have a predisposition to alcoholism, but that doesn't morally entitle him to get drunk every day. And those who were abused as children are no less guilty when they abuse their own children. In these instances the vices are, in a sense, more understandable, but they are no less sinful.

Finally, when blame and rationalization are not plausible options, we often resort to minimalization. While acknowledging that we are to blame in a situation, we downplay the significance of what we've done, perhaps remarking, "I didn't hurt anybody" or, if someone was harmed, "He'll get over it." This, too, is a tempting route to take in the face of accusation. We appear to admit our guilt before our accusers, but we do so in a way that preserves our pride. Minimalization is not, of course, a true admission of guilt but a crafty form of avoidance. It might be true that not reporting some forms of income on one's tax return "won't hurt anybody" or that a person will "get over" our harsh words. But such facts are morally irrelevant. These consequences don't change the fact that we're guilty of the sin of stealing or spite.

We must own our sin and avoid the bad faith temptations of blame, rationalization, and minimalization. It's just as important, however, that we also *disown our righteousness*. We must resist the temptation to see our sin as a mere occasional occurrence rather than as a state of being. Because of original sin we all suffer from an inborn tendency toward selfishness and rebellion against God. So my individual immoral actions are not deviations from some natural righteous condition that constitutes "the real me." Rather, my sins are an accurate representation of who I really am as a fallen human being. This biblical diagnosis of the human condition has often been criticized as harsh or pessimistic (such criticism has been especially strong during the last half century). But Scripture is clear that human beings have a sinful nature and that our individual sins are but a reflection of such.[5]

Why It Is So Hard to Be Sincere

So the first step toward sincerity, and the most important antidote to bad faith, is the recognition that we are not basically good but sinful. This realization will not only help us to more readily admit when we are wrong, but will also enable us to overcome our temptations to do wrong. Once we have recognized this moral truth, however, there remain some powerful psychological and cultural obstacles that we must fight against as we strive to be sincere people.

First, as psychological fact, we are selfish. Much of the time we're not vitally interested in other people's lives. And to the extent that we are interested, it's indirectly for our own sakes. Plato illustrated this fact in his famous discussion of the "Ring of Gyges." This story, told by Glaucon in Plato's *Republic,* concerns a shepherd who discovered a ring that had the power to make him invisible. He used this power to kill the king, seduce the queen, and take over the kingdom. Such a response, claims Glaucon, reflects a universal selfishness in human beings. He declares,

> Supposing now there were two such rings, the just man wearing one and the unjust man the other. No man is so unyielding that he would remain obedient to justice and keep his hands off what does not belong to him if he could steal with impunity in the very midst of the public

---

5.   See, for example, Genesis 6:5; Romans 3:23; and Galatians 5:16–21. It's ironic that the increasing skepticism about original sin follows the most cruel and bloody period in human history. If over 100 million murderous atrocities worldwide do not demonstrate a fundamental moral corruption in human beings, what can?

market itself. The same if he could enter into houses and lie with whom he chose, or if he could slay—or release from bondage—whom he would, behaving toward other men in these and all other things as if he were the equal of a god. The just man would act no differently from the unjust; both would pursue the same course.[6]

Glaucon's conclusion is that humans act justly only because of constraint. We act rightly only because we don't want to face the consequences of acting wrongly. As difficult as it might be to face this fact, consider how you would act if you possessed the Ring of Gyges. Would you act differently, from a moral standpoint, than you do now? What if your actions were invisible even to God? I have yet to encounter anyone, even among my most idealistic and zealous students, who could honestly declare that, with such power, they'd behave morally. This thought experiment does not demonstrate that humans always act selfishly, but it does show that many of our actions have a selfish motive. It's this selfish tendency that we must work against as we strive for the virtue of sincerity.

A second obstacle to being sincere is insecurity. Sincerity often involves vulnerability because it requires truthfulness about our own negative traits, be they moral or otherwise. Admissions of weakness or failure can be perceived as threats to our self-worth and for this reason can make honest self-appraisals difficult. Thus, a complete moral anthropology must not emphasize human sinfulness without also emphasizing the dignity and worth of human beings. We have been created in the image of God (Gen. 1:27) and endowed with capacities that ultimately reflect the divine nature, including rationality, will, emotion, creativity, and the various aspects of personality. These facts guarantee our inestimable value, irrespective of our obvious inequalities, be they physical, mental, emotional, or socio-economic. Even our fallenness does not change our worth in God's eyes, as he acted to redeem us in Christ while we were yet sinners (Rom. 5:8). Recognizing these facts does not, of course, automatically make one feel secure. Feelings of insecurity often derive from complex experiences and years of unhealthy relationships. Accordingly, long-term counseling is sometimes required to overcome certain patterns and dynamics. But a sense of self-worth and emotional security can be gradually improved and, in the process, so can one's ability to be forthright and to take responsibility for one's choices and actions.

---

6. Plato, *The Republic*, trans. Richard W. Sterling and William C. Scott (New York: W. W. Norton, 1985), 56.

A third set of obstacles to sincerity is cultural. Popular in the U.S. are the self-image mantras of advertisers (e.g., "image is everything"). These messages not only emphasize outward appearance over inner reality, but also encourage us to be something we're not. Such an attitude, when applied to the moral realm, translates into insincerity. It's ironic that the contemporary focus on improving self-image misses the mark when it comes to personal fulfillment. What we should seek is not an improved *image* of ourselves but rather an improved *self*. The latter route will always be the least popular way because it takes more work. The way of self-image improvement is an attractive but futile shortcut that not only fails to bring the happiness it promises, but at times even leads to devastating results (e.g., anorexia, drug addiction, anxiety disorders, etc.). Improving self-image is the siren song of popular culture, and because of it millions have lost their way.

In addition to the self-image gospel of advertisers, we must contend with the self-esteem gospel of self-help gurus. The self-help culture does often recognize that a simple physical makeover will not lead us to personal fulfillment. They tell us, correctly, that what we need to change is internal. They recommend, however, that we make a psychological change (i.e., in attitude and self-perception) rather than a moral change. So this approach ultimately misses the mark too, since it ignores the biblical truth that human beings are fallen. Essentially, like the self-image gospel, the self-help approach offers a therapy that is based upon self-deception. It asks us to believe a lie about ourselves, that we are intrinsically good and that any disruption in our lives is due either to poor management skills or conditions over which we had no control. So the self-help gurus deny the basic reality of human sin and consequently practice a therapy of bad faith.

Lastly, social pressures and devices tempt us to be insincere. We manage to hide ourselves in numerous ways. We engage in learned behaviors such as the false smile we use in public places which quickly disappears after we've greeted someone or engaged in a short conversation. Various trendy fashions, such as hairstyles and clothes, enable us to "fit in" with the crowd, as do some manners of speech, such as the latest catch phrases and clichés. Even some forms of humor, such as sarcasm, may be used as a cover-up. All of these are distractions or modes of hiding our real selves, usually motivated by insecurity but sometimes also by simple laziness.

The Christian subculture is far from immune to these social devices. Some forms of insincerity are, in fact, unique to the Christian community. We have our own language and set of social practices that have little to do with true spirituality. Christians hide behind formulas (e.g., WWJD) and clichés (e.g., "hate the sin, love the sinner") that we might use to excuse us from digging too deeply into threatening areas, asking hard questions, or admitting our ignorance. Even Christian apologetics may be used as a substitute for sincerity and authentic living.

How to Become More Sincere

The way of true self-improvement is essentially moral, beginning with a reassessment of ourselves and culminating in behavioral change. The enemies of sincerity are human selfishness, insecurity, popular cultural trends, and social pressures. Thus, if we are to grow morally, we must not only be aware of these things but also intentionally counteract them in our daily lives. As noted above, the starting point is owning our sin and disowning any pretenses of righteousness. It's also essential that we deepen our self-knowledge by practicing self-assessment. To some degree, improvement in self-awareness is as simple as "putting your mind to it." A person will probably become more self-aware just by resolving to pay more attention to his motives and actions.[7] Enlisting others' assistance in one's self-assessment is also helpful. Typically, such assistance is an appropriate task for our closest friends, since they know us best and are generally those we consider most trustworthy. Lastly, crucial to growth in the virtue of sincerity is humility. One must resist the temptation to see his own case as special or as deserving greater concern than others. As already noted in a previous chapter, humility is essential for Christian moral development generally and for most of the virtues individually, including sincerity.

In conclusion, two observations should be made. First, sincerity doesn't necessarily trump kindness. Speaking or acting forthrightly is never an excuse to be rude or discourteous. Sometimes it's best not to publicly speak one's mind about a person in a given situation, even when doing so would help to explain one's actions. Declaring publicly, for instance, that someone has bad breath might provide an honest explanation for some avoidance behavior but would, nonetheless, be inappropriate. Knowing just when to speak and act in certain ways, of course, pertains to yet another moral skill, namely discretion. Sincerity must be balanced with discretion.

---

7. The common Christian practice of journaling is a popular means of gaining self-understanding. But it can backfire as a tool of moral development, since it might reinforce the youthful tendency to focus on oneself. Therefore, it should be done only with great care and attention to this risk.

Second, like all virtues, sincerity takes time to develop, the reason for which relates to human development itself. As has been seen, one can only be sincere to the extent that one knows oneself, and self-knowledge takes a long time to acquire. Perhaps this is why the most sincere people I know are at least in their thirties.

Sincerity is a prerequisite for most of the virtues, as should become clear in the chapters that follow. In this sense, then, sincerity is properly considered one of the core traits of Christian character. In whatever we do, we must be forthright. To do so is to live a truly authentic life, to sign every aspect of our lives, "Sincerely yours."

5

ACTING RIGHTLY
IN THE FACE OF DANGER

The Virtue of Courage

In February 1983, a commercial jet plunged into the Potomac River in Washington, D.C. Most of the passengers were killed instantly, but a few stunned survivors treaded water in the icy river. The temperature of the water that day was just a few degrees above freezing. An unprotected human body can last only a few minutes in such temperatures before hypothermia causes unconsciousness and eventual death.

Emergency crews quickly arrived on the scene and began airlifting survivors out of the water. Because of weight restrictions, though, only a few persons at a time could be lifted out. One man helped several women and children to safety, waiting until they had all been carried off before taking his turn. But when the helicopter returned to pick him up, he was nowhere to be found. His decision to allow the others to go before him was fatal.

Elsewhere on the river, a few survivors attempted to swim to the riverbank. One woman, within fifty feet of land, was losing consciousness even as she swam. She lost her ability to move her limbs and began to bob in the water as onlookers watched in horror. Suddenly, a man on the bank threw off his coat and dove into the river. He swam out to the woman and pulled her to safety.

Today I recall the newsreels of these heroic acts as vividly as the day I watched them. I remain inspired by those who behaved so selflessly in the face of grave danger. These persons modeled courage, doing the right thing when it threatened harm to them. Living virtuously is difficult, but among the virtues, none are more difficult than those that challenge our instinct of self-preservation.

Courage, or the virtue of acting rightly in the face of danger, is a trait seldom emphasized by Christians these days, in spite of its importance in the Christian life. Jesus regarded extreme courage—that required when laying down one's life for another—as the exemplar of love. The morally serious person is frequently called to act rightly in spite of the risks or even the certain harm to herself that her right action poses. It will be worthwhile, then, to analyze this virtue to better understand from a Christian perspective just what courage is. In doing so, different forms of courage will be explored, using some biblical narratives for guidance. A few psychological features of courage will also be discussed, and its connections to other virtues will be noted. Finally, some keys will be proposed for becoming more courageous.

Biblical Profiles in Courage

Moses was God's chosen mediator to lead Israel out of Egyptian bondage and through forty years of desert wandering on their way to Canaan, the Promised Land. On the eastern bank of the Jordan River, Moses finally died, having seen the Promised Land he would never enter. God appointed Joshua as Moses' successor to lead his people into Canaan, a land flowing with milk and honey but also teeming with warrior tribes. As they prepared to cross the Jordan, God promised Joshua, "No one will be able to stand up against you all the days of your life. As I was with Moses, so I will be with you; I will never leave you nor forsake you" (Josh. 1:5). Then God commanded Joshua, "Be strong and courageous, because you will lead these people to inherit the land I swore to their forefathers to give them" (v. 6).

Joshua's cause for fear was great. His good friend and Israel's greatest leader was dead, and now he had to lead his people into an unknown territory containing violent opponents. The Lord's promise and repeated exhortations to be courageous, however, encouraged Joshua and, through him, the whole nation of Israel. Joshua led his people into Canaan, where they conquered city after city, proving the Lord's power and faithfulness as they took the Promised Land.

Joshua did his duty in the face of danger, relying not upon himself but upon the strength of the Lord. This story provides a useful model for understanding the virtue of courage. Note that the danger was real. Moreover, fulfilling the divine command made the danger unavoidable. Real and unavoidable danger seems to be a feature of any situation calling for courage. The courageous person doesn't seek dangerous situations for vanity's sake or because of suicidal motives. She would, in fact, rather avoid the danger altogether. Still, she doesn't act on that inclination but fulfills her obligation. Courage avoids the extremes of foolhardiness and cowardice, it being the virtue that lies midway between these vices.[1]

Consider some other biblical examples of acting rightly in the midst of danger. In a time of rampant spiritual dissolution, King Asa led reform in Judah. Throughout the kingdom he removed the altars dedicated to false gods and commanded the people to worship the Lord (2 Chron. 14:2–5). Like Joshua, Asa received an encouraging word from God through the prophet Azariah, who told him, "Be strong and do not give up, for your work will be rewarded" (15:7). After this, Asa "took courage" and removed all idols from Judah and Benjamin and repaired the altar of the Lord at the temple. Such radical obedience in a land of idolaters was perilous, but Asa, nonetheless, did his duty and was rewarded. After a period of constant war and conflict, the Lord blessed Judah with twenty years of peace.

The apostles Peter and John were called upon to act courageously as well. Luke records how, after Peter's healing of a crippled beggar, they were arrested and brought before the Sanhedrin (Acts 4). They asked them, "By what power or what name did you do this?" (v. 7). Peter answered directly, "It is by the name of Jesus Christ of Nazareth, whom you crucified but whom God raised from the dead, that this man stands before you healed" (v. 10). Luke notes that the Sanhedrin were astonished at the courage of Peter and John, but they commanded them not to speak and teach in the name of Jesus. To this, Peter and John replied, "Judge for yourselves whether it is right in God's sight to obey you rather than God. For we cannot help speaking about what we have seen and heard" (vv. 19–20). After the Sanhedrin had threatened them further, the two were released, but they continued to teach in the name of Jesus.

Finally, consider Paul, the apostle who suffered more than any other because of his faith. Five times he had been flogged by the Jewish authorities, three times beaten with rods by the Romans; he had been stoned and left for dead, shipwrecked, troubled by bandits and traitors, gone hungry and thirsty, and faced numerous other difficulties (2 Cor. 11:24–27). These were dangers not only faced but realized as Paul fulfilled his apostolic duties.

Respectively, the above are cases of courage in repentance (Asa), truth telling (Peter and John), and suffering (Paul). In these and other contexts the Christian is called "to be strong and very courageous" as Joshua was commanded to be. We all will face situations where we must do what is right, even though it

---

1.   Here I follow Aristotle's general conception of this virtue. See Aristotle, *Nicomachean Ethics* 3.6–9, in *Introduction to Aristotle*, ed. Richard McKeon, trans. W. D. Ross (New York: Modern Library, 1992).

means exposing ourselves to danger or, as in Paul's case, actually experiencing extreme pain and suffering. A sobering fact about the Christian life is that none of us are promised a life free of extreme physical pain and emotional hardship. On the contrary, the Bible indicates that we should expect such problems as a result of our faith commitment.[2] What *is* promised us is God's faithfulness through it all, that he will never leave or forsake us in times of danger and difficulty. As the psalmist says, "A righteous man may have many troubles, but the Lord delivers him from them all" (Ps. 34:19). This is a guarantee that God will, at the least, preserve us into eternity. As with Job, our greatest fears might be realized (see Job 3:25), but no matter what harm befalls us, if we are obedient, we'll experience no harm to our souls.

Notice that in each of the above cases courage is simply expected (or, in Joshua's case, commanded) without any recipe for removing the fear that makes courage so difficult. Frightening situations are a fact of life, and so is the need for divine assistance in facing them. The courage required is never irrational or absurd, however, because all that we risk is our temporal condition—our physical or perhaps mental well-being. These conditions will ultimately be restored. Considered in this light, one more clearly understands Jim Elliot's famous statement: "He is no fool who gives what he cannot keep to gain what he cannot lose."[3] The Christian's real fears, then, regard only short-term loss. Moreover, when one is obedient, these potential losses are parleyed into long-term gains, eternal rewards that remove all grounds for despair. Regretting one's earthly harms sustained in service to God is like regretting the loss of money spent on a winning lottery ticket. Courage for God's sake is thus clearly a rational and even self-interested thing. But since it's difficult to maintain this eternal perspective, having courage is difficult. But to the extent one can maintain an eternal point of view, one will be able to act courageously.

Foolhardiness and Cowardice

As noted earlier, courage lies between the vicious extremes of cowardice and foolhardiness. The foolhardy person runs headlong into danger, paying too little attention to the risks she takes in undertaking some endeavor. Such persons are sometimes called daredevils, because their actions are so risky as to entice forces of evil to bring about some dreadful outcome. In contrast, extreme acts of

---

2. See, for example, James 1:2–4 and 1 Peter 1:5–7.
3. From Elisabeth Elliot's *Shadow of the Almighty: The Life and Testament of Jim Elliot* (San Francisco: Harper San Francisco, 1989), 19.

courage, in which tremendous risk is undertaken, might appear to be foolhardy due to the high degree of difficulty and the improbability of a positive outcome. The difference between foolhardiness and courage lies in whether the purpose of the action is worthwhile. If there's enough merit in the end to be achieved, however remote the odds of success, then the act might still be courageous. So walking on a ledge outside of a building for the sake of amusing the crowd ten stories below would be foolhardy. Doing so to save someone stranded during a fire would be courageous. Thus, each of the biblical narratives discussed earlier features acts of true courage rather than foolhardiness.

Cowardice is a more common vice than foolhardiness because the human instinct to avoid danger is so strong. This natural desire becomes vice, however, when it involves a shirking of duty. So how dangerous does an act need to be to justify one's refusal to take a chance? Helping an injured person is a moral duty, other things being equal. But attempting to rescue someone from a burning vehicle might be so dangerous that this duty is nullified. In the latter case, the act is no longer obligatory but is supererogatory—that is, it goes above and beyond the call of duty. Shrinking from such acts is understandable, which is why those who do them anyway are regarded as heroes.

The cowardly person shrinks even from obligatory acts involving danger. Her moral failure consists in allowing the natural fear of harm to overpower her commitment to doing the right thing. Accordingly, cowardice grows from two roots, each constituting a particular vice. Most obviously, the coward lacks self-control. She might want to do the right thing in a particular situation but is overcome by the impulse to secure her own safety. The coward is ill equipped to resist these natural urges for a higher end, such as preventing a gross injustice or saving a life. As was discussed in an earlier chapter, this failure is known generally as moral weakness, the failure to do what one knows is right. Courage, especially, calls for moral strength, because it challenges a basic human drive. Consequently, when a person is prone to moral weakness, courage will be among the first virtues to wane in that person's character.

Cowardice also reveals a lack of humility. This appears to be a strange claim, but consider the nature of humility. Among other things, humility involves seeing one's own case as no more important than anyone else's. To shrink from helping someone because it involves risk is implicitly to place more value on one's own well-being than on that of the other person. It involves seeing one's own case as more important, the very opposite of humility.[4] The coward, then,

---

4. This might explain why Benedict de Spinoza says the courageous person "can hate no one, be angry with no one, can neither envy, be indignant with nor

manifests vicious pride. She demonstrates an inappropriately high self-regard, placing her own safety ahead of that of others. The courageous person, on the other hand, maintains a properly humble self-regard and readily incurs risk for a worthy purpose.

Cowardice should not be mistaken as a merely passive vice. Its manifestations can be quite active, indeed. Because cowards are so readily overrun by fear, they're prone to overcompensate with violence, at least when they're in positions of power. According to Montaigne, cowardice is the "mother of cruelty." He writes, "What makes tyrants so bloodthirsty? It is concern for their security, and the fact that their cowardly heart furnishes them with no other means of making themselves secure than by exterminating those who can injure them."[5] The notorious reign of Saddam Hussein is a recent testament to this claim (as was his meek surrender despite bold promises that he would not go down without a fight). And hundreds of other despotic rulers down through history support the idea as well. From Emperor Nero to Fidel Castro, the most ruthless leaders really might have been cowards, unable to deal with their personal fear and insecurity.

Courage and Other Virtues

Just as cowardice and foolhardiness involve other vices, courage involves other virtues. As just noted, self-control is one key prerequisite. Another important related virtue is patience, which is required when doing one's duty through long-term painful circumstances. Nelson Mandela is a striking contemporary portrait in courage. A leading opponent of South African apartheid during the 1950s and early 1960s, Mandela was arrested in 1962. He was imprisoned and remained there for twenty-seven years before his release in 1989. His courage in continuing leadership of the antiapartheid movement in his country was only possible because of his patience—a willingness to endure extreme discomfort without making it his focus. Mandela instead directed his energy toward ending South African racial injustice and helping others in their struggle against oppression. Mandela also exhibited a rare form of humility, another virtue essential for outstanding displays of courage. Mandela saw himself as a player within a drama much bigger than himself. He humbly elected to serve a cause rather than use

---

despise anybody, and can least of all be proud." *Ethics,* ed. James Gutmann (New York: Hafner, 1949), 241.

5. Michel de Montaigne, *The Complete Essays of Montaigne,* trans. Donald M. Frame (Stanford: Stanford University Press, 1948), 528.

that cause for his own advance. He did so consistently for nearly three decades of imprisonment, which is what makes his story so compelling.

Every instance of courage is also a display of humility precisely because the willingness to face danger requires that a person submit herself to some higher end. Mandela did this. So did Rosa Parks when she opposed similar racial injustice in America in 1955, refusing to give up her bus seat to a white man. The American soldiers who landed at the beaches of Normandy on D-Day during World War II did the same. So did the man who leapt into the freezing waters of the Potomac to save the drowning air crash victim in 1983. And so did Joshua, Asa, Peter, John, and Paul. These and other courageous characters are also profiles in humility. They willingly submitted themselves to causes or persons, even to the point of endangering themselves.

Finally, courage often calls for faith. This is because the dangerous circumstances in which one finds oneself are typically not under one's control. Whether attempting a rescue on a slippery mountain pass or standing up against an immoral practice by an employer, one risks great loss and cannot rely entirely on oneself for success. The trust necessary for action, then, must transcend the situation, including the physical elements and even the human beings involved. History is filled with stories of people whose bravery was essentially an exercise in faith. Having run up against the limits of their own skills and resources they could do nothing else but turn to God in total trust. Mary, mother of Jesus, marvelously exemplified this. Upon hearing the angel's report of her impregnation by the Holy Spirit, she simply declared, "May it be to me as you have said" (Luke 1:38). She trusted the Lord would protect her through whatever scandal might ensue. Martin Luther courageously refused to recant at the Imperial Diet of Worms, knowing that his refusal placed his life at risk. He trusted God would preserve him, for no one else could control the hearts and minds of those opposing him.

Some Psychological Features of Courage

Courage consists not only of moral dimensions but also features unique psychological elements.

Courage Is Contagious

In sports there is something we call momentum, a psychological dynamic that transcends rational understanding of the game situation. To some degree, courage works the same way. When we see or learn of another person's courageous feats, we are inspired. We might even resolve to be the same kind of person, if possible. To the extent that their examples effectively motivate us to be courageous, we have caught the courage contagion, so to speak. Models are not, of course, sufficient by themselves to enable a person to become courageous, but they might be a necessary element in developing courage. Surely Joshua was deeply affected by the courage he observed in Moses. Those serving under Joshua took heart and pressed forward in battle because of his courage. Rosa Parks also inspired masses of people to act courageously. Thus, to an extent, the courage of these people proved contagious.

Courage, though, ought not to be thought of as primarily an emotion. Passion can be useful, but only in service of wise commitments. Still, a proper perspective of the significance of one's commitments sometimes requires the sort of inspiring reminder a courageous act provides. To see another person's eternal perspective put into action enables us to reorient accordingly our own perspectives. For this reason, courage is perhaps less effectively argued for than modeled. There's no better moral teacher than a life well lived, especially when it comes to the virtue of courage.

Courage Is As Courage Does

I have a friend whose uncle Bob inadvertently became a war hero. While serving in Europe in World War II, Bob naïvely volunteered to run through enemy fire to carry a message to some fellow troops. The fire was so heavy, he was advised to stop, for his own safety, at various shelters to catch his breath and wait for the gunfire to die down before running again. But once he took off, he didn't stop sprinting until he reached his destination and successfully delivered the message. His actions so impressed his fellow soldiers that they regarded him as a hero. Bob's explanation was, however, somewhat self-effacing. "My shoes were oversized," he said, "and it was so hard to get moving that once I started I didn't want to stop." Bob's story shows that courage does not require feelings or self-perceptions of bravery, but only an eagerness to do what's right. Then, as the situation unfolds, courage is the result. Heroes are not those who seek heroism, but those who just do the right thing in adverse circumstances.

I recall attempts on the part of the news media to make a public celebrity out of the man who rescued the woman in the Potomac River in 1983. During one morning news show the anchorperson was rebuffed by the rescuer's unwillingness to be considered a hero. Such is typically the case with genuine heroes. They can take or leave celebrity status, finding the attention inappropriate and a nuisance. Those who seek attention usually are not the type who can act so courageously, and for a simple reason: they're self-focused, more interested in their own reputations than in the well-being of others. Courage, in contrast, involves self-denial, putting others' interests before one's own. A courageous person doesn't seek the limelight, although the limelight might seek her.

Courage Is Consistent with Fear and Sorrow

Because the courageous person is self-concerned—although not self-centered—fear of possible sorrow over real loss is appropriate. The courageous person does not take danger lightly. Otherwise, she'd be foolhardy. Jesus was so frightened and sorrowful in the garden shortly before his arrest that he sweated blood. His fear must have been compounded because he recognized that his fate could not be circumvented. He knew the outcome in advance. So it was not merely the danger of harm that distressed him; it was the certainty of it. Such anticipation is the source of a terror perhaps unparalleled in human experience. In his book *The Idiot*, Dostoevsky—through the central character, Myshkin—recounts the mental torture of preparing for execution. When Dostoevsky was a young man, he and several of his friends were arrested and convicted for an antigovernment conspiracy. They were subsequently sentenced to die. Led before the firing squad, blindfolded, the young men knew that the order to fire was imminent. Suddenly it was announced that they were not to be executed after all, but sent to Siberia. Dostoevsky described the terror as unbearable, particularly because his fate (he thought) was certain. When we consider that Jesus' execution (a much more excruciating and humiliating one than Dostoevsky faced) was certain, then we'll appreciate his courage all the more.[6]

What distinguishes the courageous person is her capacity both to control her feelings and to put them into proper perspective relative to the good that she's trying to achieve. Josef Pieper writes, "That man alone is brave who cannot be forced, through fear of transitory and lesser evils, to give up the greater and actual good, and thereby bring upon himself that which is ultimately and absolutely dreadful."[7] Courage, then, demands not only self-control but also a resolute sense of what is truly valuable.

---

6. Andre Comte-Sponville writes, "The true hero is the person who is able to face not just risks, which are ever-present, but also the certainty of death." *A Small Treatise on the Great Virtues,* trans. Catherine Temerson (New York: Henry Holt, 1996), 56–57. He is right about this, and Jesus was a true hero.

7. Josef Pieper, *The Four Cardinal Virtues* (Notre Dame: University of Notre Dame Press, 1966), 127.

Keys to Becoming Courageous

As with all of the virtues, there's no easy recipe for courage. But based on the preceding discussion, the following may be regarded as keys to becoming courageous. For one thing, maintaining an eternal perspective is essential. This world is not our ultimate home, nor does it contain our ultimate possessions. We are prone to forget this, and so we mistakenly value the things that perish as having everlasting worth. What has final value is eternal—God and his reputation, human souls, and the traits that human souls develop. This seems to be Jesus' point when he says, "Do not be afraid of those who kill the body but cannot kill the soul. Rather, be afraid of the One who can destroy both soul and body in hell" (Matt. 10:28).

Self-denial, too, is essential. To be courageous, one must deny oneself, at least from a temporal perspective. As was discussed in the chapter on self-control, self-denial is a skill and, therefore, a matter of active, intentional practice. Sacrifice yourself in the little things now, and you'll be prepared to sacrifice yourself in some big way later. Models of courage begin with small steps toward heroism. Smaller patterns of self-denial culminate in a lifetime of virtues of all kinds, and courage in particular.

Be committed to principle. A duty-first mentality is crucial for growth in courage, fostering a disciplined mind prepared for acting rightly in a dangerous context. A passions-first mentality, on the other hand, fosters an inclination to take the safest route, the nearest path away from danger. Such is the first step toward cowardice and other shameful forms of moral compromise.

Exercise wisdom in dangerous situations. As noted earlier, we ought not to seek out or create circumstances of danger. Daredevils are so called for a reason. They needlessly endanger themselves for some insignificant end, such as entertainment or personal satisfaction. Such are not noble purposes. Morally significant dangerous situations, in contrast, crucially involve the well-being of another person or an entire community. Courage demands the wisdom to know not only what actions are morally recommended but also which risks are worth taking relative to the benefits involved.

Conclusion

The moral life is not easy. Nowhere is this more apparent than when one considers the virtue of courage, which requires a complex of other moral virtues and good judgment besides. We can be thankful that plenty of historical figures, biblical and otherwise, provide vivid models of courage whom we may strive to emulate. May we ally their inspiration with the faith God gives us so we'll be prepared to act rightly in the face of danger.

6

BEING CONSIDERATE

The Virtue of Kindness

Mark Twain reportedly said, "Kindness is a language which the deaf can hear and the blind can read." His remark is a testament to the power of kindness which we all admire in people and would like to practice more consistently. But as universally appreciated as this trait is, it's not easy to define. Kindness is a general term that refers to a cluster of more specific moral skills, each of which essentially involves a special thoughtfulness displayed toward someone. In discussing what it means to be kind, then, this chapter explores some of these particular moral skills. In addition, ways to develop one's own capacity for acting kindly will be proposed.

Examples of Kindness

What sorts of acts are typically regarded as kind? A person who tenderly cares for children or animals would be described as kind. So would the person who warmly greets a stranger or who shows genuine interest during casual conversation. The person who opens doors for others or who is careful not to interrupt while others are talking also is kind. These are all rather ordinary, but no less commendable, instances of kindness observable in daily life. The characteristic these instances all have in common is that they involve thoughtfulness or considerate behavior. Kindness, then, is a demonstration of concern for others. To be kind is to be considerate, mindful of another's well-being. But exactly why is kindness a virtue?

The great American theologian and philosopher Jonathan Edwards conceived of virtue as moral beauty, a kind of symmetry or proportion displayed in one's life. For Edwards, to be morally beautiful, or virtuous, is to maintain a benevolent regard for all beings, because everything that exists is created and owned by God. It is only morally proper, then, that we think, speak, and behave in ways that show respect toward everything around us. And the more excellent a thing is, the greater respect it is due.

Edwards' analysis seems sound. Virtue is, as he puts it, "Benevolence to be-ing."[1] So to be kind is virtuous because kindness displays benevolence toward being, most importantly beings made in the image of God. This is, however, a general answer to a general question, and it leads to the further question, "What forms does kindness take?"

While an exhaustive list of the categories of kindness will not be offered here, three principle forms will be discussed: gentleness, friendliness, and courteous-ness. Each of these traits is typically regarded as a distinct virtue, but they are united under the general heading of kindness because they all demonstrate thoughtful regard for the well-being of others.

Gentleness

Gentleness is a disposition to behave tenderly toward others. The gentle person strikes the middle ground between obsequiousness and gruffness.[2] He is neither spineless nor insensitive to the needs of others. Jesus exhibits (and testifies to his having) this virtue when he says, "Come to me, all you who are weary and burdened, and I will give you rest. Take my yoke upon you and learn from me, for I am gentle and humble in heart, and you will find rest for your souls. For my yoke is easy and my burden is light" (Matt. 11:28–30).[3] These remarks are especially impressive considering the power at Jesus' disposal. His gentleness—like all gentleness—is not the result of impotence or servility. It is power in restraint. In the words of Andre Comte-Sponville, "Gentleness is strength in a state of peace, serene and . . . full of patience and leniency."[4]

---

1. Jonathan Edwards, *A Dissertation on the Nature of True Virtue*, in *The Works of Jonathan Edwards* (Edinburgh: Banner of Truth Trust, 1974), 1:122. Edwards' more complete definition is as follows: "True virtue most essentially consists in benevolence to being in general. Or perhaps, to speak more accurately, it is that consent, propensity, and union of heart to being in general, which is immedi-ately exercised in a general good will."
2. Aristotle's discussion of the virtue of "good temper" falls along these lines. See *Nicomachean Ethics* 4.5, in *The Basic Works of Aristotle*, ed. Richard McKeon (New York: Random, 1941), 995–96.
3. In Galatians 5:23, Paul also recognizes this virtue in his list of the fruit of the Spirit.
4. Andre Comte-Sponville, *A Small Treatise on the Great Virtues*, trans. Catherine Temerson (New York: Henry Holt, 1996), 186.

Although we greatly appreciate gentleness in others, most of us do not work hard to develop the trait ourselves. Consequently, we fall into patterns of harshness, the antithesis of gentleness, which are subtle enough to escape detection by us when doing moral inventory. We're harsh in our attitude when, for example, we display pessimism. To be pessimistic is to look on the dark side first, to expect the worst of people and situations, and to dismiss redemptive possibilities. The cynic is also harsh. He eagerly attributes selfish or sinister motives to others and in doing so reveals his own bitter spirit.

Patterns of harshness also emerge in conversation, particularly in the form of sarcasm and destructive criticism. Sarcasm is an indirect verbal attack used by those who would rather not be forthright. This is a convenient offensive weapon because usually it's not recognized as such. When someone is praised for some good quality, one can simply snicker and say, "Yeah, right," registering disagreement but not so as to invite a reply. The sarcastic joker appears to play peacefully when actually he makes war. The critical person, too, speaks harshly, openly tearing down others in the attempt to make himself look better. But the payoff is brief and ultimately counterproductive. Although he feels a temporary sense of superiority, his critical spirit displays his weakness. He looks worse, not better, than his target of attack.

Open violence is the clearest form of harshness. Although Christians usually don't consider themselves to be participants in violence, this might be due more to a narrowness of moral vision than to a truly peace-seeking life. One need not directly injure other persons or damage their property to be guilty of violence. Unnecessary violence toward animals or other parts of nature are also instances of this vice. Since all of creation is God's and therefore owned and valued by him, we affront God when we unnecessarily harm an animal, destroy vegetation, or pollute the environment. Such acts sometimes are justifiable, of course, but they do need strong justification. The burden of proof is upon *us* to show that taking this animal's life or damaging that ecosystem is justified. When we destroy parts of nature, we must note that it's God's creation we're acting upon. As the Lord says, "Every animal of the forest is mine, and the cattle on a thousand hills. I know every bird in the mountains, and the creatures of the field are mine" (Ps. 50:10–11).

So the gentle person avoids harshness, cynicism, or violence, and is instead hopeful, forthright, and peaceful. To be hopeful is not necessarily to expect the best possible outcome in any given situation, but it is to think and behave in a way that maximizes the chances for a good outcome. Hope envisions and works for a worthy end, recognizing whatever obstacles may emerge and developing strategies to overcome them. Hope is the gentle, rather than the harsh, approach to life.

To be forthright is to be direct and honest. When disagreeing with someone or disapproving another's behavior, the gentle person either says nothing or speaks directly to that person about the matter. He doesn't take the halfway approach of sarcasm or resort to gossipy complaints, but addresses the matter in an honest and straightforward way. Such is the gentle approach to conflict.

The peaceful person promotes life and harmony among people and between humans, animals, and the rest of creation. Although not necessarily a pacifist, he opposes violence even in its subtler forms and eagerly seeks ways to bring about harmonious resolutions to conflicts. Such is the gentle way of life.

Friendliness

Another form of kindness is friendliness, the attribute of being favorably disposed toward others, particularly strangers. We are exhorted to be friendly by the writer of Hebrews when he says, "Do not forget to entertain strangers, for by so doing some people have entertained angels without knowing it" (Heb. 13:2). Friendliness is also commended by Jesus, when he says to one of the Pharisees, "When you give a luncheon or dinner, do not invite your friends, your brothers or relatives, or your rich neighbors; if you do, they may invite you back and so you will be repaid. But when you give a banquet, invite the poor, the crippled, the lame, the blind, and you will be blessed" (Luke 14:12–14).

Like gentleness, friendliness is a quality we admire in others but which we do not always make a point of displaying ourselves. In our culture, it sometimes really takes work to be friendly. Suspicion toward strangers seems increasingly common. This suspicion derives from at least three cultural tendencies that militate against friendliness. One of these is growing violence in public places. We regularly hear reports of some random shooting or gross injustice, then we follow the stories of the sad aftermath for the victims or family members as they grieve their loss. We know that we could be the next victim, and this makes us wary. Public trust has been displaced by fear and suspicion. Such a mindset naturally leads to a presumption of distrust of our neighbors, making a favorable disposition toward strangers difficult.

Second, our culture's mobility contributes to increasing public alienation. We are a transient society, always on the move, whether it be our long commutes to work or in our jobs themselves, as we relocate every few years to take new positions on the corporate ladder. But even as we improve ourselves professionally, we damage ourselves socially and culturally. We lose our sense of public connectedness, the feeling—or even the fact—of belonging to a particular community with a distinct and stable identity. Consequently, our sense of community responsibility is also forfeited. People are naturally more inclined to reach out to those with whom they have common history or some other bond of unity, the most significant of these being religious, political, ethnic, and even geographic. We are less inclined to be favorably disposed to our neighbors, because we are less sure of who our neighbors are.

Thirdly, and more insidiously, those who would be friendly are handicapped by the culture-wars mindset. Because of rampant media attention to sharply divergent segments of society and the disproportional attention to the extremes within different social groups (e.g., liberals vs. conservatives, the religious vs. the secularists) we feel less identity with others. This exacerbates our sense of public alienation and disconnectedness. It might even foster a sense of enmity and defensiveness, feeding the warrior mentality as the "culture wars" metaphor suggests. Mass media encourage us to focus on our differences because stories about conflict, especially between those on the extremes, are more dramatic and interesting (and therefore more profitable). Consequently, we forget that we have unity simply because we're fellow human beings. We allow ourselves to see our differences as primary, rather than as secondary. Yes, we differ over religion and politics, even over very fundamental moral issues such as abortion and gay marriage. But even these differences do not justify the public animosity that is so prevalent today in our culture. Our shared humanity should be enough to favorably dispose us toward our neighbors, however different from us they might be.

Courteousness

Another form of kindness is courteousness—a trait often equated with politeness—which is the exercise of good manners. A polite person observes codes of public conduct that are not intrinsically moral (such as table manners and theater etiquette). Politeness is important because it makes us agreeable to others and helps to preserve social order by functioning as an endorsement of virtue.[5] Even when someone is "faking it" in displaying good manners, he pays respect to these standards, and this itself has moral and social value. It's true, as

---

5.   On these points, see Sarah Buss, "Appearing Respectful: The Moral Significance of Manners," *Ethics* 109 (July 1999): 795–826.

Judith Martin says, that "manners involve the appearance of things, rather than the total reality,"[6] but appearances can have significant social impact.

It's reasonable to expect people to maintain good manners. It could be said that politeness is minimally decent behavior, a kind of social respect that we owe to one another. Some forms of courtesy, of course, go beyond the obligatory into the realm of the supererogatory (i.e., above and beyond the call of duty). We might distinguish between "common" courtesy, which all of us are expected to display, and "special" courtesy, which is desirable but not expected. A person at the front of a long line who gives up his spot to someone else shows special courtesy, as does the person who stops along the roadside to help a motorist change a tire.

An excellent New Testament example of special courteousness is found in Matthew 27, subsequent to Jesus' death on the cross. Matthew records how Joseph of Arimathea approached Pilate for the body of Jesus. Pilate consented, after which "Joseph took the body, wrapped it in a clean linen cloth, and placed it in his own new tomb that he had cut out of the rock" (vv. 59–60). This was an act of supererogatory kindness on Joseph's part. He didn't have to provide his own tomb for the storage of Jesus' body, but Joseph did so. Special acts of courtesy are properly so-called because they require an extra measure of consideration for, and attention to, someone's needs. The especially courteous person does not merely respond affirmatively to a request made by a needy person. On the contrary, such gestures are usually significant enough that the person in need would not have made such a request in the first place. So special courtesy may be described as "a preemptive response to a bold request." Certainly it's a bold request to ask someone to give up his spot at the front of a long line. The especially courteous person does so without being asked. For this reason, special courtesy crosses over into the virtue of generosity, the moral skill of freely giving to others.

As with the other forms of kindness, courteousness seems less common these days. Often one hears elderly people bemoan the fact that people are not as polite or well-mannered as they used to be. These complaints can be seen as quaint, but if kindness is a bona fide virtue, then its decline in public life is a serious concern. As one seeks to explain why our culture is less courteous, several social trends come to mind. One such trend is our busyness. Courtesy takes time and is inefficient, at least as far as the discourteous person is concerned. And in a culture that stresses the bottom line and the achievement of tangible goals, polite gestures are bound to go by the wayside.

Another factor in the decline of courtesy is the informalization of public life.

---

6.   Judith Martin, *Miss Manners' Guide to Excruciatingly Correct Behavior* (New York: Warner, 1983), 13.

The past few decades have seen a slow erosion of the sense of what is personal and private. Whether on television talk shows or in other public forums, people now willingly share aspects of their lives that previous generations would have called unseemly. Even the most sordid of personal habits are now, in fact, paraded as matters of casual entertainment. What once was shamefully private is now gleefully public. A predictable consequence of this is a corresponding drop in public behavioral expectations. The shame parade has eroded our sense of decency, and without a clear sense of what is publicly decent, courtesy cannot thrive. Even worse, individual acts of courteousness will seem pointless or idiotic.

A third contributing factor to the demise of courtesy is the social alienation of our transient culture described earlier. Where once Americans lived their whole lives within a community, we now move from place to place, severing social connections almost as soon as they're made. The Internet compounds the problem of alienation, as we carry on commerce, conduct business "meetings," and even participate in worship without actually coming into direct contact with another human being. Such capacities might increase efficiency, but they foster anonymity and social alienation. Consequently, what is lost is a sense of who one's neighbors are, not to mention the loss of a sense of interest in, and moral accountability to, one's neighbors, all of which are necessary for basic courtesy to remain "common."

Finally, the narcissism of our culture naturally discourages courtesy. America's consumer mentality encourages us to satisfy our desires in the most impressive ways, without concern for our neighbor. We are, in fact, taught by advertisers that we are competing with others for attention and appeal, so we'd better work to get the upper hand (by purchasing their products, of course). In short, ours is a culture that encourages selfishness. From Wall Street to Hollywood, the centers of American public influence teach the same thing: "me first." This moral narcissism is obviously at odds with the virtue of courtesy, which causes the courteous person to experience some discomfort and forfeit the upper hand in order to help someone.

What It Takes to Be Kind

These different types of kindness all involve a special regard for the well-being of others. Displaying these virtues, though, can be very demanding. To treat others tenderly, to be favorably disposed toward strangers, and to be well-mannered requires that one live against the cultural grain of contemporary American life. It's all too easy to act unkindly without realizing it. The motorist does so when he cuts others off in traffic because, "After all, I'm in a big hurry, and I don't even know these people." The cashier is unkind when he sneers or rolls his eyes when asked a question he's been asked many times before. And the couple who ignore their neighbors because they are preoccupied with their own lives are also unkind. Such cases as these give us a clue as to what is required of us if we are to be kind. Kindness involves at least three prerequisites, and they in turn involve other virtues.

First, kindness demands a sense of public responsibility, what is sometimes referred to as civility. We're all members of a community, a collection of persons who are interdependent in diverse ways. This interdependence brings privileges as well as duties. The more fully we recognize that we have natural obligations to everyone around us and every stranger we meet, the better we will fulfill our duties of kindness toward them. Second, kindness requires a willingness to go slowly and wait without complaint, that is, to be patient. This is, of course, antithetical to the rapid pace of our culture. But therein lies good news: We have ample opportunity to practice patience, to intentionally slow down, to forestall the satisfaction of our own desires and thereby improve our ability to be patient. Third, in order to be kind one must take the focus away from oneself and one's own needs and desires and place others before oneself. To do so is to practice humility, which is, as has been already noted, central to the virtues.

So nurturing in yourself these virtues of civility, patience, and humility will also make you more kind. But it will help to focus on the particulars of kindness. Aim to be more gentle in various ways, to maintain a spirit that relaxes and disarms people. Strive to be less critical of others, less uptight and persnickety, less abrasive even when disagreeing with others. And resolve to show greater care and attention toward children, animals, and the rest of God's creation.

Strive to be more friendly. Initiate conversations with strangers and look for ways to make others, especially the less fortunate, feel more welcome in your life. Be willing to forsake time that you'd like to spend on your own interests. Consciously fight the emotional barriers to friendliness, such as bad moods and the fear of strangers. Sow peace and trust where others cause dissension and mistrust. And be critical of the forces of division in our culture.

Finally, commit yourself to courtesy. Act politely and be good mannered in public and in private, as is your obligation. But resolve to perform occasional supererogatory acts as well, going out of your way to help someone without expecting anything in return. Go above and beyond the call of duty, then in your kindness you will, in the words of Twain, use a language that even "the deaf can hear and the blind can read."

7

GIVING TO EACH ITS DUE

The Virtue of Justice

Today people clamor for justice in every sphere of American life, from commerce to health care to criminal law to personal relationships. But when people call for justice, what exactly are they demanding? What does it mean to say that a person or situation is just or unjust? It's popular to demand justice, but it's disturbing that many people could not define the term, much less agree with one another on its precise meaning.

This is no small problem, considering so many important human endeavors presuppose a shared concept of justice. For Christians, the concept of justice is doubly relevant, since the Bible repeatedly calls us to live just lives. Consider the "Micah Mandate" wherein the Old Testament prophet sums up our duties as follows: "He has showed you, O man, what is good. And what does the LORD require of you? To act justly and to love mercy and to walk humbly with your God" (Mic. 6:8). Justice is a basic requirement of human beings, a virtue we all must possess.

So what does it mean to be just? The following discussion will show why few people explain what they mean when using the term "justice." It will also reveal how important it is that we be able to do so. Simply too much is at stake. Not only is justice essential to our moral, social, and political well-being, but also powerful cultural forces constantly push us toward unjust patterns of thought and behavior. Understanding the basics of justice and what we can do to nurture this virtue will help us resist these forces.

The General Concept of Justice

In addition to the Micah Mandate, Scripture repeatedly emphasizes the duty to act justly. The proverb says, "To do what is right and just is more acceptable to the LORD than sacrifice" (Prov. 21:3). Isaiah declares, "The LORD is a God of justice" (Isa. 30:18). Moreover, Scripture recommends justice in dozens of particulars, including speech (Ps. 58:1), discipline (Jer. 30:11), guidance (Ezek. 34:16), decisions (Isa. 58:2), judgments (John 5:30; 1 Peter 2:23), punishment (Heb. 2:2; Luke 23:41), conduct in personal affairs (Ps. 112:5), kings (Ps. 72:1–2), rulers (Isa. 32:1), laws (Prov. 8:15), and treatment of the poor (Ex. 23:6) and aliens (Mal. 3:5).

Justice is a wide-ranging characteristic, applicable to a variety of contexts. What do all of these instances of justice have in common? The answer could be summed up in one word—*fairness.* A just person acts fairly, giving to each her proper due, all things considered. So just discipline or punishment is neither too harsh nor too lenient, just laws are neither too demanding nor too lax, just guidance and decisions give the appropriate amount of consideration to each relevant factor, and so on. Different situations call for different measures, and the just person gives fair treatment to the people and things in her care.

So understood, justice is nearly as broad a moral concept as virtue itself. The ancient Greeks certainly saw things this way. Plato, for instance, regarded justice as the ultimate aim of the moral life, and he devoted his most significant work, the *Republic,* to exploring the nature of justice. According to Plato, justice is a quality found both in individual human beings and in institutions, such as the state.[1] In either case, justice consists in every part of a thing fulfilling its natural function. So a civil society is just when the workers produce diligently, the soldiers protect effectively, and the rulers govern wisely. In a similar way, justice is present in an individual soul when each aspect of the soul—appetite, will, and reason, as Plato conceived it—performs its particular tasks. Justice, then, in Plato's view, is a virtue of virtues. It's the moral quality of a person whose soul displays other particular virtues, each doing its part for the whole. And injustice is "a kind of civil war of the [soul's] three principles . . . the revolt of one part against the whole of the soul that it may hold therein a rule which does not belong to it."[2]

---

1. According to Plato, the human soul is a microcosm of civil society. He uses the latter to guide his inquiry about the former: "If we found some larger thing that contained justice and viewed it from there, we should more easily discover its nature in the individual man. And . . . this larger thing is the city. . . . [T]he same forms and qualities are to be found in each of us that are in the state. They could not get there from any other source." *Republic,* in *The Collected Dialogues of Plato,* trans. Paul Shorey (Princeton: Princeton University Press, 1961), 676–77.
2. Ibid., 686.

For the purposes of the present discussion, a more narrow view of justice will be taken than that of Plato. Rather than seeing justice as more or less synonymous with virtue, this discussion conceives of it as resembling simple fairness, as noted above. This perspective is more in line with both common and biblical usage of the term. Taking this approach, however, doesn't completely simplify matters, as will be seen next.

The Different Senses of Justice

Aristotle regarded justice as a sort of proportionality, but he noted the ambiguity of the concept. He distinguished three major forms of justice: remedial, commercial, and distributive.[3] *Remedial* justice pertains to justice between persons, particularly when some harm has been done. When someone steals from another person, for example, it's only fair that the thief pay for her crime. Some remediation is called for, which may take the form of restitution, meaning that the culprit actually makes payment back to the victim, or retribution, where she pays for her crime by suffering punishment of some kind. Criminal justice systems are supposedly premised on this latter sense of justice. The ideal at which such systems aim is to make the punishment fit the crime, so far as that is reasonable and possible. Just what it means for a punishment to "fit" the crime can be at times difficult to determine (e.g., cases of rape, forgery, defamation of character, etc.). But this is the aim of the retributive approach, and one major application of the larger aim of justice—to pay to each her proper due.

Commercial justice regards fair exchange of any kind. Whether goods are purchased at an appropriate price or a worker is paid wages that fit the nature of the task performed, there must be reciprocity in due proportion. Suppose I purchase a lawn mower for $150. A just transaction would be one in which the lawn mower is actually worth $150. It starts easily, handles well, cuts evenly, is durable, etc. The mower might, of course, be worth the cost for some very different reasons. It might, for example, be entirely useless as a working lawn mower but have significant value as an antique. In any case, a just exchange of

---

3.   Aristotle recognized, with Plato, the general sense of justice as goodness itself, as "not a part of virtue but virtue entire." Nevertheless, he noted, "What we are investigating is the justice which is a *part* of virtue" (emphasis his). *Nicomachean Ethics* 5.1–2, in *The Basic Works of Aristotle,* ed. Richard McKeon, trans. W. D. Ross (New York: Random, 1941), 1004.

the item is one in which there is payment in proportion to the actual value of the thing.[4]

Aristotle's third category is *distributive* justice, the fair distribution of wealth and honor among citizens. Today we might define distributive justice more broadly to include services and responsibilities. However understood, "To whom should society's resources go?" is the perennial question of distributive justice. It is controversial because this question has several possible answers, each of which has been vigorously defended in some quarters. To make matters more difficult, each answer is plausible, as each uses a criterion that appeals to common sense.

One major approach to distributive justice is premised on the criterion of equality. Popularly known as egalitarianism, this view says wealth should be doled out equally among citizens, the philosophical basis being that human beings are themselves of equal value. Our physical and psychological differences are morally irrelevant; we ought not be credited or penalized for them. A person's innate intelligence and trained abilities to read, write, and do math are the result of natural gifts and educational opportunities she did not earn. And a handicapped person is not responsible for her limitations. Such factors, from a human standpoint, are quite random. Yet one's gifts or defects either help or hinder her in the workplace. Thus, the argument goes, unequal outcomes in the distribution of goods are unfair, since they allow morally irrelevant differences to determine who is wealthy and who is poor, who thrives and who suffers. The egalitarian therefore advocates a social system that corrects these natural injustices. Goods should be redistributed at least approximately equally.

Christian egalitarians point out that their view enjoys scriptural support. A biblical mandate for care of the poor is found in Proverbs 14:31: "He who oppresses the poor shows contempt for their Maker, but whoever is kind to the needy honors God." Old Testament civil law makes special provisions for the

---

4. Another school of thought prefers to make commercial justice a more subjective matter, defining a just transaction as one in which both the buyer and seller are satisfied, irrespective of the actual worth of the item purchased. As a friend of mine likes to say, "I received a fair deal if the lawn mower I bought is worth more *to me* than my hundred-and-fifty dollars. If I would rather have the mower than the money, then I got a good deal, period." Such a view is problematic, though, since it implies that any transaction is potentially just. If someone purchases a book of matches for a million dollars, for instance, then it's a fair deal if the purchaser is happy about it. Such a view strains common sense, to say the least.

less fortunate, such as is found in Leviticus 19: "When you reap the harvest of your land, do not reap to the very edges of your field or gather the gleanings of your harvest. Do not go over your vineyard a second time or pick up the grapes that have fallen. Leave them for the poor and the alien. I am the LORD your God" (vv. 9–10).[5] In the New Testament, we find the early church modeling an egalitarian approach to their personal property. Luke notes, "All the believers were together and had everything in common. Selling their possessions and goods, they gave to anyone as he had need" (Acts 2:44–45).[6]

These passages do not imply a full-fledged egalitarian system, but they do support wealth redistribution on a local basis. Christian egalitarians argue that approximately equal redistribution would be the best response to the biblical mandate to help the poor. Critics are quick to point out, however, that the Old Testament civil law does not apply to us today, since it was intended specifically for the nation of Israel. As for the apostolic church, their redistribution of wealth was strictly voluntary, not dictated by any civil authority.[7] Moreover, Luke merely describes the early Christians' life together. His narrative does not *prescribe* how Christians should act.

Nevertheless, the biblical passages above reflect a serious divine concern for the poor that Christians should reflect in their conduct. But a less extreme approach than egalitarianism is needed. Some prefer to conceive of distributive justice according to the criterion of need, that people should have access to goods and services based upon their needs. As we look closely at the above passages, we find that this, not total redistribution of wealth, is their focus. The Old Testament laws provided for the needs of the poor and aliens, but were not meant to give them wealth equal to that of all their neighbors. The Israelites were told, "Be openhanded toward your brothers and toward the poor and needy in your land" (Deut. 15:11). And in the book of Acts the believers "gave to anyone as he had *need*." Furthermore, this approach fits the ethic of Jesus, as he advised that we "give to everyone who asks" (Luke 6:30). One may assume that generally people will ask us for things that they really need.

Using the criterion of need, then, seems more consistent with the spirit of biblical teaching about the poor, but it's not without problems. How are we to understand need? Surely, basic needs (e.g., food, water, shelter, clothing, basic medical assistance) must be met. But how much beyond this ought to be con-

---

5. See also Deuteronomy 15:4–11 and Galatians 2:10.
6. See also Acts 4:32–35.
7. The early church therefore practiced a form of communitarianism rather than what is commonly known as socialism.

sidered matters of need rather than mere desire or even luxury? Is transportation, for example, a genuine need? Certainly the one billion malnourished and starving people in the world would not consider it so. How about high-tech medical resources, such as MRIs, arthroscopy, and CAT scans? Are these needs? Again, the idea is hard to defend, when billions of people worldwide do not even enjoy basic medical assistance such as immunizations and antibiotics. These facts provide perspective on the popular claim in our country that there is a basic right to even sophisticated medical resources.

Notwithstanding these complications, there does seem to be a biblical duty to help the poor and address their basic needs. That is, Christians have an obligation to contribute to efforts to feed the hungry, house the homeless, and provide clothing and basic medical care for those who have such needs. Presumably, the proximity to us of the needy is irrelevant. Scripture teaches that all human beings are our brothers and sisters. So the fact that a starving child is five thousand miles away in no way diminishes our duty to help. This should give us pause as we consider the amount of money we spend each year on entertainment and other luxuries, money that might have been used literally to save lives. Such talk, of course, makes us uncomfortable. None of us want to admit that we're potentially conspirators to the problem of world hunger, that our laziness and inattention costs lives.

A third approach to distributive justice uses the criterion of desert. A just distribution of wealth, in this view, is one in which each individual obtains what she deserves. A person might be thought to deserve goods and services, for instance, because of her contributions to society. Nearly every major profession can be understood as a means of contributing to the social good: Physicians heal the sick, carpenters build homes, artists create beautiful objects, teachers educate, etc. These and hundreds of other tasks improve society and enrich individual lives in some way. Consequently, those who perform them deserve payment. Moreover, it is argued, they have the right to use their wages as they see fit.

Understanding desert in terms of actual contribution to society might be too strict, however, since some persons' work might provide little quantifiable societal benefit but still be thought worthy of financial reward. The purely theoretical research of some scholars, for example, might have little practical application. (This is true in some areas of the humanities and sciences.) Yet we generally regard such research as deserving of reward. Such is a looser application of the concept of desert, appealing to achievement rather than contribution.[8] In either

---

8.   For such a reason, athletes might be deemed worthy of a high wage for their accomplishments. How significant are the societal benefits of someone pitching

case, whether one appeals to achievement or contribution to society, the desert approach defines a just distribution of goods as a situation in which each person receives what she earns.

Biblical defenders of this view point to the plain words of Jesus that a "worker deserves his wages" (Luke 10:7). Paul assumes as much when he argues that ministers of the gospel, like other workers, ought to be paid for the services they provide (1 Cor. 9:7–12). The concept of desert also helps to make sense of the biblical work mandate, expressed in Paul's counsel to the Thessalonians to "keep away from every brother who is idle and does not live according to the teaching you received from us" (2 Thess. 3:6). He then reminds them that "when we were with you, we gave you this rule: 'If a man will not work, he shall not eat'" (v. 10).[9]

Granting the biblical significance of considerations of desert, problems nonetheless arise when defining distributive justice entirely by this criterion. First of all, Scripture places moral limits on personal gain. The Israelites were commanded, for example, not to charge interest when lending money (Exod. 22:25; Lev. 25:35–37). Secondly, and most importantly, the biblical duty to the poor precludes our using all our income, however well deserved, for our own purposes. Clearly, Christians who have no outstanding basic needs are required to give to those who do.

So where does this leave us? Which, if any, among the three perspectives on distributive justice is, from a Christian standpoint, the correct one? A look at history shows that no one of them has been successful by itself. This is certainly true of the criteria of equality and need. Marxism is a vivid example of a politico-economic philosophy that takes these principles to their logical conclusion. "From each according to his ability to each according to his need," is the Marxist motto.[10] Much of the devastation of the twentieth century is a tragic tribute to the failure of this maxim as a standard for social justice. What Marx did not recognize, and what all egalitarian systems overlook, is that socialism works only in a morally perfect world. Human beings are, however, morally crooked. Our selfishness naturally leads us to be lazy rather than productive

---

a no-hitter or winning a major golf tournament? Probably very little. The value attached to them is, in fact, contrived, invented like the games themselves. But since these are significant achievements within the worlds of these sports, we tend to believe they deserve financial reward. Just how much reward they deserve is, of course, another matter entirely.

9.   See also 1 Thessalonians 4:11–12.

10.   Karl Marx, *Marx and Engels on Religion* (Amsterdam: Fredonia Books, 2002), 203.

workers if we know the fruit of our labor will be redistributed evenly. Consequently, socialist philosophies like Marxism lead not to universal thriving but social stagnation and, ultimately, further oppression of the very people they aim to help.

Applying the criterion of desert in isolation from considerations of need, however, is no more promising. Historical cases of this approach have proven to be as ruthless as socialism. Adam Smith, the father of modern capitalism, proposed that individuals buying and selling in a self-interested manner would lead to economic efficiency and the meeting of basic needs throughout society. Social justice would be ensured by an "invisible hand," where individuals pursuing their private interests benefit the whole society. Less is more when it comes to economic policy, according to Smith. Leave the market alone, and society will thrive. Like socialism, however, free market capitalism only works so well on paper. In the actual world, such *laissez faire* systems result in appalling social inequities. The upper economic stratum of society enjoys millions of dollars of wealth, while the lower stratum is homeless, hungry, and unhealthy. Smith's "invisible hand," it seems, is not entirely reliable. One need only walk the streets of any major U.S. city to see the disparity between economic classes, and ours is not a pure capitalism but a somewhat guided market.

The reasons for the failure of pure capitalism are plain. First, it takes money to make money. The poor lack sufficient capital to improve their lot, while the rich have abundant capital to invest and gain yet more wealth. Second, the wealth of the rich does not "trickle down" all the way to the poorest segments of society, nor does it trickle evenly. The real socio-economic world is just too messy and cruel to be left alone. Pure capitalism, again like socialism, fails to adequately account for the flaws in human nature. While it ingeniously exploits human selfishness and greed (and to this extent is an improvement on socialism), a totally free market does not provide a buffer against these aspects of our nature. Guidance, therefore, is necessary to ensure social justice for the lower classes.

It seems, then, that criteria of desert and need are both essential for distributive justice in society. There must be rewards for the contributions of hard workers, but the basic needs of all citizens must be met. The vices of laziness and greed alike must be combated in any civil society if it is to thrive. Attention to the criterion of desert will ward off the former vice, while heeding the criterion of need will discourage the latter vice. No economic or political philosophy, of course, can bring moral reform or ensure perfect distributive justice. Nevertheless, some systems are better than others, and we must all do our part in promoting those laws and policies that are most just. In the U.S., there's little danger of failing to emphasize the criterion of desert. We probably overemphasize it, such that we fail to address the needs of others, ignoring unfair social and economic conditions. The plight of millions of Americans (not to mention one billion people worldwide) is a testament to this fact.

So the Christian must keep in mind that she cannot hide behind a *laissez faire* economic policy any more than she can opt for socialism. Nor can the biblical duty to the poor and oppressed be ignored. Civil society is tremendously complex, however, and the political, social, and economic issues involved are seemingly endless. Perhaps, though, a balanced approach will help us deal with the issues we encounter in our daily lives: A Christian perspective on distributive justice will work within a basic framework in which we consider both desert and need, as both criteria are biblically founded. The difficulty, of course, is to work this out in actual practice.

The complexity of the preceding discussion reveals the foolishness of simply clamoring for justice without clarifying what one means by the term. Because the term is so ambiguous, to speak generally of justice may only confuse matters. As explained, the term *justice* has to do with fairness, giving to each her due. We've seen a variety of ways in which this might be understood. A balanced approach to the difficult issue of distributive justice has been proposed, an approach that seeks to be sensitive to considerations of both desert and need. Moving from the societal to the personal level, we may conclude that each of us should strive to be fair in these ways to our individual neighbors. This means giving to people what they deserve and what they need.

Each of the major categories of justice discussed above has, too, its personal equivalent. When we pay what we owe when making a purchase, we act justly in the commercial sense. When we discipline our children for misbehaving, we act justly in the remedial sense. When we reward our children for some accomplishment, we exhibit distributive justice, according to the criterion of desert. And when we sponsor a child through a world hunger relief organization, we exhibit distributive justice by the criterion of need. In these and many other routine ways, we act justly in our personal lives.

Favoritism and Other Forms of Injustice

As Christians seeking fairness in a harsh world, we must be alert to ways in which we may be drawn unknowingly into patterns of injustice. One major category of injustice is favoritism, a circumstance that the Bible strongly cautions against. Paul tells Timothy to carry out his instructions impartially and "to do nothing out of favoritism" (1 Tim. 5:21). James rebukes those who give special attention to the rich, saying, "If you show favoritism, you sin and are convicted by the law as lawbreakers" (James 2:9).[11]

The problem of favoritism is a timeless one. By nature we tend to favor the wealthy and attractive. They represent power and prestige and, by their very presence, make *us* feel important. Even unthinkingly we can find ourselves going out of our way for them, while passing over those less fortunate. The fact that we can slip unintentionally into favoritism is what makes it so insidious. Thus we must actively war against this social inertia. The old saying "out of sight, out of mind" describes a sad truth about the human condition: We can easily forget the plight of the poor because of their remoteness from us, especially those in other countries. Our inattention to the unattractive is ensured by the fact that we simply find the physically beautiful more pleasant to look at. In both cases, continual self-reminders are necessary to resist slipping into favoritism.

Our culture incessantly reinforces the idealization of wealth and physical beauty, through advertisements, television programs, and pop music. These forces of popular culture condition us to think success consists in being rich and beautiful or at least in hanging out with such people. Even Christians, who supposedly believe that only internal and moral qualities really matter, often fall into the trap of placing inordinate value upon possessions and outward appearance. When these become the primary life values of these people, they actually have shifted worldviews. It's no wonder, then, that Western culture is experiencing such moral demise. If even the couriers of biblical values are trading true virtue for superficiality, then the slide to paganism will be sure and swift.

Why is it wrong to show favoritism? First, favoritism flouts the equal inherent worth possessed by all people due to our having been created in God's image. When I'm partial to a wealthy person, I treat others as if they're beings of lesser value and declare by my actions that they're not equally divine image bearers. Consequently, favoritism mocks God himself by subverting the value structure he has instituted. Second, favoritism harms those we favor by reinforcing the false notion that it *is* the external features—possessions and physical appearance—that are most worthwhile about them. It positively reinforces their reliance upon things that have essentially nothing to do with who they really are as persons. Why should they strive to be more virtuous when their money or beauty get them all the attention they want? So our partiality has the

---

11.   See also Leviticus 19:15 and Malachi 2:9.

effect of discouraging them from developing their own character traits. In short, when we favor people, we morally handicap them. Perhaps this explains why wealth is such a spiritual snare, as Jesus indicates: "It is hard for a rich man to enter the kingdom of heaven" (Matt. 19:23). Third, favoritism harms those whom we disfavor. Our partiality communicates to them that they are less valuable than those we dote upon. And, as with the favored, it undermines morality in the eyes of the disfavored: Why bother with moral improvement when wealth and beauty, rather than qualities of character, are most richly rewarded? So favoritism is wrong for several reasons. It harms the favored and disfavored alike, it undermines morality, and it affronts God himself. No wonder Scripture so strongly condemns it.

Another pervasive injustice in Western culture consists in honoring trivial pursuits more than significant ones. We prize the work of entertainers and athletes, not only economically but also by exalting them as role models. Even by the criterion of desert, the wealth of some of these people is scandalous. Can any reasonable person argue that an entertainer or an athlete deserves millions of dollars because of what she contributes in playing a role in a movie or in the effort she exerts in playing a sport? The idea is absurd. More significantly, the honor we as a culture bestow upon those who excel at these activities is grossly out of proportion to their inherent, and even instrumental, value. Physicians, fire fighters, educators, and research scientists surely deserve more recognition and praise, if not financial reward, for their contributions to society. Yet entertainers and athletes dominate the minds of Americans and for doing much less inherently significant things.[12] "Celebrity" has been defined as someone who is famous for being famous. This definition not only applies to America's most well-known athletes and entertainers but also reveals the inherent injustice in our cultural "star" system.

Athletes benefit society, George Will once said, by providing us with clear examples of excellence. It's unfortunate that the vast majority of Americans and most athletes themselves don't view sports with such moral keenness. The "winning is everything" mentality is dominant in our culture. But consider the absurdity of this attitude (and I say this as a serious amateur athlete myself). If you're not playing for a reward (e.g., a trophy, cash prize, dinner), then you're really just playing for the right to say you won. What value does that have? It can have no value beyond pride itself. The old dictum, "It's not whether you win or

---

12.   It's sad that some of the most popular athletes and entertainers today not only fail to do inherently significant things but, in fact, do demonstrable harm to society by the poor examples they set.

lose but how you play the game," though very much in line with biblical values, is implicitly rejected these days, even by some Christian athletes. While it's true that winning is often the result of pursuing excellence, the goal of winning has overwhelmed the simple striving for excellence. The latter is most often seen as a mere means to winning. And proper moral conduct in sports has taken a backseat, again even among many Christians. This is one of the more disturbing examples of how the church has conformed to popular culture as opposed to transforming it.

A final pervasive cultural injustice is found in lotteries. Anti-lottery arguments based upon negative social consequences are well-known, and a conclusive case against lotteries likely can be made based on these considerations alone. But the moral and psychological harm caused by the mere existence of lotteries goes unnoticed, and it involves injustice. Lotteries, as we all know, are based on sheer luck and blind chance.[13] One day you're an ordinary working class person—the next you're a millionaire. As unlikely as are one's chances of winning the lottery, many Americans pin their hopes on it.

So what's the harm of doing that, as long as people use only their expendable income to purchase tickets? The problem is the mind-set it produces. By encouraging a short-cut-to-wealth mentality, lottery systems undermine the virtues of diligence and perseverance in one's work. Lotteries, too, invite people to envy those who win (although the results of winning big cash prizes are often anything but enviable), and as lottery players fantasize about their possible winnings, they are encouraged to disdain their present conditions. More relevant to the present discussion, lotteries are based in a basic injustice. Winners do not deserve their prizes, in the usual sense of having merited them through some achievement or significant contribution to society. Nor, presumably, do they have a basic need for the money (or else they shouldn't be playing).

From the standpoint of distributive justice, then, lotteries are morally irrational. They redistribute wealth blindly (that's the point), without any regard to desert or need. Lottery defenders argue, of course, that proceeds from lotteries provide significant social benefits, such as supporting public education. But less harmful means, such as using tax revenue, can accomplish these ends.

---

13. Some Christians might take exception to my use of the terms "chance" and "luck." I use the terms, however, as the philosophers Aristotle and Hume did, to refer to *hidden causes* rather than to events that have no cause and are uncontrolled even by God. My own view, consonant with historic Christian belief, is that there are no events that fall into the latter category.

The Virtues Required by Justice

As with most of the virtues discussed so far, to be personally nurtured justice requires humility. To be a fair person, one must see other people's concerns and situations as being as important as one's own, which is the essence of humility. A humble attitude is a natural boon to personal justice, because it prevents a person from acting with partiality to herself. One must possess, of course, the self-control to resist the temptation of favoritism, particularly given the powerful forces of Western culture that militate against fair treatment of persons. We all must daily resist the temptation to treat her best who can benefit us most in return. Also, a just person must be wise and discerning. One must know what counts as fair and equitable in a particular situation and keep in mind relevant persons and factors that might be more remote from view than some other considerations. One's discernment must transcend personal affairs and apply also to broader social and cultural issues. The just mind critically assesses popular culture so as not to participate in its systematic injustices. Lastly, the just person must be considerate, sensitive to the needs of others. All of us may affirm the importance of attending to people's needs, but the ability to recognize those needs when they're not immediately apparent is a special moral skill. Humility, self-control, discernment—all are traits crucial to the development of the virtue of justice. A person who has these qualities will be better equipped to act fairly, giving to each her due.

8

HILARIOUS GIVING

The Virtue of Generosity

Milton Hershey was considered to be a fool by his wealthy contemporaries. His chocolate company brought him millions of dollars, but he used most of it to invest in a school for homeless children (now known as the Milton Hershey School) and other charitable causes. Meanwhile, his millionaire contemporaries built giant mansions, sparing no expense to surround their families with luxuries. The children of these other families of fortune, however, encountered endless personal troubles, while the Hershey family thrived. These early twentieth-century entrepreneurs are testaments to a biblical truth: Those who horde their wealth suffer for it, while the generous are rewarded.

Generosity is a disposition to give to others, a willingness to go beyond what justice requires when it comes to sharing one's resources. Although generosity is universally admired in those who display the trait, few manage to consistently display it. This chapter, then, looks closely at what it means to be a generous person, what this virtue involves, and the factors that motivate generosity.

Biblical Models of Generosity

The virtue of generosity is explicitly recommended in Scripture. The psalmist notes that the righteous "are always generous and lend freely" (Ps. 37:26). Paul tells Timothy to "be generous and willing to share" (1 Tim. 6:18), and elsewhere he declares, "God loves a cheerful giver" (2 Cor. 9:7). It's interesting that the term translated as "cheerful" in this passage could as easily be rendered "hilarious," which expresses a particular exuberance about giving. Scripture teaches that generosity is also good policy from a practical standpoint. We're told that "a generous man will prosper" (Prov. 11:25) and that "good will come to him who is generous" (Ps. 112:5).

Human Generosity

One of the more outstanding examples of generosity in the Old Testament regards the queen of Sheba. After hearing of the wisdom of king Solomon, she decided to visit him and see for herself. She tested him with hard questions and discovered that his reputation was well deserved, even exceeding the reports she had received. In response, the queen gave to Solomon enormous quantities of gold, precious stones, and more spices than Israel had ever seen (1 Kings 10:1–13).

It is one thing, of course, for a wealthy queen to freely share her abundance; it's quite another for impoverished people to give generously. This is precisely what we find modeled by the first-century Macedonian churches. Paul reports,

> Out of the most severe trial, their overflowing joy and their extreme
> poverty welled up in rich generosity. For I testify that they gave as much
> as they were able, and even beyond their ability. Entirely on their own,
> they urgently pleaded with us for the privilege of sharing in this service
> to the saints. (2 Corinthians 8:2–4)

Perhaps most remarkable about this passage is not the Macedonian Christians' giving so freely in the midst of their poverty, but that they considered it a privilege to do so. The attitude here is one that sees giving itself as a source of great joy. They certainly displayed the cheerfulness Paul refers to later in the same epistle.

Divine Generosity

The best examples of generosity come, of course, from God himself. The apostle James remarks that God "gives generously to all without finding fault" (James 1:5). Given what Scripture teaches about God's gifts to humankind in spite of our fallenness, this is a dramatic understatement. Truly, God's generosity knows no bounds. Nature itself is the most basic form of divine generosity. God need not have created anything, but he did. He need not have made conscious beings such as ourselves, but he did. And he need not have blessed us with such abundance, but he did. He generously made us stewards of a spectacular physical world, featuring a plethora of living organisms to admire and use. We've been given not just enough to get by, but an endless array of foods to eat, animals to train as helpers and pets, and natural resources for fashioning clothes, homes, tools, and endless varieties of merchandise for bettering and entertaining ourselves. We could have survived without all of these things, but God gave them to us anyway. Nor is the beauty of creation a practical necessity, but a bonus. God blesses us with tremendous natural aesthetics, from an exquisite sunset to a terrifying volcano, from a delicate butterfly to a fearsome tiger. The wealth of beauty surrounding us, not to mention the amazing human body itself, are testaments to the generosity of God.

God gives particular gifts as well to particular people. He gives generously to individuals by endowing us with various talents and aptitudes, from natural intelligence to artistic and athletic abilities. He also gives to whole nations, from ancient Israel to the United States. On individual and national levels, God has blessed most of us with much more than we need to survive.

Finally, and most wondrously, God has shown supreme generosity by providing a means of salvation for a wicked and rebellious human race. He would have been just in allowing us all to perish in our sins. Yet instead of treating us with the wrath our sin deserves, he extended grace to us, providing atonement through the perfect work of Christ, adopting us as his very sons and daughters, and lavishing upon us the bounty of heaven, an afterlife in his presence for all eternity. This is unspeakable generosity.

The ministry of Christ is remarkable for it's multifaceted generosity. In terms of salvation, Jesus could have redeemed us without giving us the additional blessings of miracles and detailed sermons on how to live. He need not have extended himself so deeply and regularly, denying himself what was rightfully his for the sake of others. He need not have associated with those outside his natural social circle, persons who, in many instances, posed risks to both his reputation (e.g., tax collectors and prostitutes) and physical well-being (e.g., lepers and angry opponents). Jesus extended himself in these ways for the good of other people, including us today as we benefit from his words and example. None of this was necessary for our salvation. He preferred to far exceed what was necessary, even relative to the excessive grace of atonement for sins.[1]

Vices Opposing Generosity

So the essence of generosity, whether displayed by mortals or God himself, is a giving disposition, a general readiness to give to others. This seems to involve giving more than one is required to give and doing so with a cheerful attitude, rather than begrudgingly or with a sense of compulsion. The generous person

---

1. On this theme, see Stephen H. Webb's *The Gifting God: A Trinitarian Ethics of Excess* (New York: Oxford University Press, 1996).

recognizes that he owns nothing that has not been graciously given, so he lets his possessions flow freely and gives with hilarity.[2] The begrudging giver, in contrast, resents having to give (or the amount he must give). Since, from a Christian point of view, intentions are crucial to true virtue, such resentful giving is morally equivalent to not giving at all. The attitude of the begrudging giver not only cancels the merit of the gift but also blocks joy and divine blessing, the normal consequences of generous giving, as shall be seen below.

The twin vices on either side of generosity are stinginess and prodigality, which denote tendencies to under-give and over-give respectively. Stinginess involves holding tightly to more than one needs, an unwillingness to part with luxuries. The stingy person is typically petty, foolishly attentive to and preoccupied with the trivial aspects of his possessions. The stingy person, too, is selfish, for he clings to resources that could be easily used to meet the needs of others.

Greed is a cousin to stinginess. Whereas the stingy person is a reluctant giver, the greedy person pursues more than he needs. Like stinginess, greed is grounded in selfishness but greed is of more sinister repute than stinginess, because it usually applies to those who hoard real wealth. In these cases, the injustice of greed is more pronounced. Rather than meeting significant needs that would not discomfort him in any way, the greedy person prefers to use his surplus for his own luxury. Thus, it's been said, "Money is like manure. If you spread it around, it does a lot of good. But if you pile it up on one place, it stinks like hell."[3] One of the more disturbing illustrations of this point occurred in 1986 when President of the Philippines, Ferdinand Marcos, was driven from power. He and his wife, Imelda, lived lavishly while much of the population suffered in poverty. The Marcos' greed was typified by Imelda's shoe collection—1220 pairs, mostly expensive foreign brands.

The other vice opposing generosity is prodigality. A much less common vice than stinginess, prodigality involves giving away more than is prudent. A prodigious gift is imprudent because either the amount given threatens one's own well-being (where the giver can no longer meet his own needs) or the amount given threatens the recipient's well-being (where the gift goes so far beyond meeting

---

2.   A person's generosity, Descartes maintained, "has only two components. The first consists in his knowing that nothing truly belongs to him but [the] freedom to dispose his volitions, and that he ought to be praised or blamed for no other reason than his using this freedom well or badly. The second consists in his feeling within himself a firm and constant resolution to use it well." *The Philosophical Writings of Descartes,* trans. J. Cottingham, R. Stoothoff, and D. Murdoch (Cambridge: Cambridge University Press, 1985), 384.

3.   Clint W. Murchison, quoted by his son Clint Murchison Jr. in *Time,* 16 June 1961.

needs that it tempts the recipient to complacency and laziness). That the vice of prodigality is so uncommon, at least in the West, is partly explained by the consumer mind-set prevailing today in our culture. But, as Aristotle notes, it's probably also due to stinginess' being less dangerous than prodigality, and people naturally incline away from danger.[4] It's likely, in fact, that stinginess is sometimes motivated by a concern for personal safety, if only in the financial sense.

The Other Side of Giving: The Moral Skill of Receiving

A song by the band, Over the Rhine, features the line "There is nothing harder, than learning to receive."[5] Since human beings are naturally selfish, this might seem paradoxical, but it takes great skill to receive well, to be a gracious recipient of grace. It's a skill that constitutes the other side of the moral coin of generosity, and it's a challenge because we Americans usually think in terms of desert. We want to have earned all that we have, lest we be indebted to someone, an attitude probably linked to our lust for freedom. If we owe someone, then we're subject to him in some way, and this bothers us.[6] So to receive is in some sense to submit to another's act of grace, which is humbling. Thus it's hard to receive and is perhaps one of the main reasons why it goes against human nature to accept God's gracious gift of salvation through Christ.[7]

When Jesus attempted to wash Peter's feet, the disciple initially resisted. Jesus warned him, however, that he had to receive this gift or have no part of him (John 13:8). This exchange only seems odd when we interpret it in literal terms. The whole event is actually a profound metaphor for the gospel, a gift so great that it's quite difficult to receive. It's too good to be true, a story of such monumentally hopeful proportions that it seems to be a fairy tale.[8] Before I came to Christian faith, such

---

4. See Aristotle *Nicomachean Ethics* 2.9, in *The Basic Works of Aristotle,* ed. Richard McKeon, trans. W. D. Ross (New York: Random, 1941), 1004.
5. Over the Rhine, "All I Need Is Everything," from the album *Good Dog Bad Dog* (Milwaukee, Wis.: Back Porch Records, 2000).
6. It's ironic that this psychological fact is pervasive in a country in which credit card debt is an epidemic problem.
7. We sometimes forget, however, that this salvation was earned. It just wasn't earned by *us.* So, strictly speaking, Christianity does teach salvation by works, but it is the work of Christ, not that of any mere human, that earns this salvation. What *is* unique about the Christian religion is the vicarious atoning work of Christ and that it's applied to us on the condition of faith.
8. J. R. R. Tolkien discusses the fairy tale quality of the gospel in his essay "On Fairy-Stories," in *The Tolkien Reader* (New York: Ballantine, 1966).

was my perception. I thought it would be nice if the gospel was true, but it seemed to make the truth about the world . . . well . . . too happy. As foolish as that thought appears to me now, it made sense for me to think in such terms, given my general outlook on life. The same can doubtless be said of millions of others.

The Preconditions of Generosity

In that the gracious reception of a gift is itself a sort of gift to the giver, it's a quality directly relevant to generosity. To the extent that one learns how to receive, one will be a better giver. The reverse is true as well. And to the extent that one practices certain other virtues, one will be more generous. Several such characteristics either are required for generosity or motivate one to be generous.

One prerequisite of generosity is contentment. The generous person is happy with what he has, with a proper perspective on what is needful and, hence, not petty. He senses his ultimate personal security and so is not afraid to part with what he gives away. By contrast, the acquisitive and greedy are insecure. They, like everyone else, seek security, but they manifest this desire viciously. Their method hurts both themselves and others. Even great wealth is not a psychological balm, but a source of anxiety and stress. Moreover, wealth is a moral and spiritual handicap. Paul says, "The love of money is a root of all kinds of evil" (1 Tim. 6:10). Anyone who has spent significant time among the wealthy knows the trouble they see. Money, it seems, brings out the worst in people. Rather than making them more generous, it makes them more selfish, a possible explanation for the inversely proportional relationship between people's financial wealth and the percentage of income they give. The more money a person makes, the smaller proportion of resources he's likely to give to churches and charities.

Justice is another prerequisite for generosity. Augustine maintained that the virtuous person maintains a proper *ordo amoris* (ordering of one's loves).[9] All of us devote ourselves to the people and things in our lives with a certain order of priority. This ordering more or less conforms to the biblical ideal (God, others, oneself). To love out of order (such as by putting oneself before others or by putting anyone before God) is unjust and fails to give proper due to God or to other people. When we do give proper due to others, we'll give more to them

---

9. Augustine writes that a good man "neither loves what should not be loved nor fails to love what should be loved; he neither loves more what should be loved less, loves equally what should be loved less or more, nor loves less or more what should be loved equally." *On Christian Doctrine,* trans. D. W. Robertson Jr. (New York: Macmillan, 1986), 23.

than is our natural inclination, since our natural inclination is to keep much more than we need. So the just person will be a giving person.

Generosity also demands self-denial. More specifically, the moral discipline of living simply and limiting one's unnecessary possessions is called frugality. The frugal person is able to be more generous toward others because he's voluntarily stingy toward himself. His financial self-denial enables him to better assess what is needful and what is superfluous. What others greedily pursue as necessities, the generous person regards as luxuries to be given away.

Chief among the motivating factors for generosity is gratitude. The more thankful a person is, the more eagerly that person will give, not just to those who give to him, but to everyone. Just as the vice of resentment negatively affects a person's behavior toward everyone, gratitude has a positive effect on a person's generosity and on his behavior toward others. Indeed, this is as it's meant to be, as Jesus tells his disciples: "Freely you have received, freely give" (Matt. 10:8), without making it a condition that they receive from others first. They had already received so much from God that indiscriminate generosity was the only appropriate response as a gesture of gratefulness. This is no less true for us today.

The virtue of faith begets generosity. Active trust in God is, in fact, the most fertile moral soil for generosity. The generous Christian makes his eternal, rather than his material, possessions his focus, for these are not susceptible to loss or deterioration. As Jesus recommends, "Store up for yourselves treasures in heaven, where moth and rust do not destroy, and where thieves do not break in and steal" (cf. Matt. 6:20). Jesus also teaches that good deeds, especially those of deep sacrifice, are rewarded in heaven. So, with an eternal view in mind, a paradoxical principle applies to personal possessions: The more they are shared, the more they multiply in the life of the one who shares.

Lastly, joy is both a motivator and reward for generosity. The cheerful giver gets a kick out of giving because he's discovered the thrill of generosity. His love for others enables him to empathetically experience the joy of giving the gift, while at the same time, and in addition, receiving a gift of divine blessing. This double benefit (i.e., the joy of giving and the divine blessing) explains the logic behind the biblical principle that "it is better to give than to receive." For when one gives, one receives in return—twice.

Practical Applications

Consider some practical ways in which you could become more generous. Like all the virtues, generosity is a skill that is improved with practice. One becomes more generous, in part, by doing generous things. While this will not guarantee the development of a natural disposition to give, the joy that comes from generous acts does increase one's genuine desire to give. One might focus giving in three major areas.

First, give to the church. Begin by tithing, giving ten percent of your income, as is the biblical standard. Faithfulness in this area will almost certainly improve your financial situation, and in time you'll be able to give a higher percentage. Second, give within your local community. Remember that generosity doesn't involve just money and material possessions, but time and other less tangible resources as well. Strive to give time and energy to your family, as your first circle of influence, then to friends and others in your local community, such as at work and in your neighborhood. Finally, give globally, to people elsewhere in the world who are undernourished or otherwise impoverished. While it's easy to forget the plight of millions of people because they're invisible to us in our daily lives, the very act of committing to give to a hunger relief organization helps to alleviate this problem. If only through the monthly reminder of writing the check and reading the organization's literature, the experience raises the giver's awareness and sensitivity to others less fortunate than ourselves.

But how much should one give? I can think of no better answer than that given by C. S. Lewis:

> I do not believe one can settle how much we ought to give. I am afraid the only safe rule is to give more than we can spare. In other words, if our expenditure on comforts, luxuries, amusements, etc., is up to the standard common among those with the same income as our own, we are probably giving away too little. If our charities do not at all pinch or hamper us, I should say they are too small.[10]

If we're honest with ourselves, these are hard words to accept, let alone put into practice. None of us wants to be hampered. What is more, this general approach to generosity applies not only to our finances but presumably to our other resources, even that most precious to us—our time. All human relationships, within families and between friends, involve time commitments. The generous person sacrifices his time to the most important people in his life, denying comforts to himself in regular and tangible ways. Nowhere is this more essential and demanding than in parenting. The best parents I know have made sig-

---

10.   C. S. Lewis, *Mere Christianity* (New York: Macmillan, 1952), 81–82.

nificant sacrifices in terms of personal finance and professional careers, to spend time with their children. One of my colleagues, for example, set aside a promising writing career so that he could spend more time with his three boys. Twenty years later, his sons are admirable Christian men whose characters bear the unmistakable marks of their dad's time investment. And I know many mothers (and some fathers) who've opted to stay home with their kids during the formative years, rather than take a job. They are to be admired for recognizing that time spent with their kids is more valuable than additional financial resources (which are often negligible anyway, given the costs of daycare, transportation, and other expenses related to work).

Finally, the Christian is expected not only to be generous with his time and money, but also must exhibit generosity of spirit, which is grace. The gracious person gives morally, in the form of mercy and forgiveness, in spite of whatever harm he's suffered at the hands of his neighbor (see chap. 14). This latter is the most difficult form of generosity. And as shall be seen, it's also the most important.

9

SEEKING HARMONY

The Virtue of Peace

Jesus said, "Blessed are the peacemakers, for they will be called sons of God" (Matt. 5:9). This beatitude recalls the peaceable kingdom described by the prophet Isaiah:

> The wolf will live with the lamb,
>> the leopard will lie down with the goat,
> the calf and the lion and the yearling together;
>> and a little child will lead them.
> The cow will feed with the bear,
>> their young will lie down together,
>> and the lion will eat straw like the ox.
> The infant will play near the hole of the cobra,
>> and the young child put his hand into the viper's nest.
> They will neither harm nor destroy
>> on all my holy mountain,
> for the earth will be full of the knowledge of the LORD
>> as the waters cover the sea.
>
> —Isaiah 11:6–9

The peaceful relations among the people and animals described in this passage are so striking as to be almost comical. It's difficult to imagine such situations as safe and serene rather than hazardous and violent. But here is a prophetic promise that claims this very thing will happen, the biblical portent of a final and lasting *shalom*. The causal source will be the great Peacemaker himself. So dramatic a work, as Jesus says, is truly that of a son of God. As his followers, called to be peacemakers as well, we have a mandate to act as sons of God in the making and preserving of peace.

SEEKING HARMONY   103

But what exactly does it mean to be a peacemaker? What, indeed, is peace? And how does one go about nurturing peace, both in one's own life and in the lives of others? None of us are able to change the nature of a snake or lion, as Jesus evidently will. But, presumably, we must be about the business of making peace some way or another. So it would be well to look into this matter of peace and peacemaking.

The Essence of Peace

We may think of peace positively or negatively. In the latter sense, peace is simply an absence of strife, as is often thought of in a civil or political sense. Two countries, for example, enjoy peaceful relations when they're not at war. They may or may not pursue the same political ends or have productive trade relations, but to be at peace with one another, it is enough that they don't fight. But such a condition is only minimally sufficient for peace. In the fuller, positive sense, peace is the presence of real harmony between two parties, and this is so for two reasons. For one thing, to define peace as a mere lack of hostility is to understand it solely in terms of symptoms rather than as an abiding, underlying condition. Two individuals might distrust or even despise each other and so avoid one another. So long as they succeed in not making contact, no actual strife or conflict occurs between them. But this can hardly be called peace. It's more like détente, where tensions are eased but only through avoidance.

The second reason for preferring the conception of peace as positive harmony between parties is more complicated, derived from our understanding of what it means to be virtuous. Augustine conceived of evil as a privation of good, that is, the absence of something.[1] Vice, then, is the absence of some good character trait, the lack of a particular excellence in a person's life. Accordingly, peace cannot just be the absence of something vicious, such as hostility, but must be the presence of something positive, such as harmony. And the absence of harmony—strife among individuals or war between nations—is vicious. Yet it's not enough just to avoid strife and war. We must ally with others, both civilly and personally.

---

1. Augustine's doctrine of evil follows from these facts: God made everything, and everything God made is good. So Augustine says, "We must conclude that if things are deprived of all good, they cease altogether to be; and this means that as long as they are, they are good. Therefore, whatever is, is good; and evil . . . is not a substance, because if it were a substance, it would be good." *Confessions* 7.12, trans. R. S. Pine-Coffin (New York: Penguin, 1961), 148.

Harmonious relations between people, then, are essential to peace. One qualification remains, however, for a complete definition of this virtue. People cooperate with one another for various reasons, and not all of these are noble. History shows that people can unite for the sake of evil in a most harmonious way. During World War II, the Axis powers joined forces to pursue world dominance; during the first century, Herod and Pilate bonded as "friends" through their shared opposition to the Jews. Were these truly peaceful relationships? On the contrary, because they united on merely pragmatic grounds, whatever harmony they enjoyed was not genuinely peaceful. Such bonds are easily broken and give way to strife of an especially bitter sort, because they are set-ups for treachery. Why remain in an alliance when another becomes more profitable?

So peace is not mere harmony between people or nations, but must be something more. It is properly based upon a shared aim that is not merely practical but good in itself. That aim must also be secure, immune from the threat of being trumped by a still greater aim. We must conclude that true peace is forged upon goodness, for a bond is only as secure as its foundation, and nothing is so stable as goodness itself. True peace, then, whether between individuals or nations, is a harmonious relationship founded upon a stable, shared commitment to the good. Thus, a peaceful relation is an alliance in goodness.

International Peace

The conception of peace as harmony can be applied to three general spheres of human life—international, interpersonal, and intrapersonal. While the first of these contexts is somewhat removed from the arena of moral virtue as typically understood, beginning at this level will illuminate the present analysis of the personal realms, where peace is pertinent to virtue.

With regard to international peace, two or more nations enjoy peaceful relations in the fullest sense when, as noted earlier, they work together toward worthy ends. International freedom, justice, security, and the fair, effective distribution of world resources are examples of such worthy ends toward which nations might strive. The shared pursuit of these ends, however, demands that nations enjoy a degree of mutual trust. Trust between nations, though, is a delicate thing. It takes a long time to build and can be destroyed in an instant. Diplomacy is a painstaking art and demands constant attention to all the vicissitudes of public life, across the domains of politics, economics, rhetoric, science, and even sports. A few words from a government spokesperson can significantly reduce or exacerbate international tension. An unexpected turn in a diplomatic meeting or Olympic event can help unite or alienate nations.[2]

That lasting peace between nations requires so much effort and attention is, without doubt, an unmistakable sign of our fallenness as a race. Peace, it seems, is not our natural state. Rather, enmity is fundamental to the human condition. The much ballyhooed pessimism of philosopher Thomas Hobbes is more realistic than most of us care to admit. If left ungoverned, Hobbes said, human beings would find themselves in a constant condition of war, and life for every one of us would be "solitary, poor, nasty, brutish, and short."[3] This truth applies to entire nations, as well as to individuals. Peace must be actively nurtured, pursued creatively and with close attention to detail. Tremendous sacrifice and forms of compromise that hurt are demanded in the process.

When two or more nations are unwilling to take the effort or make the sacrifices necessary for peace, war is often the tragic result. It's ironic that the costs of war almost always exceed the costs of peaceful compromise. Even when executed with tactical precision, war is chaotic and harmful to all sides. Consequently, some take a pacifist view which rejects war as an illegitimate response in all cases. According to this perspective, military force only makes things worse and is, therefore, always wrong. So a thoroughgoing pacifist will shun war even in cases where a nation is attacked without provocation, such as in response to Japan's attack on the U.S. in 1941, or to prevent a despot such as Hitler from achieving world dominance. It's always better, says the pacifist, to attempt diplomatic negotiation than respond with military force.

Proponents of the "just war" perspective see things differently and, perhaps, more correctly. Although chaotic and even socially devastating, war is sometimes just. But, as just war theorists argue, important criteria must be met for a war to qualify as just. First, a justifying cause must be present, such as self-defense, defense of the helpless and innocent, or enforcement of justice. Second, the means must be proportionate to the end (e.g., destroying a major city in retaliation for an attack on a military unit would be unjustly disproportionate). Third, the war must be declared and executed by a competent authority, such as the government of a sovereign state. And, fourth, war must be a last resort after exhausting all other means of peaceful resolution, such as negotiation. In a given

---

2. Some Olympic events have impacted international relations in dramatic ways. Jesse Owens' triumphs during the 1936 Olympics are an example. And the controversial victory of the Russians over the U.S. in the 1972 basketball competition further soured relations between our two countries during the Cold War.

3. Thomas Hobbes, *Leviathan* (New York: Macmillan, 1962), 100.

situation, though, it can be quite difficult to tell if some of these criteria are satisfied. But these guidelines do seem to be reasonable for determining when, if ever, military action is appropriate.

If a nation can justly wage war, such as in response to unprovoked attack, then—notwithstanding some popular rhetoric to the contrary—it is not inconsistent for a country to simultaneously commit to peace and prepare for war. Preparation for war can, in fact, effectively deter despotic regimes. Such was the common sense wisdom behind Theodore Roosevelt's maxim that the U.S. "speak softly and carry a big stick." So long as it is possible, a nation should work harmoniously with other nations. Only when the cause is clearly just should war be entered into, and then only as a last resort. This seems to be both a practically and biblically sound approach to the pursuit of international peace.[4]

Interpersonal Peace

At the interpersonal level, the pursuit of peace is less complex but the personal effort required can be just as taxing as achieving and preserving peace between nations. The same basic force is at work in both arenas: fallen human nature. Consequently, as Hobbes noted, our natural state is enmity. We display an inertia toward conflict and enter easily into a condition of war with others, whether that takes the form of physical violence or verbal assaults. The latter, of course, may be direct or indirect, as in the case of slander or gossip. About these forms of interpersonal warfare, more will be said shortly.

Our Christian duty is, paradoxically, to make war against this warlike tendency, to strive for harmony in all our personal relations. Paul says, "Do not repay anyone evil for evil. Be careful to do what is right in the eyes of everybody. If it is possible, as far as it depends on you, live at peace with everyone" (Rom. 12:17–18). Numerous other passages echo this exhortation, which constitutes the challenge to act like real sons of God.[5] As in the international context, the

---

4.   Immanuel Kant was among the first to propose a formal federation of nations as a solution to the perennial problem of international discord. His proposal has been somewhat realized in the United Nations. Opinion is mixed, of course, as regards the usefulness of this international agency of peace. Kant writes, "Without a contract among nations peace can be neither inaugurated nor guaranteed. A league of a special sort must therefore be established, one that we can call a league of peace. . . . [T]his idea of federalism should eventually include all nations and thus lead to perpetual peace." *Perpetual Peace and Other Essays*, trans. Ted Humphrey (Indianapolis: Hackett, 1983), 117.

5.   See, for example, Ephesians 4:3; 1 Thessalonians 5:13; 1 Timothy 2:2; and Hebrews 12:14.

interpersonal peacemaker must exercise tremendous discipline and attention to detail, mindfully avoiding careless remarks or actions that might offend someone. The peacemaker will also prod others to be careful in these respects. Interpersonal diplomacy is costly, demanding steadfast commitment and a willingness to sacrifice and compromise. These are the prerequisites for true harmony—effective cooperation rather than mere détente. We see now why Jesus called peacemakers "sons of God," for their work calls for no small measure of self-denial. And as was noted in earlier discussions of humility and self-control, self-denial is the essence of Christlikeness.

But is physical violence ever justified on an interpersonal level? If we follow the model for international peace sketched above, it would seem we should avoid it except as a last resort when all peaceful means have been exhausted and only when just cause is clearly present. Further biblical considerations, however, support a more strict approach. In the Sermon on the Mount, for example, Jesus famously declares, "Do not resist an evil person. If someone strikes you on the right cheek, turn to him the other also" (Matt. 5:39). From this remark, considered along with Paul's command not to repay evil for evil, what are we to conclude? Should we be personal pacifists, avoiding violence regardless of the situation? This seems to be an unwarranted extreme for much the same reason that war pacifism is unwarranted. Sometimes living peacefully with others is not possible because of the choices they make. One can be placed in a situation where violence is simply unavoidable, such as when an intruder threatens to kill one's entire family. In this case one may, of course, avoid killing the intruder by stunning or maiming the person instead. Such a response would certainly satisfy the criterion of proportionality noted above in the context of just war.

Even granting that some rare situations do call for force, it should be emphasized that the way of Christ places strong limits on its use. Jesus calls us to a higher standard. So it is the peacemaker who is strong, and violence is the weapon of the weak. As a sign of just how much strength peacemaking requires, consider how difficult it would be to live the life of peace as Jesus did. Symptomatic of our weakness is our devolving, on occasion, into uses of force when it's not necessary. The violent person gives in to her impulses rather than controlling them, as the morally strong manage to do. She's impatient, refusing to search out through personal diplomacy a solution to conflict. A person might, of course, see nothing wrong with use of violence to achieve certain ends, in which case the person is not weak so much as brutish.

We also make war on one another in less direct ways, such as by creating or reinforcing unjust systems and oppressive social patterns. Laws and economic policies that unfairly exclude or disadvantage minorities or the underprivi-leged are examples, as are social practices that arbitrarily alienate certain people. Such instances militate against harmony between people and thus undermine peaceful relations. It's no surprise that women and minorities have sometimes resorted to social disturbance in their quests to rectify social injustices. But as in cases of literal war, violence tends to beget violence. Defeating violence through peaceful means demands great resolve and ingenuity. History shows, however, that this route is not only feasible but also most effective in over-coming oppression, as the approaches of Ghandi and Martin Luther King dem-onstrate.[6] The initiatives of these two peacemakers continue to benefit the world.

Racist attitudes disturb the peace as well. These can be so entrenched in a person's psyche that she hardly notices them. Racism is a universal phenom-enon, explained by the fact that it grows out of two universal qualities of fallen human nature: ignorance and fear. To some degree, the latter grows out of the former as well, since we tend to be afraid of what we don't understand. Thus, education is crucial in rooting out racism. To gain deeper understanding of a people or culture necessarily reduces ignorance, which in turn reduces fear. More-over, when we seek to understand others, their experiences, and their cultural ways, we're likely to develop genuine interest in them. Understanding, too, helps us to overcome our ignorance about ourselves and our own cultural ways (along with our self-favoring biases). These steps are essential to the pursuit of harmo-nious race relations. The peacemaker seeks mutual understanding among those who differ. And she celebrates, rather than merely tolerates, those who differ from herself.

Language, too, can be used to work against peace. James likens the tongue to fire in terms of its destructive power (James 3:6). Through insults, name-calling, jokes, labels, and stereotyping clichés, we may diminish individuals or entire groups. These tactics are so tempting because they can usually be employed without immediate repercussions. The peacemaker avoids any such efforts to alienate others, however popular or seemingly innocuous they might be.

---

6. Martin Luther King described his approach as achieving a middle ground be-tween complacency and violence: "I have tried to stand between these two forces, saying that we need emulate neither the 'do-nothingism' of the complacent nor the hatred and despair of the black nationalist. For there is the more excellent way of love and nonviolent protest." "Letter from a Birmingham Jail," in *Why We Can't Wait* (New York: Harper and Row, 1964), 87.

The peaceful person also avoids divisive argumentation, as Paul cautions:

> Avoid foolish controversies and genealogies and arguments and quar-
> rels about the law, because these are unprofitable and useless. Warn a
> divisive person once, and then warn him a second time. After that, have
> nothing to do with him. You may be sure that such a man is warped and
> sinful; he is self-condemned. (Titus 3:9–11)

Paul's advice for dealing with such people is interesting. He seems to say that you just can't win with them, so don't bother trying. His counsel is reminiscent of the proverb, "Do not answer a fool according to his folly or you will be like him" (Prov. 26:4).

Perhaps the most damaging of all uses of language is also the most subtle. Gossip is especially harmful because its effect multiplies through repetition. Gossip is the interpersonal analogue of a radioactive dirty bomb that detonates at a particular time and place but continues to contaminate long afterward. Items of gossip cannot be withdrawn or undone, even if the gossiper repents. Like radiation, the gossip's poison can never be retrieved.

Intrapersonal Peace

The most intimate domain of peace is intrapersonal, the psychological realm within each of us. From a Christian point of view, intrapersonal peace is the seed from which all other peace grows. Individual human minds are moral-spiritual battlegrounds, and as those battles go—for good or ill—so go human interpersonal and international relationships. Such a claim is controversial in certain quarters where some see institutions and social dynamics as the primary carriers of evil in the world. Society corrupts, according to this perspective, so our primary concern should be to mend institutions, which will lead to individual moral health. While it's true that society may corrupt individuals, the more basic movement is from the individual to the collective. Such is the biblical model for the original occurrence and proliferation of evil, as Adam and Eve sinned individually. Moral corruption spread throughout all human communities from there, permeating every social structure from families to entire nations. This model seems also to hold true today in diverse spheres of human life, as problems in businesses, schools, governments, and churches are traceable to the moral failures of individuals within those institutions. This intuition regarding the moral primacy of the individual is the source of some common critiques of institutional approaches to curing social ills. Institutions bear the symptoms of evil, but they are not the primary vectors. The most basic cause is the individual human heart.

Intrapersonal strife comes in many forms. Psychological problems, such as bipolar disorder or depression, are especially distressing and debilitating. This is so because the sources of such troubles are not always evident. The causal dynamics of a particular person's development and current situation are so complex that diagnosing a mental illness and developing an effective treatment regimen can be a formidable challenge.

In many cases, though, the causes of psychological disorders are clear, such as in cases of abuse. The tragedy is that abusive behaviors tend to run in patterns—persons who as children had been physically or sexually abused are more likely to abuse as adults, and so the cycle continues down through the generations. Even where such behavioral patterns are brought to a halt, an individual might face long-term internal struggles with shame, anxiety, regret, fear, self-loathing, or temptation. These are some of the psychological wages of sin, and they are paid by perpetrators as well as victims. While psychological and behavioral conditions often must be addressed to reduce a person's internal conflict, such is not the whole story. From a Christian perspective, the most important matter is a person's moral-spiritual condition. No lasting inner peace can be reached until one ends her warfare with God and allies herself to goodness. This is done by seeking forgiveness in Christ and repenting of one's sinful behavior.

What are the signs of Christian inner peace? Or, better, what does peace with God *feel like,* from an internal standpoint? Since the attainment of inner peace is a gradual process—because one's moral-spiritual condition is not fixed suddenly—it's best to describe it in terms of a process. Peace, then, is either more or less present. So as one's inner peace grows one notices a reduction of internal unease and psychological disruption accompanied by an increase in feelings of serenity and calmness of mind. One also experiences improved clarity of thought and a sense of purpose and direction in one's life. Behaviorally, inner peace improves one's ability to conduct oneself rightly, to more consistently act on one's commitments. This in turn brings a greater sense of ease and calm, since living well is so satisfying. Thus, the peaceful life begets even more peace. We might call this a virtuous cycle.

Inner peace is a condition that is difficult to describe and must be experienced to be truly understood. This resistance to literal description is probably due to the nature of its cause. Because Christian peace has a transcendent source in Christ it will also be immune to circumstances and even defy rational comprehension at times. Paul says that the peace of God "transcends all understanding" (Phil. 4:7). Anyone who's been a Christian for a while will testify to this. The believer experiences a calm and prevailing sense of well-being that she enjoys even through great trials and deep sorrows. This is the paradox of peace, and it's a perennial invitation to poets, artists, and songwriters to communicate imaginatively what cannot be captured in straightforward, literal descriptions.

Living As a Peacemaker

One's behavior follows from one's internal condition. Thus outward hostility is always an indicator of internal strife. The person who resists conflict, on the other hand, is someone within whom peace resides. Moreover, the peaceful person actively sows peaceful relations. So what does this look like? How ought the true peacemaker to live? In short, the peacemaker is one whose entire life is oriented toward the fulfillment of the peaceable kingdom, the sort of concord described in Isaiah 11, the passage with which this chapter opened. The peacemaker seeks harmonious relations not just between herself and others but among all human beings, even among all living things. The whole of creation was originally intended to be peacefully inhabited by God's creatures. As redeemed people whose lives properly aim toward the reinstitution of that original peace, we ought to seek concord among all aspects of creation.

From a social-political standpoint, any discord, whether visited upon humans or other living things, ought to be addressed by the Christian. This is particularly true when that discord involves unnecessary violence, for such militates against the peaceable kingdom to which our lives must always point. The Christian peacemaker is not just a mellow pacifist, though, ready with a hug and a smile. She actively engages issues and people with a purposeful energy aimed at realizing God's kingdom on earth. She's alert to contemporary thought forms and public policies that undermine social welfare and justice. And she offers her input as to how these sources of discord can be overcome. Overall, she pursues the good in the public sphere as a natural extension of her pursuit of the good in her own life.

From a more local standpoint, the peacemaker seeks harmony in all of her family relations, friendships, and casual relations. Because we are more tightly bound to family and close friends, maintaining harmony in this context can be our biggest challenge. There is some truth to the phrase "familiarity breeds contempt." We tend to let our guard down around those whom we know best and whom we trust. We feel more comfortable with them, so we speak our minds more readily and are less likely to edit our actions so as not to offend them. This cavalier attitude leads, of course, to trouble. Eventually we say or do something that crosses the line, and conflict ensues. The key to peacemaking among one's more intimate associates, then, is to resist the tendency to be *morally* casual with them. Note that this is not the same as not being *socially* casual with them. One may be relaxed and comfortable socially without letting down one's moral guard, especially regarding such virtues as self-control, humility, discretion, kindness, and wit.

The peacemaker is sensitive to conflicts between others in her social group. Some people are more naturally adept at discerning tension between people, but all of us can develop this skill. The main component of this ability is simple attentiveness. When a conflict between people does develop, the peacemaker will encourage resolution through careful communication, confession, and forgiveness. This requires tact—as feelings can be tender—and diligence, because mending relationships usually takes time. A good sense of justice is also required if the peacemaker is to reliably direct the parties involved.

So, as has been seen with many of the other virtues, peacemaking involves the employment of several different virtues. Harmony between people is achieved only through kindness, self-control, discretion, justice, and diligence. Those who possess these traits are blessed indeed, and those who use them for the advancement of God's peaceable kingdom are all the more so. It's easy to see why they should be called sons of God.

10

LIVING ARTFULLY

The Virtue of Creativity

Christians believe in a creative God. They also confess that human beings are made in God's image, having been endowed with many divine capacities, including creativity. And yet even Christians who write about the virtues seldom discuss creativity. One can only presume that these writers either consider it to be a morally neutral trait or not sufficiently important to consider. Both of these opinions are seriously mistaken. That creativity is a fundamentally divine characteristic confirms its moral significance for the Christian. More than this, creativity is, as will be seen, a trait that enriches every aspect of a person and enhances his ability to display many other good qualities, moral and otherwise. What could be more essentially moral than that?

Divine Beauty and Creativity

A discussion of creativity might well begin by focusing on the divine attribute of beauty. Scripture speaks strongly and often of this important divine characteristic, expressing it in a variety of ways such as the Lord's being praised for his glory, splendor, majesty, and excellence. Jehoshaphat, for example, exhorts his people to "sing to the LORD and to praise him for the splendor of his holiness" (2 Chron. 20:21). The psalmist writes, "One thing I ask of the LORD, this is what I seek: that I may dwell in the house of the LORD all the days of my life, to gaze upon the beauty of the LORD and to seek him in his temple" (Ps. 27:4). And elsewhere, the psalmist declares, "O LORD my God, you are very great; you are clothed with splendor and majesty" (Ps. 104:1). Literally hundreds of other passages praise God for his beauty or else describe him in aesthetic terms.

From a historical standpoint, the greatest of Christian theologians have recognized the attribute of divine beauty. Augustine exclaims in prayer, "I have learnt to love you late, Beauty at once so ancient and so new! . . . The beautiful things of this world kept me far from you and yet, if they had not been in you, they would have had no being at all."[1] The last statement in this passage is the most striking, as Augustine affirms all earthly beauty to be derivative of divine beauty. In a similar way, Jonathan Edwards asserts,

> For as God is infinitely the greatest Being, so he is allowed to be infinitely the most beautiful and excellent: and all the beauty to be found throughout the whole creation, is but the reflection of the diffused beams of that being, who hath an infinite fulness of brightness and glory.[2]

Since all being either is God or is derived from God, all that is beautiful either *is* him or comes *from* him. Consequently, any aesthetic satisfaction—whether of objects, animals, or other humans, and however seemingly remote from the divine—is ultimately an enjoyment of God. For not only is God beautiful in his being, he creates beautiful things.

God is the cosmic artist, and his artwork authentically reflects his nature. Nature serves as an unmistakable self-expression of God. As the psalmist writes, "The heavens declare the glory of God; the skies proclaim the work of his hands. Day after day they pour forth speech; night after night they display knowledge" (Ps. 19:1–2). Paul notes that "since the creation of the world God's invisible qualities—his eternal power and divine nature—have been clearly seen, being understood from what has been made, so that men are without excuse" (Rom. 1:20). God's cosmic art clearly bears the indelible marks of a powerful, intelligent, wise, and loving being, so we have no excuse for not recognizing their source.

In Genesis 1 we're told, "God created man in his own image" (v. 27). To be created in God's image suggests, of course, that we share some essential ultimate capacities with the divine nature. Among these are the abilities to reason, will, perceive, love, and emote. More important for our present purposes, humans reflect God's image in the capacity to create and to do so with intentionality. Like our Creator, human artists properly execute according to a plan, aiming toward a definite, preconceived outcome. And just as God's creativity is self-revelatory, the human artist reveals something of himself in his art. Just as many divine attributes are manifested in God's creation, as Paul notes in Romans 1, so

---

1. Augustine, *Confessions* 10.27, trans. R. S. Pine-Coffin (New York: Penguin, 1961), 231–32.

2. Jonathan Edwards, *A Dissertation on the Nature of True Virtue,* in *The Works of Jonathan Edwards* (Edinburgh: The Banner of Truth, 1984), 1:125.

the personal attributes of artists are known by their works. Creation, it seems, is essentially an act of self-expression.

The Bible and the Arts

So what does the Bible teach us about the arts and artistic endeavor *per se?* Scripture speaks to these matters both by example and by direct injunction. Scripture declares the importance of the arts in that the books of the Bible are works of literary art. From Genesis to Revelation, we find epic narratives (tragic and comic), proverbs, poems, hymns, oratory, and apocalyptic literature, the artistic tools of which include allegory, metaphor, symbolism, satire, and irony. Comparatively little of the biblical material is strictly didactic, and where this is the case, such as in the book of Romans, the logical rigor itself is, indeed, elegant (an aesthetic quality).

God himself, then, chose an artistic medium—literature—as his primary vehicle of special revelation. Such by itself ought to persuade us to place a special premium on the arts. But the Bible also speaks explicitly to some specific art forms. With regard to music, the Bible is replete with injunctions to "sing to him a new song" (Ps. 33:3; 98:1), to praise him using a variety of instruments (Ps. 98; 150), and to "play skillfully" in doing so (Ps. 33:3). Dance, too, is encouraged in the Psalms: "Let Israel rejoice in their Maker; let the people of Zion be glad in their King. Let them praise his name with dancing" (Ps. 149:2–3; see also 150:4). The Bible sanctions dramatic arts as well. In Ezekiel 4:1–3 the prophet is instructed to execute a drama portraying Israel's sad fate due to her disobedience. Scripture also speaks to the visual arts. The most celebrated example appears in Exodus 35:30–35, regarding the construction of the tabernacle, where Moses declares the Lord's selection of Bezalel and Oholiab to be the chief artisans for the project because of their special divine gift of craftsmanship.

What conclusions are we to draw from this? First, it's clear that beauty is an important biblical category. This is true of the nature of God in two ways. God himself is beautiful in his being and creative in his actions, bringing other beautiful beings into existence. His works are excellent, displaying technical genius. They are original in the ultimate sense, as he creates *ex nihilo.* They display authenticity, serving as expressions of himself, declaring aspects of his nature. And his works are intentional in that he purposes details, and works toward an end, bringing glory to himself. Second, the Bible has much to say regarding artistic endeavor and aesthetic considerations. Both implicitly and explicitly, then, the Bible sanctions the arts. These aesthetic matters are important not merely for their practical utility but for the immediate glory of God.

A Christian Model of Creativity in the Arts

In the previous section, it was noted that because we bear the image of God, humans have the capacity to create. It might even be said that, since we are called to mimic God, we have a duty to be creative. But what exactly does this mean? How ought we to pursue the fulfilling of this biblical aesthetic mandate? Some specific suggestions follow, which are based upon the biblical doctrine of beauty that has been developed thus far.

Technical Excellence

For every skill there are proper and improper methods. There's a right way to hold a brush while painting, to position actors on a stage in a drama, and to enhance dynamics in the performance of a song. Each artistic domain has its proper methodology, and while the results are different depending upon the art form (and even between genres within art forms), technical precision is always of the first importance. Thus, artists must attend to the established guidelines of their craft. Abiding by such standards maximizes the desirability of the outcome of the creative process. It should be noted, however, that in the fine arts a reasonable allowance must be made for free and spontaneous play of the imagination. This is especially the case in the process of poetic and musical composition, but also in the performing arts. In any case, the artist should strive for efficiency with proper method or technique being essential.

Veracity

The artist must be both truthful and authentic. To the extent that the artist makes truth-claims in a particular work, he must take great care. He should strive to accurately depict events, faithfully portray persons, and insightfully expound upon important ideas. Artistic works must also be authentic in the sense that they effectively display the artist's unique perspective. If, as noted above, creative activity is properly self-revelatory, the content of a work of art should faithfully represent the artist's particular beliefs and feelings about the subject matter. With regard to style, it's appropriate that the artist's personality be apparent in his work. Included here is the practice of genuine personal vulnerability, something often lacking in contemporary Christian art.[3]

While strong theological reasons can be offered for identifying veracity in artistic expression as an aesthetic value, human self-understanding is also an important incentive. Leland Ryken remarks that the arts "are the most accurate index to human preoccupations, values, fears, and longings that we possess." He adds, "The arts are therapeutic and corrective: They at once call us to the essential patterns and values of life."[4] If such is the case, then the more truthful and sincere an artist's expression, the more his work has to teach us regarding the human condition and the greater moral service it can provide.

Originality

Like our Creator, artists should strive to be innovative in the content of their works. Stylistically, they should show imaginative resourcefulness in depicting events, portraying persons, addressing issues, expressing feelings, and communicating truths or values. However, no artist, particularly the Christian artist, is an island of innovation. Art happens in, and partly for, community, and the history and tradition of that community will properly find expression in pieces of art the members produce. But just as communities evolve and advance, so must their artistic expressions. Thus, to maximize their aesthetic potential, artists must constantly strive to push boundaries—both in terms of the techniques of production and the content of their works. Artistic exploration serves to vitalize and nourish a community's corporate imagination, awakening persons to new truths and enabling them to see old truths from a new perspective.

Moral Integrity

All human endeavors should reflect a commitment to biblical moral standards, and art is no exception. The artist must create works that are not only consistent

---

3.   Leo Tolstoy's Christian aesthetic recognized the communication of genuine feeling as essential to artistic expression, which he explains as follows: "Art is a human activity consisting in this, that one man consciously by means of certain external signs, hands on to others feelings he has lived through, and that other people are infected by these feelings and also experience them." *What Is Art?* (Indianapolis: Bobbs-Merrill, 1960), 51. Tolstoy defends a strong "expression" theory in aesthetics, but one need not share his definition of art to recognize the validity of stressing authentic communication in art.

4.   Leland Ryken, *The Liberated Imagination* (Wheaton, Ill.: Harold Shaw, 1989), 132.

with a Christian ethic but also display moral coherence, speaking with one voice regarding its moral messages. No work of art should be caustic or demeaning toward a person or institution in the name of Christ, but rather should always strive for redemptive themes. Artistic criticism of false ideas or worldviews is appropriate and at times even necessary, but should always be done not in a spirit of combat but of service, not to glibly censure but to imaginatively persuade and enlighten.

This idea of the moral responsibility of artists is one of the distinctive features of a Christian aesthetic. Nicholas Wolterstorff notes, "Where the Christian sees the artist as a responsible agent before God, sharing in our human vocation, Western man in the Gauguin-image sees him as freed from all responsibility, struggling simply to express himself in untrammeled freedom."[5] In an ironic twist, the Christian claims that true artistic freedom begins with the recognition of the moral responsibility of the artist, for in living morally humans are at their best, fulfilling their earthly purpose. And a biblical ethic constitutes the true ground of moral responsibility.

Intentionality

The Christian artist ought to be thoughtful about his work in the fullest sense. First, one must attend to proper technique and mechanical execution. As discussed earlier, this is a practical axiom for excellence in any endeavor. Second, critical reflection about the nature of one's artistic labors is necessary. Because every work of art falls within some specific genre, the artist must be critically aware of the standards for excellence within that genre if he is to excel.[6] Third, the intentional Christian artist is a student of the history of that genre and is capable of emulating the worthy artistic methods of its experts. Fourth, some minimal awareness about art theory is essential. The Christian artist must be aesthetically literate, having developed a basic definition of art, a view on the nature of the creative process, a conception of the biblical view of art, and the various purposes of artistic expression. Regarding these matters the artist should be conversant with others in the Christian community, drawing upon them for the sake of moral and theological accountability.

5.   Nicholas Wolterstorff, *Art in Action* (Grand Rapids: Eerdmans, 1980), 78.
6.   T. S. Eliot takes this a step farther: "What I believe to be incumbent upon all Christians is the duty of maintaining consciously certain standards and criteria of criticism over and above those applied by the rest of the world; and that by these criteria and standards everything what we read must be tested." "Religion and Literature," in *The Christian Imagination* (Grand Rapids: Baker, 1981), 153.

The guidelines discussed above are surely prerequisites of creativity, traits that the artist should strive to emulate. Enemies of creativity, however, are to be avoided. Some of the more common aesthetic vices are as follows:

Laziness

The lazy artist is too easily satisfied with (a) flawed technique (e.g., poor acting, writing, singing), (b) unauthentic art that addresses issues in the abstract, (c) unoriginal productions that merely offer cheap rip-offs of what is popular and trendy, and (d) work that shows little or no sign of critical reflection on the part of its creator. While some maintain that it's the message that matters or that good theology can compensate for aesthetic mediocrity, such an attitude forgets that aesthetics *is* a theological concern. As Madeleine L'Engle says, "If it's bad art, it's bad religion, no matter how pious the subject."[7]

Banality

This vice deadens the sensibilities of the lay person who is not aesthetically keen enough to recognize it but is, nonetheless, harmfully affected by it. The banal annoys the aesthetically aware person to distraction, or else it puts him to sleep. In short, any significant lack of imagination is banal. In written or lyrical compositions the vice of banality consists in the use of platitudes, clichés, and trite moralizing. Musically it is exhibited in dull, excessively repeated choruses or a failure to sufficiently diversify musical styles. A bland visual atmosphere, displaying little or no artistic expression is another example. This is not to say that simplicity in art is aesthetically vicious. On the contrary, a beautiful artwork can be simple, provided it is imaginatively so.

Artificiality

This aesthetic vice is opposed in certain respects to both originality and authenticity. It represents a failure to take seriously the psalmist's injunction to sing a new song and to do so in new and original ways. Various forms of popular kitsch, including T-shirt designs, jewelry, posters, bumper stickers, and coffee mugs are often instances of artificiality. The vice has more subtle manifestations as well, such as the use of hackneyed formulas in music (e.g., a key change toward the end

---

7.   Madeleine L'Engle, *Walking on Water* (Wheaton, Ill.: Harold Shaw, 1980), 14.

of the song) and maudlin dramas that oversimplify the complexities of real life moral problems and dilemmas (e.g., "Yes, Jane, your pregnancy out of wedlock is a serious problem, but if you just trust the Lord . . .").

Aesthetic Utilitarianism

In one sense this vice opposes the virtue of intentionality. Christians manifest aesthetic utilitarianism in the common notion that art is used properly only for evangelistic purposes. This perspective runs counter to the biblical idea that excellent creative endeavors bring *direct* glory to God and need not be used as a means to save souls in order to be valuable and pleasing to God. It also subversively affects even the capacity to successfully use art as an evangelistic tool. Accenting the salvific effects of a work of art, thereby demoting aesthetic concerns, invariably results in a lower grade art object that an audience will consequently find less compelling. The ironic result is that prioritizing the evangelistic purpose of art compromises the artist's ability to connect with persons outside the Christian community.

The Value of Creativity Outside the Arts: The Teaching Method of Jesus

The Christian has a responsibility to be creative, but the display of creativity need not be limited to the art world. Ways can be found to display creativity in our daily lives, even if only in the way we communicate with one another. No better example of a creative communicator can be pointed to, of course, than Jesus, who modeled the virtue of creativity every living moment.

Consider some of the sayings of Jesus. What do each of the following have in common?

- "You are the salt of the earth" (Matt. 5:13).
- "You are the light of the world" (Matt. 5:14).
- "If you're right eye causes you to sin, gouge it out and throw it away" (Matt. 5:29).
- "Do not give dogs what is sacred; do not throw your pearls to pigs" (Matt. 7:6).
- "Enter through the narrow gate. For wide is the gate . . . that leads to destruction" (Matt. 7:13).
- "The harvest is plentiful but the workers are few. Ask the Lord of the

harvest, therefore, to send out workers into his harvest field" (Matt. 9:37–38).

- "Whoever does the will of my Father in heaven is my brother and sister and mother" (Matt. 12:50).
- "Be on your guard against the yeast of the Pharisees" (Matt. 16:6).
- "Take and eat; this is my body" (Matt. 26:26).
- "No one can see the kingdom of God unless he is born again" (John 3:3).
- "My food . . . is to do the will of him who sent me" (John 4:34).
- "The bread of God is he who comes down from heaven and gives life to the world" (John 6:33).
- "I have come into this world, so that the blind will see and those who see will become blind" (John 9:39).
- "My sheep listen to my voice. . . . No one can snatch them out of my Father's hand" (John 10:27, 29).
- "I am the true vine, and my Father is the gardener" (John 15:1).

All of these sayings are figurative expressions, not to be taken literally. These are just a sampling, of course, of Jesus' figurative language. When one reviews the gospel discourses with an eye for Christ's literary devices, it's easy to see why he is sometimes regarded as a poet. He used symbol, oxymoron, simile, hyperbole, irony, humor, and parables. But Jesus had a special fondness for metaphor, as is evidenced in most of the passages quoted above. Along with the use of parables, metaphor is a hallmark of Christ's teaching style. He regularly took common physical objects, often from the agricultural world, and parleyed them into vehicles of spiritual truth. Sheep, bread, salt, light, trees, eyes, and childbirth are among his favorite tools for helping his hearers understand the connection between what he called the "kingdom of God" (yet another metaphor) and this world.

In many instances, though, his expressions served to baffle rather than enlighten his hearers. Even the learned Nicodemus didn't get the point when Jesus told him that a person has to be "born again." He replied, "Surely he cannot enter a second time into his mother's womb to be born!" (John 3:4). We smile at this response, recognizing that Nicodemus has made the mistake of taking Jesus literally. The expression is intended as a metaphor for spiritual renewal. And a vivid picture it is, so vivid that the Pharisee couldn't get past the picture itself, as perhaps none of us would have had we been in Nicodemus' sandals. We privately patronize him, forgetting that the only reason we "get it" is because others have made it clear to us what Jesus meant. Expressions like this one are very peculiar, even bizarre. But today we scarcely notice this because of our over-whelming familiarity with them. Yet since Jesus' teachings are so often processed through our contemporary popular thought-forms, we might not understand them as well as we think we do. In trying to understand Jesus and his words, the church has often resorted to generalization and formula (e.g., the "sinner's prayer"), be it popular or scholarly. The fact is, much of the time Jesus is *very* difficult to understand.

A particular saying of Jesus found in John 16 deserves special focus. The context is Jesus comforting his disciples. He had remarked that soon he was "going to the Father"; this confused the disciples. After promising them that their grief will one day turn to joy, Jesus makes this comment:

> Though I have been speaking figuratively, a time is coming when I will no longer use this kind of language but will tell you plainly about my Father. In that day you will ask in my name. I am not saying that I will ask the Father on your behalf. No, the Father himself loves you because you have loved me and have believed that I came from God. I came from the Father and entered the world; now I am leaving the world and going back to the Father. (John 16:25–28)

Here we have Jesus describing his own language as figurative, which appar-ently came as a great relief to the disciples, who responded to this admission and further clarification as follows: "Now you are speaking clearly and without figures of speech. Now we can see that you know all things and that you do not even need to have anyone ask you questions. This makes us believe that you came from God" (v. 29–30). This response is perplexing in itself, perhaps even incoherent. But what I find most peculiar is that the disciples do not ask what appears to be an obvious question (or at least John did not record it): "Why, Jesus, do you use figurative language at all?" Given his decided preference for metaphor and parables, this seems to be a reasonable query. So what would Jesus have said in response? Surely he had his reasons, and they must have been good reasons, especially given that when Jesus speaks plainly, as he does (at least in the opinion of the disciples) in John 16:25–30, faith in his hearers is evoked.

Without putting words into Jesus' mouth, several good reasons can be sug-gested that go beyond the obvious fact that metaphors and parables are more easily memorized than literal statements. (Some of the benefits of figurative language might be considered benefits of creativity in general.)

First, the use of metaphor, parable, and other nonliteral devices avoids reductionistic distortions of spiritual truth. It seems to be human nature to try to "boil things down," to "simplify," and to reduce things to the "essentials" or "fundamentals." But when one is dealing with such profound and lofty matters as human nature, the meaning of life, and the nature of God himself, this impulse can be dangerous. Seldom did Jesus reduce or simplify spiritual truth. One significant exception—known as the Golden Rule—had to do with our moral duty before God: Love your neighbor as yourself. It's interesting to note that, notwithstanding the Golden Rule, Christians who are called "fundamentalists" do not typically emphasize it today as strongly as some other points (some of which—such as special creationism and biblical inerrancy—are not even addressed in the Bible).

A second benefit of figurative language is that it respects the mystery of godliness. Metaphors and parables are indirect vehicles of truth, hitting their targets in roundabout, unexpected ways. As literary devices they are themselves, in many ways, mysterious. Sometimes it's difficult, if not impossible, to explain precisely why an image or phrase "works" poetically, such as Emily Dickinson's line "I felt a funeral in my brain / And mourners, to and fro" or Eliot's phrase, "When the evening is spread out against the sky / Like a patient etherized upon a table."[8] Poets respect the mysteries of the human condition by their figurative expressions. If they must resort to images to effectively convey human emotions and experiences, then how much more so the whole matter of relating to God and striving to live well before him? Paul says, "Beyond all question, the mystery of godliness is great" (1 Tim. 3:16). Figurative descriptions, such as those given to us by Jesus, respect that mystery while helping to partially unveil it. If Jesus is difficult to understand because of his use of metaphor and parables, he has only matched form to content. The mystery of his subject is reflected in the mystery of his method of communicating it.

Another benefit of figurative language is that, when used properly, it inspires an audience to deeper inquiry. A good metaphor or symbol forces a person to do some work. Like a good brainteaser, it begs to be figured out. The hearer must solve it or wait unsatisfied. If the teacher is clever enough, he will prompt a student to ask, "Okay, will you just tell us the answer?" But the most effective teacher will not satisfy even this request but rather provide another clue, a further teaser to whet even more the searcher's appetite. Jesus was the master of

8.   These lines come, respectively, from Emily Dickinson, "I Felt a Funeral in My Brain," in *Emily Dickinson: Selected Poems* (New York: Random, 1993), 140; and T. S. Eliot, "The Love Song of J. Alfred Prufrock," in *The Complete Poems and Plays* (New York: Harcourt Brace and World, 1971), 3.

this technique, and his dialogue with Nicodemus in John 3 offers an intriguing example. The rebirth metaphor is only the first stage. From there, after Nicodemus' request for clarification, Jesus answers with more metaphorical language, this time regarding water and wind, both metaphors for the Spirit of God. "How can this be?" the old Pharisee asks. Jesus explains the gospel to the Pharisee (John 3:11–21) but not without tantalizing him with further images and similes. No doubt Nicodemus' thirst for the truth was only deepened even as he began to have it quenched.

So Jesus deliberately conceals things from his hearers. How strange, we might think. Strange, yes, but it seems to be the way of God generally, not just during the ministry of Jesus. Isaiah says, "Truly you are a God who hides himself, O God and Savior of Israel" (Isa. 45:15). And the Proverb says, "It is the glory of God to conceal a matter; to search out a matter is the glory of kings" (Prov. 25:2). An old rule of fiction—"show, don't tell"—seems to be endorsed by God himself; illustrating with an action impacts more deeply than simple description. Jesus certainly followed this rule in his teaching method, as does God the Father, by embedding moral-spiritual truths in natural objects and events.

This suggests a fourth significant function of Jesus' use of figurative language. It trains us to look for spiritual truths in obscure places or in common circumstances we don't usually explore to find a divine message. Jesus' references to so many elements of nature in his metaphors and parables surely did not exhaust all the ways that the kingdom of God may be symbolized. Could it be that everywhere in creation, lessons of God are pouring forth? Might each of the millions of life forms in the plant and animal kingdoms conceal some moral-spiritual lessons waiting to be unpacked by discerning minds? Are we living in the midst of potential parables every moment, whether we're farming, driving, eating, or chatting with friends? Perhaps if we simply train ourselves to be more alert about the situations in our lives and the natural world around us, we'll find ourselves making significant connections and discoveries about moral-spiritual truth.

I recently made one such observation. While leveling an old, overgrown garden I discovered that the weeds were taller than the plants. As I pulled the weeds, I noticed that they came out much easier than the plants. I also found the stems of the weeds were hollow. Soon the moral-spiritual metaphors came to mind, echoing the Bible's own language about the similarities between weeds and the wicked. As with the weeds in my yard, the wicked are initially very impressive and often quickly rise to prominence in this world. But they are morally hollow with shallow roots that are easily torn from their foundation. Moreover, the wicked bear no fruit and are, like many weeds, harmful upon contact. Such powerful metaphors or "types" of moral-spiritual truths are embedded in creation all around us. Early modern scientists used to say that God wrote two books, the Bible and the book of nature. While this conviction has fallen out of fashion, perhaps it should not be forgotten.

A final benefit of Jesus' use of figurative language is beauty. Intrinsic value resides in the aesthetically excellent, whatever external purpose a thing may also serve. Jesus' metaphors and parables are indeed beautiful, and he displayed genuine artistry in devising them. Such creativity is compelling in and of itself, independent of the actual content of the teaching. Combine the transcendent truth of *what* Jesus taught with the aesthetic genius of *how* he taught it, and it's little wonder that he is the most influential human being that ever walked the planet, although he didn't leave any writings and never traveled more than a few hundred miles from his birthplace. If one virtue of Christ is ignored more than any other, it is creativity. And among those who do acknowledge the importance of this virtue, there is too little recognition that concealment, subtlety, and tantalization are vital aspects of creativity. That the American church has managed to make the gospel boring and predictable to the rest of our culture is sad testament to this lack of recognition. Today, more than ever, we need a resurgence of the creative Christian mind, to intrigue, enthrall, and captivate, to show more than tell, to draw outsiders into asking, with Nicodemus, "How can this be?"[9]

---

9.   In recognizing the figurative nature of Jesus' language we do not thereby diminish concern for truth in all that he said. On the contrary, I believe we exalt truth ever higher, recognizing that it transcends straightforward and literal expressions and even language itself. There are some truths that can only (or best) be expressed through poetic devices and other art forms. Jesus was the master at using such techniques to show us spiritual reality and motivate us to a deeper faith and commitment to God. Let us strive to emulate him even in this.

11

JOKING AROUND

The Virtue of Wit

So this horse walks up to the bar, and the bartender looks at him and says, "Why the long face?" This is one of my favorite jokes. I've been telling it for years, and people usually laugh at it. Why? What makes jokes funny (when they are funny)? And what's the moral significance of humor? Does wit have anything to do with virtue? This chapter makes the connection clear while defining wit, revealing its moral significance, and discussing some prerequisites for being a witty person.

The Bible and Humor

Biblical references to laughter are scant. The psalmist declares, "The Lord laughs at the wicked, for he knows their day is coming" (Ps. 37:13). Abraham laughed when God told him that his elderly wife would bear him a son (Gen. 17:17). Neither of these cases feature a jest of any kind but actually regard quite serious matters. Perhaps the only biblical reference to laughter at good humor is general and indirect, where the proverb says, "A cheerful heart is good medicine" (Prov. 17:22). Nowhere in the Bible do we find jokes, pranks, or one-liners. Many biblical narratives, however, have a humorous dimension. The Israelites choice of the term "manna" to name the edible flakes that appeared daily on their campground is amusing since it literally means "What is it?" Jesus' use of hyperbole and irony in his teaching, too, is often comical. When, for instance, he says, "Do not throw your pearls to pigs" (Matt. 7:6) and when he asks "Why do you look at the speck of sawdust in your brother's eye and pay no attention to the plank in your own eye?" (Luke 6:41), the images are humorously absurd.[1]

---

1. Even some of Jesus' miracles were amusing. His feeding, for example, of thousands of people with a few fish and loaves of bread has a droll quality about it.

In an earlier chapter, it was noted that the virtue of humility is essentially ironic, the opposite of what one would expect. Irony is often a significant source of humor. So when we find ironic biblical events and characters, we may also find cases of humor. David's defeat of Goliath is morbidly comical, and an amusing quality is couched in the raising up of such flawed figures as Moses and Peter for leadership of Israel and the apostolic church, respectively. Such developments as these strike us as laughable precisely because they are so ironic.

Three Theories of Humor

Both in Scripture and in everyday life we find a range of humor. Many different things can make us laugh, but why do we find funny the things that we do? Three basic theories have been proposed to answer this question: superiority theory, incongruity theory, and relief theory. Superiority theorists, such as the philosopher Thomas Hobbes, maintain that we find an event funny when we experience a sudden sense of superiority to someone. Laughter, says Hobbes, "is a kind of sudden glory."[2] The humor is especially strong when the person involved normally enjoys a revered status or is otherwise exalted in our minds. So when one's boss or a well-known public official slips on a banana peel or leaves his fly open, we find this amusing. We suddenly feel superior to them, and our natural response is to laugh. Jokes about presidents and political candidates, too, are readily explained by the superiority theory. People of public renown are normally regarded as "above us," so a joke that cleverly humbles them is funny.

Another perspective—one defended by the philosopher Immanuel Kant—sees incongruity as the central element in humor. Kant says, "Whatever is to arouse lively, convulsive laughter must contain something absurd."[3] So we find humor in something out of it's proper context or when two things are unnaturally juxtaposed. The more incongruous, the funnier a thing is likely to be. We laugh, for instance, at a man in a dress or a woman wearing a fake mustache. These gags combine elements not ordinarily brought together. One need not, of course, pull Vaudevillian stunts to observe cases of comic incongruities. More ordinary examples occur frequently in casual conversations. Many people laugh, for instance, when they learn that as a child Albert Einstein was a poor student

---

2. In contrast, Hobbes explains weeping as the result of sudden dejection. See Thomas Hobbes, *Leviathan* (New York: Collier, 1962), 52.
3. Immanuel Kant, *Critique of Judgment,* trans. Werner S. Pluhar (Indianapolis: Hackett, 1987), 203.

or that Babe Ruth was a successful pitcher early in his baseball career. Each case features an odd combination of facts that strikes the listener as humorous.

The third view accounts for humor as a sudden liberation from restraint. A classic example is the child who struggles to stifle her laughter when hiding from a playmate who walks right by without noticing. As adults we experience something similar when a veiled insult is made about someone in her presence. The urge to laugh results from the psychic tension created by the situation. Sigmund Freud, a proponent of the relief theory of humor, maintained that laughter is often the release of repressed impulses.[4] This explains the popularity of jokes involving sexuality, violence, or ethnicity. Social expectations and moral guidelines forbid the expression of certain thoughts and feelings, and jokes are a means (as are dreams, according to Freud) by which we vent this pent up energy. Gags that poke fun at sacred things, too, are probably popular for the same reason.[5]

Each of the above theories explains some kinds of humor better than others. So rather than affirm one of these theories of humor as the single true account, we may prefer an eclectic view affirming each as explaining different categories of comedy. Superiority theory makes the best sense of slapstick humor and physical comedy. It also explains why we laugh when recalling our own most embarrassing moments. Although anything but funny at the time, we can laugh when looking back because we feel superior to who we were at the time. Incongruity theory, too, seems to make the best sense of a large category of humor. The humor of most puns seems due to a unique juxtaposition of contexts, such as my favorite: "Time flies like arrows, but fruit flies like bananas." And Gary Larson's *Far Side* cartoons are almost exclusively premised on dramatic incongruities, such as when a polar bear, taking a bite out of an igloo, says "Oh, I just love these things—crunchy on the outside with a chewy center." Relief theory, too, adequately accounts for laughter in situations where neither an incongruity nor a sudden sense of superiority reveals itself. Finally,

---

4.   Sigmund Freud, *Jokes and Their Relation to the Unconscious,* trans. James Strachey (New York: W. W. Norton, 1960).

5.   It is worth noting that as social pressures against profane jokes diminish, more extreme sacrilege and bawdiness is required to elicit laughter. This is borne out in popular culture today. Fewer things are regarded as socially forbidden, so popular comedians strike at more sacred things to get a laugh. Lenny Bruce, the first popular "dirty" comic in the U.S., had a routine that is tame by today's standards. But his jokes crossed a line that has been continually redrawn until it was eventually erased altogether. Today, comics can use any language and make fun of anything they want, however delicate or sacred the subject matter. This is a clear example of a law of diminishing returns when it comes to profane humor.

relief theory best accounts for body function humor and the so-called "shaggy dog" stories, which feature long drawn-out, tension-building narratives that end abruptly and disappointingly, usually with an empty punch line (e.g., "Hey, that dog is not so shaggy").

Examples of each form of humor can be found in Scripture, although in most cases the contexts in which they occur are serious. In the book of Esther, Haman's hanging on his own gallows is humorous, albeit darkly, because as empathetic readers we experience a sudden superiority to this villain when he gets his due. Many scriptural narratives feature humorous incongruities. The impregnation of Abraham's elderly wife, Sara, is a good example. The idea certainly tickled Abraham, as he fell facedown laughing when God gave him the news (Gen. 17:17). And as for biblical humor falling into the relief category, the most well-known and shocking example is probably Paul's remark about the Judaizers in Galatia, who preached circumcision and other aspects of the law. About them Paul says, "I wish they would go the whole way and emasculate themselves!" (Gal. 5:12). This harsh quip is especially funny, Freud would say, because it's content is both sexual and violent.

Bores, Buffoons, and Social Propriety

It's safe to say that all of the basic forms of humor are, in general, morally legitimate. Like any aspect of human life, though, abuses of comedy are to be avoided. And as with all the virtues, vicious extremes reside on either side of wit, specifically those of being a bore or a buffoon. A bore is someone who is dull or tiresome. Dull people lack social spirit, while tiresome people use their social energy in tedious ways. The dull person doesn't say much, and the tiresome person says too much that really amounts to nothing. In either case, the person lacks wit and could benefit from some comic spice in her manner.[6] The buffoon, on the other hand, indulges excessively in comedy, either by making jokes too frequently or in socially offensive ways. Such a person needs to scale back or refine her witticisms to make them more appropriate.

---

6. Aristotle regards boorishness as the vice of insufficiency when it comes to wit. See Aristotle *Nicomachean Ethics* 2.7, in *The Basic Works of Aristotle,* ed. Richard McKeon, trans. W. D. Ross (New York: Random, 1941). A boor is someone who is socially clumsy or ill-mannered, even rude. She lacks a certain social grace that sets other people at ease. I disagree with Aristotle here. It seems to me that boorishness is the vice of excess, while reclusiveness is the vice of insufficiency, relative to the virtue of refinement.

How does one avoid being a bore or buffoon? Most importantly, a person must take a sincere interest in others. If there's one thing that the bore and buffoon have in common it is that they are selfish. The selfishness of one is manifested in not bothering to make herself more interesting, while the other's selfishness is manifested in making herself the center of attention with all her joking. Also, one must have a sense of the socially appropriate. To avoid being a bore, it's obvious that one must use one's sense of humor, but to avoid being a buffoon, one must know when to make witty remarks. Even good things (assuming the jokes are good) can become annoying, but once the joker crosses the line of what's considered good, a gag that might have been merely annoying, becomes offensive.

So which topics, from a moral standpoint, are appropriate for humor? First, which topics are *not* appropriate to joke about? A good starting point might be to rule out as morally legitimate, all forms of mocking. To be specific, we should avoid mocking persons—for to do so is cruel—as well as sacred things—for to do so is profane. Jokes that belittle faith or poke fun at God are irreverent and obviously wrong. To mock a fellow human being indirectly insults God, since we all bear God's image. Moreover, mockery is painful to the person mocked. It's a form of contempt and is wrong, no matter how many laughs one might elicit. This doesn't rule out teasing that's done in good fun and doesn't hurt feelings or belittle a person. Teasing might be a nuisance to the person teased, but it's not humiliating. The difficulty here is that it's not always easy to know when one has crossed the line from teasing into mockery. Such knowledge requires discernment and an understanding of those involved. For this reason, it would be well to avoid entirely making fun of people, or at least one should do so in a way and to an extent that is safely away from mockery.

Teasing is only appropriate between persons who know each other well. Attempt to tease a stranger and you'll almost certainly come off as a mocker. This explains why ethnic jokes (in addition to making unfair stereotypes) tend to be cruel. When you poke fun at a whole race of people, it cannot possibly be considered teasing because most people in that group—in any ethnic group, including your own—are strangers to you. Necessarily, then, ethnic jokes are a form of mockery and are rarely appropriate.[7]

Wit has much social value when used appropriately. Humor can be useful to restore proper perspective when we're taking a situation or ourselves too seri-

---

7. I do think some instances of ethnic humor are both appropriate and edifying, assuming such jokes are used to educate or encourage people. An excellent example of this is to be found in the film *Mr. Saturday Night,* in which Billy Crystal's character (a stand-up comedian) routinely jokes about his Jewish culture. The effect is endearing rather than humiliating.

ously. Recently, my softball team was badly trounced, and we all felt a bit down about our performance. Then someone said, "Well, at least we weren't fighting for our country." This remark brought some smiles back to our faces as it put the loss of a softball game into better perspective. Wit calls for a certain amount of objectivity, which enables a person to see situations in their proper light and not become overwhelmed. For this reason, wit is an antidote to stress. If we make people laugh when they're feeling down or uptight, the improved perspective we provide is calming. This literally helps them physically, as stress contributes to numerous medical problems. No wonder the proverb describes the cheerful person as "good medicine."

Humor also is a valuable means of stimulating thought and critical thinking. Puns in particular are useful in this way. An example is, "Why did the fly run really fast across the top of a cereal box? Because the box said, 'Tear here along dotted line.'" Such jokes challenge the hearer to think abstractly and make verbal connections. Perhaps this is why it's been said that puns are the highest form of humor. Because humor has the ability to stimulate thought, it is actually a powerful educational device. One of the texts I use in my introductory course features over five hundred cartoons, all of which are both amusing and insightful. Like many of the goofy illustrations and puns I myself use in class (e.g., "don't put Descartes before the horse"), cartoons are easily recalled, which helps to seal even difficult concepts in students' memories.[8]

Finally, humor has social value because it creates connections between people and reveals commonalities they might not realize. To share a joke is to share something of yourself and become vulnerable. Depending upon the nature of the joke, it may also reveal something about your values. So where there's hearty laughter, or at least a positive response, the joke teller is affirmed personally and perhaps even in terms of her opinions on some matter. Humor, too, eases tensions in formal situations, a reason why preachers and other public speakers often begin their sermons and lectures with a joke. It sets people at ease, relaxes the mood, and enables the audience to better concentrate on the message.

What It Takes to Be Funny: Prerequisites of Wit

In the past, Christians have often been criticized for being uptight and overly serious. We've been accused, essentially, of lacking wit and being bores. And to

---

8. The educational value of humor is well understood by political journalists; since the mid-1800s, cartoons have played an important role in public dialogue about politics.

some degree the criticism has been on the mark. Certainly, the Puritans epito-mized a deep seriousness about moral conduct that inclined them to fall short in the department of wit. One of Jonathan Edwards' personal resolutions was "never to utter anything that is sportive, or a matter of laughter, on a Lord's day," a self-restraint that strikes us today as extreme.[9] For all their theological insight and high moral standards, the Puritans, in general, probably were too serious, taking a comparatively narrow view on the appropriateness of wit. To-day, Christians in general take a more balanced view and recognize that it's okay, even edifying, to joke about certain things.

It's one thing, though, to start telling a few jokes; it's quite another to strive for true wit. Like all the virtues, wit is a trait that one does not simply will into existence. It takes time and intentional exposure to the right sorts of influences to develop it. Moreover, wit requires a complex of other characteristics, each of which we should strive to nurture in its own right. The witty person must be imaginative. She must possess a trained ability to come up with new or creative connections between objects, contexts, and persons. Doing so requires knowl-edge about various subjects, but just as important is an aesthetic sensibility. It's no accident that the study of humor falls within the domain of aesthetics, the philosophy of art. Humor is artistic, and one might say that the witty person is skilled at the art of making people laugh.

Wit also calls for discernment. Earlier, it was noted that in order to avoid being a bore or a buffoon, one must be able to discern when a joke is socially appropriate. A person must be discerning in yet another way in order to be witty: One must have the insight to detect subtle ironies in events and to spot absurd aspects of ordinary objects and inappropriately revered people and prac-tices. This type of discernment requires critical thinking skills and a set of val-ues that one actively uses to evaluate one's culture and environment.

Another important trait is versatility. Witty people expose themselves to a wide variety of subjects and experiences. The more topics about which one is conversant, the more connections she will be able to make. It's hardly a coinci-dence that so many well-known comedians studied philosophy, the most di-verse and interdisciplinary of subjects. The list is impressive: Steve Martin, David Brenner, George Carlin, Joan Rivers, Martin Mull, and Woody Allen, to name a few. Philosophy might, in fact, be the ideal pre-comedian major. In addition to training in critical thinking and linguistic analysis, philosophy involves a broad exploration of issues in most other disciplines. All of this comes in handy for

---

9.   Jonathan Edwards, *Memoirs of Jonathan Edwards*, in *The Works of Jonathan Edwards* (Edinburgh: Banner of Truth, 1974), 1:xxi.

the comic. The reverse, of course, might also be true—that the comic sensibilities of these people led them to philosophy. In any case, variety and depth in
understanding only enhance one's ability to be humorous.

Lastly, humility is important for the development of wit, as it is for most
other virtues. The social risk and vulnerability involved in making a joke demands that a person not take herself too seriously. The most endearing humor
is, in fact, self-deprecating. Rodney Dangerfield made a career out of jokes about
himself. ("I tell ya, I don't get no respect. Yesterday, I stuck my head out of my
car window and got arrested for mooning.") The appeal of such humor is easily
explained: When people make fun of themselves, we feel the sudden sense of
superiority described by Thomas Hobbes. A humble perspective equips a person to use herself as the butt of jokes and gives others that sudden sense of
superiority that makes them laugh.[10]

Conclusion

Kierkegaard called humor "the last stage of existential inwardness before
faith."[11] I have no idea what this means, but it sounds cool. Just kidding. His
point is that since humorists spend much time pointing out absurdities in life,
they are well prepared to embrace the absurd aspects of (in Kierkegaard's
judgment) the Christian faith. Such aspects of Christian doctrine might be better
described as paradoxical or ironic, but Kierkegaard's point still stands. A further
link can be made between wit and faith: Humorous people are primed for faith
by their refusal to take themselves too seriously. Such humility is a prerequisite
for placing faith in someone. This is not to say that wit is necessary for faith—
that some Christians are humorless proves otherwise. Rather, it suggests that an
important aspect of wit—humility—is also crucial for faith. Which by itself
might be sufficient reason to take humor seriously.

---

10. If humility is a prerequisite for good humor, this explains why witty people
     tend to be less easily embarrassed than other people. Embarrassment pivots on
     vanity and pride, traits the humble person lacks.
11. Søren Kierkegaard, *Concluding Unscientific Postscript,* trans. Howard Hong and
     Edna Hong (Princeton: Princeton University Press, 1992), 1:259.

12

KEEPING SECRETS

The Virtues of Discretion and Modesty

Human beings are social creatures. Our nature is to live in community and to relate to one another, buying and selling, teaching and learning, working and playing. This characteristic of human nature presents both benefits and challenges. Among the difficulties is that of keeping private what is inappropriate for public display. Some things just should not be shared with many people while still others are properly kept entirely to oneself. The ability to keep secrets is one of the marks of the virtuous person, a moral skill that takes many forms. This chapter discusses two of these: discretion and modesty.

Discretion, or the Keeping of One's Confidences

An old adage says, "Don't tell your friends what you don't want your enemies to know." This piece of wisdom is echoed by the Old Testament prophet Micah: "Do not trust a neighbor; put no confidence in a friend. Even with her who lies in your embrace be careful of your words" (Mic. 7:5). This counsel would surely seem like paranoia if its wisdom were not borne out repeatedly by human experience. Apparent friends may become turncoats, and the most intimate lover can be treacherous. What at the moment might seem an innocent, off-hand remark can come back to haunt a person—sometimes for years.

If it's important to guard one's mouth for one's own sake, the stakes are that much higher when keeping another person's confidence. Here, the reputation or welfare of others might be on the line, and for this reason the temptation to break confidence is stronger. The allure of divulging secrets derives from various dynamics, one of which is the sense of superiority it can bring. When a person confesses something to us, we might privately sigh, "I'm glad I didn't do that." And to share that person's confession with a third party can bring a perverse exhilaration. Another lure to break confidence is the sheer drama it creates, if only in the emotional response that divulging the secret might elicit. In addition, a person might stand to gain in some way by breaking confidence or might stand to lose something by keeping the secret. It's no wonder, then, that the psalmist lauds the ability to resist such temptations, saying the God-fearing man "keeps his oath even when it hurts" (Ps. 15:4).

Keeping secrets is a significant element of the moral skill of discretion. The discrete person has a good sense of the appropriate when it comes to what is said and left unsaid. He's careful not to air information that places others at risk, whether personally or professionally. He weighs his words carefully so as to avoid embarrassing, undermining, or falsely implicating himself or others. And he succeeds in doing so even when emotions run high. A romantic interlude might tempt one to make a declaration or promise that goes too far. Or a comical context might invite a crass remark to draw a good laugh. Discretion will refrain from such and, in the process, perhaps save someone's feelings or even a reputation. For this reason Shakespeare called discretion "the better part of valor."[1]

The point of discretion is the preservation of trust between people.[2] Properly motivated by interest in people's welfare, discretion should not be confused with wholly negative attitudes, such as fear of reprisal if one says the wrong thing. Clearly, nervousness about crossing certain lines can be a boon to discretion but is not virtuous in itself. Nor ought discretion be confused with disinterest in the subject of a secret. A person should be willing to handle an issue carefully as a matter of principle, whether or not that person finds interest in it. Only this commitment will guarantee that a person will guard a confidence even when it hurts.

A major vice opposing discretion is gossip, which is essentially the sharing of others' secrets. When I share a secret that a person has told to me, I place it in the "confidence" of yet another person. Doing so not only breaks the original confidence but also proves me to be untrustworthy. What's worse, it invites others to also share the secret. Speaking is a public act, and all public acts are implicit

---

1. William Shakespeare, *King Henry the Fourth* 1.5.iv, in *The Complete Works of Shakespeare* (New York: Walter J. Black, 1937), 493.
2. David Hume notes, "The quality . . . most necessary for the execution of any enterprise is discretion, by which we carry on a safe intercourse with others, give due attention to our own and to their characters." He adds, "In the conduct of ordinary life, no virtue is more requisite, not only to obtain success, but to avoid the most fatal miscarriages and disappointments." *Essential Works of David Hume,* ed. Ralph Cohen (New York: Bantam, 1965), 228–29.

recommendations, invitations for others to do the same. So gossip is, by its nature, contagious. And, like any contagion, it spreads exponentially, as one "just between you and me" becomes two, then four, then eight, and so on. Before long, a secret is public knowledge and what was whispered from ear to ear might as well have been proclaimed from the rooftops.

The real poison of gossip lies in the distortions it creates. Stories passed through the grapevine are inevitably embellished, and truth gradually morphs into falsehood. In the worst cases, the result is outright slander.[3] And public lies about a person, however unintentional, may be no less devastating. An old story powerfully illustrates this. In a certain community a rumor about a rabbi was carelessly spread by a young man who failed to take the time to confirm the facts about the story. Only after the rumor had spread throughout the community was the young man corrected. He went to the rabbi and apologized. The priest accepted his apology but then took the young man to the highest hilltop in the region, where he released a bag of feathers into the wind. After this, the rabbi told him, "Now, go and gather all the feathers for me," to which the young man replied, "That's impossible." The rabbi said, "Nor can you or anyone else retrieve the lies you've spread about me." This anecdote illustrates just how extensive and lasting the effects of gossip can be. A word spoken cannot be withdrawn, and the damage it may bring to a reputation often cannot be altered. Hence the saying that "loose lips sink ships."

The flip side of gossip is flattery. Whereas gossip typically involves saying something negative about a person that you wouldn't say in that person's presence, to flatter is to say something *positive* about someone in his *presence* that you wouldn't say in his absence. Flattery is indiscreet in an ironic way, as it superficially appears to edify and advance a person's welfare. But since it exaggerates or even falsifies a person's real qualities, it winds up harming rather than helping. Flattery is really a form of mockery, as it draws attention to the contrast between the praise lavished on the person and his actual qualities.

The temptation to flatter basically lies in the favor that one's praise may elicit. When I flatter someone—assuming he doesn't see through my remark—he naturally thinks better of me. While it's true that kind words tend to elicit friendly responses, lying to bring about such a response is not justifiable.

---

3.   Immanuel Kant writes, "We can have either an honest or treacherous enemy. The fawning, clandestine, deceitful enemy is far baser than the open one, even though the latter be violent and wicked. We can defend ourselves against the latter, but not against the former." *Lectures on Ethics,* trans. Louis Infield (London: Methuen and Co., 1930), 215.

So gossip and flattery are equal but opposite symptoms of indiscretion, each motivated by the same perverse desire to appear or feel superior to others. The gossip aims to achieve superiority by lowering the public estimation of another person. The flatterer tries to achieve this by increasing another person's estimation of himself. Discrete persons resist this self-serving impulse, preferring to tell only the truth about others and to do this only when it's appropriate.

As with all virtues, discretion is a skill built through practice. By experiencing diverse social situations, one gains a feel for what is and is not appropriate to talk about. Self-training in discretion is possible as well. The spiritual discipline of secrecy is especially relevant to the development of discretion. Secrecy involves the practice of voluntarily keeping secrets when it's not morally required. One might resolve, for instance, to keep private one's good deed or accomplishment that one would otherwise enjoy sharing. This builds the self-discipline required for discretion, much in the same way that fasting builds bodily self-control. Saying "no" to one's natural desires when there's nothing at stake morally strengthens one's ability to stand firm when faced with real temptation.

Modesty, or the Keeping of Bodily Secrets

If keeping one's confidences is important, keeping one's bodily secrets is no less so. The virtue pertaining to the latter is modesty, the moral skill of maintaining physical privacy and, in particular, exercising public restraint in the area of sensuality. Persons who display this virtue have a strong sense of decency and, consequently, a capacity for both shame and embarrassment when certain standards of behavior have been violated. Although not identical with purity or chastity, modesty overlaps them. It is, one might say, the public expression of these traits.

Behaving modestly is a special challenge in today's American culture. Ours is an increasingly pornographic culture in the sense of the Greek root of the term, *porneia,* which refers to sexual deviancy of any kind. The notion of deviancy refers to deviation from a standard, and the moral standard of sexuality from which our culture is steadily departing is that of lifelong monogamous commitment between a man and a woman. Promiscuity and homosexuality are on the rise today and are likely to become more prevalent in the future. More significantly, in regards to the present topic, these deviations from the biblical ideal have been mainstreamed in and by the media and entertainment industries in dramatic ways. Hollywood films, television programs, and even commercials routinely feature sexual images and situations. The net effect on our culture is a rising threshold of sexual shame and embarrassment.

In her book, *A Return to Modesty,* Wendy Shalit observes how the widespread "war on embarrassment" being waged in our culture (from the entertainment industry to sex education programs in public schools) has contributed to the rise of promiscuity and sexual violence in our society. In a culture where modesty is respected as a virtue, men must show themselves worthy of a woman's affection. Where women's boundaries are relaxed, the moral demands on men are relaxed as well. "How can we expect men to be honorable," Shalit asks, "when a large number of women consistently send them the message that they do not have to be?"[4] Many liberal feminists, in the interest of advancing women's rights, have played a significant role in the deconstruction of modesty as a virtue. It is thus ironic that in their work to liberate women from sexual repression they have removed the most effective shield against male aggression. The cure is now worse than the disease.

A second factor that militates against modesty is our culture's devotion to personal autonomy, the basic value of self-determination. The notion that each person should be free to decide his own path in life for himself is deep-seated in the American psyche. The assumption is so basic that it's rarely stated explicitly in public discussions, and to question its validity would be unthinkable to most people, including many Christians. Understood politically, perhaps nothing problematic lies in this idea, but problematic from a Christian perspective is the extension of the concept of autonomy into the ethical realm. When such occurs, people are thought to be free to select their own moral values. The historic Christian conviction, by contrast, is that human beings are bound by the moral norms expressed in Scripture, and violating these is both wrong and impractical. It's sad to see this conviction continue to wane in contemporary American culture with a consequent loss of any grounds for moral shame, be it sexual or otherwise.

These factors—the mainstreaming of sexual deviancy and the widespread belief in the moral autonomy of human beings—combine to create a cultural atmosphere in which the virtue of modesty is a relic. Where deviancy is normalized, modesty cannot be seen as having any practical value. Where moral absolutes are rejected, the concept of shame, upon which the concept of modesty crucially depends, is unintelligible. Today the moral tables have completely turned. The modest are frequently lampooned as prudish, hung-up, or old-

---

4.   Wendy Shalit, *A Return to Modesty: Discovering the Lost Virtue* (New York: Simon and Schuster, 1999), 105.

fashioned. It's not uncommon for the trait to be represented as a character flaw or as symptomatic of a psychological problem. Among the virtues, none is portrayed as a vice in our culture more often than modesty. So it's important to dispel some misconceptions and confusions that enable the critics of modesty to ridicule this virtue.

Modesty is *not* bashfulness. The modest person freely chooses to keep certain things private and he does so out of respect for others as well as himself. The shy person's timidity, on the other hand, is not a choice. He keeps things private inadvertently, out of fear. So his real concern is not others but himself. Whereas the bashful person finds revealing himself in public uncomfortable, the modest person keeps a thing out of public view for the sake of others, even if he would personally be comfortable revealing more.

Modesty is *not* shame. To be ashamed of one's physical characteristics is a psychological problem and has nothing to do with modesty. If anything, it militates against the real display of the virtue. Modesty is motivated by self-respect and appreciation for one's own body, and it's because of this bodily self-respect that the modest individual keeps it private. The ironic nature of this virtue might tempt some to confuse it with shame but, in truth, they are very different traits.

Modesty is *not* symptomatic of sexual hang-ups. To be modest is not to oppose sexual expression but the vice of lasciviousness. In a sex-obsessed culture, the healthy balance will necessarily appear unhealthy, as when modest behavior is characterized as a sign of sexual repression. But the sexually-repressed person covers up compulsively, not by a choice to respect others and himself. The modest person, in fact, proves his psychological health in so far as he demonstrates self-control and a keen sense of public decency.

But, some have complained, isn't modesty at least anti-erotic? Nothing could be farther, in fact, from the truth. As Shalit's study so powerfully demonstrates, modesty is actually *necessary* for the erotic. In researching her book, she studied nudist colonies and found that in such communities the prevailing attitude toward human nakedness was not excitement but boredom. The constant public presence of genitalia served to defeat eroticism rather than stimulate it. By contrast, she found that in those cultures and epochs—such as in America's modest past—the erotic flourished precisely because so much was hidden. Sexuality was kept private, and the secrecy functioned to arouse sexual interest. Here we find the reverse dynamic of that prevailing in nudist colonies; to hide a thing is to preserve mystery. Since mystery is essential to eroticism, those communities where modesty is practiced are naturally more erotic than those where it is not. Shalit sums up the point: "Modesty is the proof that morality is sexy. It may even be the proof of God, because it means that we have been designed in such a way that when we humans act like animals, without any restraint and without any rules, we just don't have as much fun."[5]

So it seems that you can't lose with modesty. On the one hand, keeping one's bodily secrets naturally prevents unwanted and unhealthy sexual encounters, but by preserving an erotic sense of mystery it enhances one's sex appeal.[6] This significant point is lost, however, on contemporary American culture in its self-defeating erotic quest. Still, we who are serious about maintaining a Christian ethos can work to encourage modesty in our communities. We can personally model this virtue by the way we dress, speak, and behave, even to the point of pursuing an obviously countercultural lifestyle in each of these areas. For young women, especially, choices regarding clothing are crucial. An outfit need not be scanty or tight fitting to be immodest. Any style of dress that calls undue attention to one's body can be immodest. Hard and fast rules in this area are, of course, hard to come by, but at least we should be thinking critically in this area, scrutinizing the choices we make about our attire and behavior. Developing critical awareness is more than half the battle in the pursuit of modesty.

Along these lines, another important thing we can all do is consciously redirect our thinking toward what really matters about people and our lives together. Consider what dominates your attention throughout the day. Is it your physical appearance and the physical appearance of others? When you're drawn to people, is it because of their intangible personality traits or because of the way they look? Are you more likely to compliment someone regarding a character trait (e.g., "You have a great sense of humor!") or a physical feature (e.g., "You look great!")? Scripture tells us not to conform to worldly patterns of thinking but to be "transformed by the renewing of your mind" (Rom. 12:2). In our society, this exhortation must be heeded with special attention to the topic at hand. American culture is obsessed with the superficial, especially physical attractiveness. We must take active steps to resist this preoccupation.

One especially disturbing symptom of our culture's preoccupation with physical appearance is the widespread phenomenon of eating disorders, such as anorexia and bulimia. Even at the Christian college where I teach, these disorders are problems on campus. In spite of our shared belief that a person's real value transcends her physical appearance, young women become obsessed with losing weight to achieve a certain "ideal" look (as defined by popular culture). It's tragic

---

5. Ibid., 193.
6. John Peck argues brilliantly for this point in his essay "Sex in Art: Is There a Place for an Erotic Christian Imagination?" *Cornerstone* 30 (2001): 33–38.

that some women are willing to compromise their health and endanger their lives to do so. Clearly, a principal cause of this pervasive hyper-concern with body image traces to women's bodies being constantly on display in our culture. And, of course, the visibility of women's bodies directly influences the way we think and what we talk about. Men and women alike openly discuss their bodies in ways today that would have been disgraceful just a few decades ago. Our immodest conversation is a function of our physical immodesty. Could it be, as my wife has proposed, that a woman's body is simply not an appropriate topic of public conversation? Might the way we talk about our bodies be as damaging as the way we display them? Just as pornographic images are immoral because they represent women as mere objects, our conversations can be similarly immoral, representing women's bodies as objects. Given the prevalence of such patterns of speaking, it's no wonder that so many young women are obsessed with body image.[7]

So how does one resist the onslaught of immodesty in popular culture? As noted in another chapter, I gave up television several years ago and doing so has significantly impacted my family and me. One of the many benefits of this decision pertains to my sense of modesty. Without television, I'm spared the constant influx of sexual images that flood other people's homes. This has sensitized me to the sexual images I do encounter and has given me a fresh sense of just how ridiculously fixated our culture is on all things sexual. The TV-less life has assisted me tremendously in the transforming of my own mind (not to mention the time I've saved!).

In addition to changing our ways of thinking, we can encourage modesty by overtly recommending it to others when appropriate. This can be a tricky matter, however, as such encouragement can be taken as an insult and might, in fact, be intrusive, depending upon the context. Worse yet, recommending modesty might seem to imply that one has a dirty mind. For these reasons one should take great care when addressing immodesty in others. One route is to look for general or indirect ways to encourage modest behavior. A personal anecdote illustrates what I mean. A few years back my wife and I allowed a male student, whom I'll call Jeff, to stay at our house for several weeks during the summer. He was a terrific young man, and we greatly enjoyed his presence, except that he had a habit of going shirtless around the house. We didn't relish the idea of just telling Jeff to stop this, because we didn't want to hurt his feelings. So we looked

---

7. G. F. Schueler suggests that what makes immodesty a vice is that it reveals a "hollowness of self," that is, a preoccupation with the approval of others. See Schueler, "Why IS Modesty a Virtue?" *Ethics* 109 (July 1999): 835–41.

for an opportunity to allude to the fact that going without a shirt annoyed my wife, Amy. That opportunity came when, in a playful moment, Amy sprayed me with water through the kitchen window while Jeff and I were painting outside. "Okay, Amy," I said, "this means I'll have to go shirtless until you get me a dry shirt." I smiled mischievously at Jeff and whispered, "She can't stand it when I don't wear a shirt around the house." Jeff smiled, and we both returned to our painting. But Amy and I noticed that Jeff never again went without a shirt in our house. No confrontation was needed, just a passing reference, which Jeff probably never figured was intended for him.

Reverence As the Root of These Virtues

The proper keeping of secrets is a constant challenge in the moral life, particularly in a culture that celebrates indiscretion and immodesty. The Christian must commit himself to these virtues nonetheless. It's been noted that discretion is a kind of quiet valor, establishing one's trustworthiness by silence on some matters. Something similar is true of the modest person. As Jean de la Bruyere once noted, "Modesty is to merit, what shade is to figures in a picture; it gives it strength and makes it stand out."[8] Along these lines, we might say, the discrete and modest person exhibits a certain personal subtlety and understatement, which highlights his overall goodness.

This chapter has proceeded on the assumption that the practice of "keeping secrets" is the common essence shared by the virtues of discretion and modesty. The deeper moral root might be the virtue of reverence, the moral skill of paying appropriate respect. The reverent person respects God, people, animals, and even places and things, according to their worthiness. So, of course, God is due most respect, followed by human beings, and so on. Discretion and modesty are demanded by the virtue of reverence, as the disclosure of spoken and bodily secrets is disrespectful.

Gossip and immodesty, then, are each doubly irreverent. The gossiping man disrespects the person whose secret is shared, but he also shows disrespect to himself as a worthy confidant. In breaking confidence or perpetuating gossip he declares to the world, "don't trust me." And being untrustworthy, as we all know, is a transferable trait. When we don't trust someone's ability to keep a secret, we don't trust him in most other respects. In a similar way, immodesty is doubly irreverent. By dressing or acting in a provocative way, the immodest

8.   Jean de La Bruyere, *Characters,* trans. Henri Van Laun (New York: Howard Fertig, 1992), 44.

woman disrespects others by—at least—distracting them and—at worst—enticing them to focus upon her as a sexual object. She fails to revere herself by displaying publicly what is worth keeping private. Her behavior or manner of dress declares to the world, "This is not worth waiting for." And, often, others take notice and respond accordingly, treating her disrespectfully.

So the irreverence of the immodest rebounds back upon oneself. As the old adage goes, what goes around comes around. One should not expect any more respect than what one doles out, even to oneself.

13

WEATHERING THE STORMS

The Virtue of Perseverance

William Faulkner wrote, "a man is the sum of his misfortunes."[1] Faulkner's observation states a profound truth. We are the product of our sufferings. Our pains forge our souls. The grief we've borne drapes our mental landscapes, and our moral characters are the direct result of how we've responded to suffering. The moral skill that is both a requirement *and* a result of suffering is perseverance. As one manages to "keep the faith" through suffering, one grows even stronger to deal with whatever further suffering one may experience.

To internalize this from a Christian perspective is a great challenge. Our thinking about suffering is steadily infiltrated by cultural influences, so we must resist the temptation to conform to worldly patterns of thought as we reflect on the subject. Indeed, to present a biblical view on suffering is to highlight just how countercultural it is.

Three Sorrows

I don't pretend to be an expert sufferer. Yet I'm no stranger to suffering. My first major sorrow came in my youth when my family moved from Detroit to Jackson, Mississippi, wrenching me away from my siblings, my friends, and all that was familiar to me. To disorient me even further, puberty struck at the same time, and the hormonal confusion compounded the pain. I fell into a clinical depression that lasted several months. It is said that the grief of the young is especially deep because youth lack the experience to know that time heals. "This too shall pass," my mother told me repeatedly during that first cruel summer in Mississippi. She was right, but I couldn't comprehend her meaning. And to this day that sorrow remains the worst I've ever known, if only because I was so helpless to deal with it.

---

1. William Faulkner, *The Sound and the Fury* (New York: Modern Library, 1956), 129.

Nearly a decade ago as a new instructor at Taylor University, I experienced a major trial that took the form of betrayal. My first wife was unfaithful to me and had no interest in repenting or reconciling. The emotions I experienced were wide ranging, but all of them were excruciating, from rage to shame and everything in between. Even with the perspective of adulthood, I found it difficult to imagine full recovery when in the throes of my divorce. But the friends and colleagues God provided me were ever-present helps in that valley, and with the passage of time, healing did come. Today, my new wife, Amy, and our three children are constant reminders of just how wondrously excessive the grace of God can be.

My third major life trial to date came with the passing of my father in the summer of 2001. His death was actually only the bitter culmination of a decade long sorrow. For years my dad battled emphysema, a degenerating lung condition that slowly and mercilessly suffocates the person. He was a good dad—dedicated to his family, faithful to his wife, and a wild fan of his four sons, each of whom he convinced was his favorite. But because of a long train of hypocrisies he'd witnessed, he had no use for anything religious, particularly of an organized sort. When he nearly died in the summer of 1997, he finally gave in to my urgings that he start reading the Bible. He read the entire New Testament and some of the gospels repeatedly. In the end, he did believe in God but could not bring himself to believe in miracles—including, of course, the virgin birth of Christ and his resurrection. Death caught him before that belief ever came. Having prayed for two decades that he'd embrace these things, I always figured it would eventually happen. But apparently it didn't, at least not on this side of the grave.

So I've experienced being displaced, betrayed, and bereaved. But I'm not unique. Most of us have our stories of loss, despair, and deep disappointment. And for those who do not, they eventually will. Many struggle with mental illness or know the grief of miscarriage or infertility; some experience devastating physical injuries or even the death of a child. Worldwide, suffering is, of course, rampant, even gruesome in some cases. Tens of thousands have been tortured at the hands of cruel people in Bosnia, Rwanda, Iraq, and other countries. Even now innocent people are becoming victims of genocide, systematic rape, child slavery. These things happen daily all over the world. Truly, Dostoevsky was right when he said, "The earth is soaked from its crust to its center" with the tears of humanity.[2]

---

2.   Fyodor Dostoevsky, *The Brothers Karamazov,* trans. Constance Garnett (New York: William Heinemann, 1945), 224.

The Gift of Suffering

Friedrich Nietzsche is supposed to have said, "What does not kill me makes me stronger." Like Faulkner, Nietzsche glimpsed a significant truth, although it tells only part of the story. Some people are crushed by their suffering, although they do survive it. But for those who are able to sustain faith through their suffering, the experience often does make them stronger. This is the crucial biblical truth that should inform all our thinking on suffering. Suffering is one of God's preferred means to build the strong soul, and that strength occurs in at least three areas: in moral maturity, in empathy, and in the way to the inner life of God.

First, suffering is the way to *moral maturity*. This theme emerges repeatedly in Scripture. James says, "Consider it pure joy, my brothers, whenever you face trials of many kinds, because you know that the testing of your faith develops perseverance. Perseverance must finish its work so that you may be mature and complete, not lacking anything" (James 1:2–4). Here James directly links the attainment of moral maturity to suffering trials. Peter does the same thing when he writes, "Though now for a little while you may have had to suffer grief in all kinds of trials. These have come so that your faith—of greater worth than gold, which perishes even though refined by fire—may be proved genuine and may result in praise, glory and honor when Jesus Christ is revealed" (1 Peter 1:6–7). Peter connects suffering with the building of faith itself. And the prophet Isaiah makes a similar point in passing when he asserts that "the Lord gives you the bread of adversity and the water of affliction" (30:20). These metaphors suggest that adversity and affliction actually provide spiritual nourishment. In these and many other biblical passages the point resounds: Suffering has a purpose for the person of faith. And that purpose is the building of moral maturity, a better character.

If that's not enough motivation to endure suffering with joy, consider this: We take our characters with us into the next world. God doesn't form our souls from scratch again once we arrive in heaven. Otherwise, we wouldn't be recognizable for who we are when we get there! So the stakes are high; the payoff of obedience and perseverance through suffering is for the *real* long term, even eternity.

So I'm grateful for the suffering I've experienced. Today, I already glimpse many of the moral benefits that it's brought to me. From my displacement I gained greater understanding of the world and different cultures. The experience also increased my appreciation for people who are different from me, and it built my capacity to endure hardship. Through my betrayal I learned better how to trust God even through blinding pain. I gained a whole new dimension of understanding with regard to his faithfulness. In my bereavement I learned that my perplexity over God's ways in no way tells against his justice. I found, too, that his peace is mysterious and transcendent, beyond what reason can plumb.

James, Peter, and Isaiah just might be correct after all! Our trials form the very road to moral maturity. What a sad irony, then, that we so resent our suffering, that at times we'll do all we can to resist or avoid it. The poet Rainer Maria Rilke comments on this fact: "We wasters of sorrows! How we stare away into sad endurance beyond them, trying to foresee their end! Whereas they are nothing else than our winter foliage, our somber evergreen, one of the seasons of our interior year—not only season—they're also place, settlement, camp, soil, dwelling."[3]

Not only is suffering the way to moral maturity, it's the way to *empathy* toward others who suffer. Paul's words are, in fact, explicit: God is the "Father of compassion . . . who comforts us in all our troubles, so that we can comfort those in any trouble with the comfort we ourselves have received from God" (2 Cor. 1:3–4). He further says to the church at Corinth, "If we are distressed, it is for your comfort and salvation; if we are comforted, it is for your comfort, which produces in you patient endurance of the same sufferings we suffer" (v. 6).

Empathy makes grace contagious and does so in two related ways. It enhances our *ability* to help others as well as our *desire* to do so. We tend to want to help those with whom we can emotionally identify, and such identification is a function of the degree to which we have shared their experiences.

Here's another way of making the same point: the moral core of our faith is the Golden Rule—Do to others as you would have them do to you. Your ability to apply this maxim is only as strong as your capacity to understand your neighbor's point of view. Suffering through a variety of difficulties broadens your perspective on the human experience and provides new points of identification with others. This in turn enables you to imagine what your neighbor would want in a particular situation. You know because, as they say, you've been there and done that. Consequently, you're better at applying the Golden Rule—which is to say, you're a better Christian. And all because you've suffered.

---

3.   Rainer Maria Rilke, *Duino Elegies*, trans. J. B. Leishman and Stephen Spender (New York: W. W. Norton, 1963), 79.

As an aside, growth in empathy is one of the reasons art is morally valuable. It enables us to enter into other people's experience, to see things from their point of view and thus to empathize. It follows, then, that those who reserve little place in their lives for the arts are morally impoverished. They've blocked out of their lives a rich bank of insight into the human experience and so much empathy that goes with it. On the positive side, it also explains why artists themselves—musicians, sculptors, painters, etc.—tend to be empathetic people. Have you ever heard of a racist poet?

My own sorrows have made me a more empathetic person. My displacement has made me more sensitive to those who are cultural aliens, social outcasts, or misfits. It's also made me more sympathetic toward oppressed people, whether due to their race, sex, or beliefs. My bereavement has made me more sympathetic with those whose loved ones have died. My betrayal has softened my heart toward those who go through divorce and other humiliating trials. Consequently, I'm better equipped to help them through it, as I've done several times and as I did recently with one former student. I'll call him "John." A year or so ago his wife left him, and John tried to recoup. But, he said,

> The thing is, I can't seem to get over it. I can't move on. It's so hard to think that someone you loved and you thought loved you could do such a thing. I have absolutely no self-esteem. I can't sleep. Every day I wonder what any of this crazy life is for. What are we supposed to be or how are we supposed to be? She didn't even think twice about our breakup. To her it was like a high school relationship ending. I live with this guilt every day that I should have been a better husband, that maybe if I was she wouldn't have left. This guilt and sorrow pushes against my chest every day, trying to steal my breath.

The sense of despair John shares here—loneliness, humiliation, self-doubt, shame—these feelings I know from the inside. I once occupied that room in the earthly hell that is divorce. He knows this and has told me that my words of encouragement mean more to him than they otherwise would.

The redemptive power of suffering was clearly glimpsed by the twentieth century's greatest saint, Mother Teresa. She observed that Jesus shared "our life, our loneliness, our agony, our death. Only by being one with us has he redeemed us. We are allowed to do the same." Notice how her language suggests suffering is a privilege. She continues, "All the desolation of the poor people, not only their material poverty, but their spiritual destitution, must be redeemed, and we must share it, for only by being one with them can we redeem them, that is, by bringing God into their lives and bringing them to God."[4]

Not only is suffering the way to moral maturity and the way to empathy, it's the way to the inner life of God. Paul declares his desire "to know Christ and the power of his resurrection and the fellowship of sharing in his sufferings" (Phil 3:10). As Paul saw it, a natural, even necessary, connection linked Christ's mission and means. So for those of us who intend to share in his mission, we must welcome the similarly painful means as well. Thomas à Kempis writes, "No man so feels in his heart the passion of Christ as he who suffers."[5] This explains why suffering so powerfully motivates Christian faith and devotion. As we feel what Christ felt, we begin to see with his eyes and eventually to will as he wills, which is, of course, our calling.

It should be clarified that the sort of suffering to which biblical writers and Thomas à Kempis refer is not mere discomfort or unfulfilled desire for luxury. Not getting what you want is not suffering; it's just a normal part of life. Some students on our campus, for example, have recently complained about being denied off-campus housing. A few of them have remarked that the experience has caused them deep grief. To label it as such grossly cheapens the concept. Imagine what some Rwandans, Bosnians, Asian Indians, or even the destitute in America would think of so describing such petty disappointments. They'd be incredulous and rightly so, because not getting what you don't need is not suffering and is no cause for grief.

Intimacy with God is a popular subject today among Christians. That's good, at least to the extent that the concept is understood biblically. But it's rarely understood so. More times than I can count I've heard Christian speakers talk passionately about intimacy with Christ. Seldom, if ever, do they mention that such intimacy must involve suffering. How strange, since the New Testament writers stressed this fact, as did Jesus himself when he declared that to follow him we must each take up our cross, and as Paul does when he says, "It has been granted to you on behalf of Christ not only to believe on him, but also to suffer for him" (Phil. 1:29).

What I glimpsed of the inner life of God through my trials was his agony in Christ. Through my displacement, I better understand how Christ agonized in the self-emptying that Paul describes in Philippians 2. Through my betrayal, I better see the agony of Christ in being betrayed by his friend. Through my

---

4.   Malcolm Muggeridge, *Something Beautiful for God* (New York: Harper and Row, 1971), 68.
5.   Thomas à Kempis, *Of the Imitation of Christ* (Pittsburgh: Whitaker, 1981), 87.

bereavement, I taste the agony of feeling forsaken by God and something of the agony of death itself, a face-to-face encounter with the cruelest darkness—all things experienced by Christ at Golgotha. In the measure of agony I share with Christ, we touch. Through my sorrows I know something of his own. Suffering is the road to the inner life of God and what Catholics have called "beatific vision," that is, a means by which we behold aspects of divine beauty otherwise hidden to us. Perhaps this is why Peter says, "He who has suffered in his body is done with sin" (1 Peter 4:1). To glimpse such beauty is to be changed.

False Perspectives on Suffering

The Christian perspective on suffering, then, is that it's a God-ordained means of maturing us, making us more empathetic, and disclosing to us his inner beauty. It's no surprise if you've never thought about suffering in this way, given our cultural mindset that suffering is intrinsically evil. Even some theologians have made this error, in spite of the plain biblical evidence to the contrary. Where, though, did the idea that suffering is an intrinsic evil come from? Its ultimate origin is found in ancient Greek philosophy. Plato and Aristotle regarded the emotions generally as lower grade faculties of the soul. So suffering, as an emotional phenomenon, was naturally viewed as essentially a defect. This notion was passed on to the Stoics who idealized the very opposite of emotion: apathy and resignation. Through Augustine, this low view of emotion, and suffering specifically, was transmitted to Christian theology.

Today in the twenty-first-century Western world, the view that suffering is evil is reinforced by medical science. The history of Western medicine is characterized by a slow but steady expansion of its aim—from seeking remedy for illness and injury to easing all pain (note that the two are *not* equivalent). The same trend has occurred in the fields of psychology and counseling. The original legitimate aim to maintain mental health and address mental disorders has expanded into the broader goal of easing all psychic pain. But perhaps most disturbing has been the intrusion of this mindset into the realm of ethics. It is now common even for Christians to use pain avoidance as a primary guideline for conduct. The consequences of such an approach are, of course, morally devastating.

Suffering is most emphatically *not* an intrinsic evil, as proven by the fact that Scripture affirms it to be God's will in many cases, such as Isaiah's declaration regarding the coming Messiah: "It was the LORD's will to crush him and cause him to suffer" (Isa. 53:10). And if ever a final statement was made about

God's sovereignty over suffering, it is the book of Job. Here is a case that illustrates acute suffering, often dismissed by Christians as simply the work of the Devil. Those who do so appear to have overlooked the summation found in the book's last chapter. The writer notes that Job's brothers, sisters, and friends "comforted and consoled him over all the trouble the LORD had brought upon him" (Job 42:11). Note how the text says the *Lord* brought Job's troubles upon him. Satan, evidently, was a secondary cause, a mere lackey. So it goes for all our suffering. Although it may result from the sinful choices of wicked people or Satan himself, God purposes our suffering to benefit us. Thus, it is not intrinsically evil.

In regard to this plain teaching of Scripture, it would be appropriate here to address a couple of unbiblical responses—the twin errors of asceticism and apathy. The ascetic response is that since suffering is such a valuable means to sanctify us and make us more Christlike, then we should actively inflict pain upon ourselves to accelerate this process. "After all," says the ascetic, "if God can purpose suffering for my good, then why can't I?" It should be noted first that while asceticism has been popular in other cultures and other times in Christian history, it's not much of an issue among American Christians today. Still, this opinion deserves a response. The problem with asceticism is twofold. For one thing it's narcissistic. The person who actually seeks pain for her own benefit maintains a too narrow moral focus. Even the ultimate hope that one's moral growth from ascetic practice will benefit others does not justify the preoccupation with self that it involves. Also, asceticism is self-defeating, because such artificial, self-imposed pain necessarily subtracts the most edifying element of suffering: the thwarting of one's will. If you get to choose precisely how and when you experience pain, then you haven't suffered in the full sense. True suffering goes against one's will. So asceticism should be rejected because it is both self-serving and self-defeating.

The other objection regards our response to the suffering of others. It's expressed in these questions: "If suffering is ultimately a benefit, then why alleviate others' pain? How can we justify comforting other people who suffer?" Again there's a twofold reply. We should help others who suffer because, frankly, we are commanded to do so. More than being commanded, it is assumed by biblical writers that we will do so (such as by Paul in 2 Cor. 1). So, notwithstanding that suffering can help others, we should seek to comfort them. And by doing so, we edify the victims all the more, because we are being Christ to them. Our service provides a further avenue for growth for those we comfort, as they see God's provision in our help and are thus encouraged in their faith. A second reason to help others who suffer is the Golden Rule. We appreciate it when others help us, so we should help others and leave the positive use of suffering to God. As the owner of all that is, it is God's prerogative to bring suffering into the lives he chooses for his own purposes. As his servants, who have been told to alleviate suffering and comfort those in pain, we should do so.

The biblical approach to suffering can be summed up in the following three points:

1. We should expect suffering (as Peter says, there is nothing strange in it, but it is natural to our fallen condition).
2. We should minister to those who suffer (because we've been commanded to and because we'd want others to minister to us).
3. We should think about suffering under the aspect of eternity, as God's chosen means to bring about greater goods in the world, including our moral growth, increased empathy, and union with God.

Admittedly, the necessity of suffering and our mandate to relieve suffering creates something like a moral paradox (analogous to such doctrines as the Trinity, the divine incarnation, and the predestination of free human actions). But it's biblical truth.

An attempt has been made herein to clarify this third point, that we should think about our suffering under the aspect of eternity. We must evaluate our own theology of suffering with a special alertness to what Scripture has to say on the topic. In the process we'll not only gain a more biblical outlook on the matter but also discover greater inner peace. To embrace God's making suffering our lot is to surrender the unrealistic and destructive craving that we can find final and lasting comfort on this side of paradise. The lasting joy of which the Bible speaks will come only in the next life. The joy we have now is very real and blessed, but only a dim reflection of what awaits us. Moreover, our joy on earth is destined to intermingle with our blessed sorrow.

It seems appropriate to close this chapter with the words of William Blake, an individual who was on intimate terms with grief. He put it this way:

> Man was made for joy and woe;
> And when this we rightly know,
> Through the world we safely go.
> Joy and woe are woven fine,
> A clothing for the soul divine;

> Under every grief and pine
> Runs a joy with silken twine.[6]

God will keep his promise that we must suffer, in small ways and great. But our suffering is a means of grace. He has ordained pain and sorrow as teachers. This is the hard Christian truth. Let us resist our culture's tendency to blind us to it. Moral maturity, empathy toward others, beatific vision: suffering is the way of passage to some of God's richest blessings.

6.   William Blake, "Auguries of Innocence," in *Poetry and Prose of William Blake*, ed. Geoffrey Keynes (London: Nonesuch Library, 1956), 76.

14

SHOWING MERCY

The Virtue of Forgiveness

Perseverance might be the most painful virtue to learn, but there's no greater moral challenge than learning to forgive. More than most virtues, forgiveness is a matter of attitude and inner feelings.[1] Such things are not easily controlled. So when it comes to forgiveness, we much prefer to focus upon God's forgiveness toward us, as opposed to our forgiving others. Because God has shown us mercy and grace, however, we must extend the same response to those who wrong us. We're expected to "pay it forward." But what does it mean to forgive someone? Why is it so important that we forgive others? When do we have a duty to forgive? And how do we know when we have succeeded in forgiving someone? These are some of the questions that will be addressed below.

Forgiveness, Gratitude, and Grudges

If forgiveness has to do with a changed attitude toward someone who's wronged us, what sort of attitude change does it involve? The ethicist Jeffrie Murphy proposes that to forgive is to renounce one's "vindictive passions." Forgiveness, he says, involves "the overcoming . . . of the intense negative reactive attitudes—the vindictive passions of resentment, anger, hatred, and the desire for revenge—that are quite naturally occasioned when one has been wronged by another responsible agent."[2] This definition is a good one, as far as it goes,

---

1. Here I follow Joseph Butler's general account of the virtue. See Joseph Butler, "Sermon IX," in *Sermons of Joseph Butler,* ed. W. E. Gladstone (Oxford: Clarendon Press, 1897), 127–41.
2. Jeffrie G. Murphy, "Forgiveness, Reconciliation, and Responding to Evil," in *Ethics for Everyday,* ed. David Benatar (New York: McGraw Hill, 2002), 720. Some have

but it's entirely negative. True forgiveness seems also to involve a positive aspect as well. Accordingly, some have preferred to understand forgiveness more as "reacceptance" of the offending party.[3]

However we define it, forgiveness does seem to be a matter of the heart, as is clear from Jesus' teaching on the subject. In Matthew 18, we find Peter asking, "'Lord, how many times shall I forgive my brother when he sins against me? Up to seven times?' Jesus answered, 'I tell you not seven times, but seventy-seven times'" (vv. 21–22). Then he tells the following story:

> The kingdom of heaven is like a king who wanted to settle accounts with his servants. As he began the settlement, a man who owed him ten thousand talents [millions of dollars] was brought to him. Since he was not able to pay, the master ordered that he and his wife and his children and all that he had be sold to repay the debt.
>
> The servant fell on his knees before him. "Be patient with me," he begged, "and I will pay back everything." The servant's master took pity on him, canceled the debt and let him go.
>
> But when that servant went out, he found one of his fellow servants who owed him a hundred denarii [a few dollars]. He grabbed him and began to choke him. "Pay back what you owe me!" he demanded.
>
> His fellow servant fell to his knees and begged him, "Be patient with me, and I will pay you back." But he refused. Instead, he went off and had the man thrown into prison until he could pay the debt. When the other servants saw what had happened, they were greatly distressed and went and told their master everything that had happened.
>
> Then the master called the servant in. "You wicked servant," he said, "I canceled all that debt of yours because you begged me to. Shouldn't you have had mercy on your fellow servant just as I had on you?" In anger his master turned him over to the jailers to be tortured, until he should pay back all he owed."

---

complained that Murphy's definition is too narrow. Norvin Richards asks, "What if a person's response to mistreatment is not vindictive but simply sadness or disappointment? Isn't forgiveness still appropriate here?" For this reason, Richards broadens Murphy's definition to include overruling other negative feelings toward the wrongdoer. See Norvin Richards, "Forgiveness," *Ethics* 99 (October 1988): 77–93.

3. Aurel Kolnai takes this approach in his "Forgiveness," *Proceedings of the Aristotelian Society,* (1973–1974): 91–106.

> This is how my heavenly Father will treat each of you unless you
> forgive your brother from your heart. (vv. 23–35)

This parable is disturbing mainly because it ends with a threat—or, rather, not so much a threat as a scary promise. Unlike most of Jesus' promises, however, we hope it will *not* be fulfilled in our lives. In examining the unmerciful servant, his actions seem absurd to us. He's been forgiven millions of dollars of debt but cruelly demands the few dollars his fellow servant owes him. What's wrong with this picture? Why is he unwilling to forgive even a fraction of the debt he was forgiven? The answer is obvious. He's an ingrate. He's not sufficiently grateful for the grace his master showed him. It's not that he's *unaware* of how much he's been forgiven—no doubt he's cognizant of the grace he's been shown. What's missing is a heartfelt appreciation for the gift he's received. He suffers from amnesia of the heart, and his severe treatment of his fellow servant is the symptom. The moral vice that grips him is ingratitude, and so long as he remains ungrateful, he'll remain unforgiving.

All this suggests a basic principle of moral psychology: *forgiveness is motivated by gratitude.* The forgiving person remembers his own canceled debts and responds in kind. Moreover, a person's willingness to forgive will be more or less proportioned to that person's gratitude for his own forgiveness. This principle is underscored in Luke 7 where a "sinful woman" weeps at the feet of Jesus, anointing them with her tears and perfume. Her lavish behavior is scorned by a Pharisee, but Jesus rebukes him, noting that the one who's been forgiven much loves much, while "he who has been forgiven little loves little" (v. 47).

As the parable of the unmerciful servant shows, however, this proportional forgiveness is only a general rule. And those who are exceptions to this rule are the most hard-hearted of people. Immanuel Kant regarded ingratitude as having "the essence of vileness and wickedness."[4] From a Christian standpoint, Kant's estimation might not be an exaggeration, because the vice of ingratitude is wrong at so many levels. The ingrate, for instance, is unjust. Justice involves giving to each its proper due. The ingrate does not justly regard his gifts with appropriate thankfulness. Also, the ingrate exhibits moral insensitivity, taking for granted the goodness of others. And ingratitude pollutes a person's whole character, deadening that person's capacity to exhibit other virtues. Until you appreciate

---

4.   Immanuel Kant, *Lectures on Ethics,* ed. Lewis White Beck (New York: Harper and Row, 1963), 218.

the grace you've been shown, you won't be prepared to be gracious to others, whatever form of virtue that takes. So we must especially beware of ingratitude, as it is the mother of many vices. In the opposite way, the virtue of gratitude begets many other virtues. To be truly thankful for the unmerited favor of God will make a person more generous, more patient, more kind, more compassionate, more humble, and more forgiving. So the person who's serious about virtue will nurture his thankfulness.

There is truth in Shakespeare's line that "to forgive is divine." Forgiving others is a sign of divine grace in one's own life, as all grace originates with God. For the Christian, the willingness to forgive is a barometer of one's understanding and experience of grace. For this reason, an unforgiving spirit is a sign that a person is not a Christian. When Jesus says, "This is how my heavenly Father will treat each of you unless you forgive your brother from your heart," he is not saying that holding a grudge is an unforgivable sin. Rather, he is saying that those who are persistently unforgiving cannot really have experienced grace. Simply put, chronic unforgiveness is a sign that one is not yet forgiven.

Jesus tells us to pray, "Forgive us our debts, as we . . . have forgiven our debtors" (Matt. 6:12). If this doesn't make us morally self-conscious, nothing will. Sometimes when I pray this, I wonder, "What if God answers this prayer literally? If God really forgave me as I forgive others, would I be saved from hell?" Salvation, after all, demands the forgiveness of *all* my sins. Based on a literal reading of the Lord's Prayer, if I hold a grudge against someone and refuse to forgive him, then God might hold a grudge against me for just one of my sins. Since even one unforgiven sin lands a person in hell, any grudge I hold against someone else would doom me. This is a terrifying thought!

Here, I comfort myself with the thought, "This is just a prayer. God will not really answer this prayer literally and forgive me just as I forgive others." But the way out isn't so easy. First of all, most of the requests in the Lord's prayer simply affirm what God does anyway and are not conditioned upon his responding affirmatively to our petition. So it's natural to assume the same is true of our request that God forgive us as we forgive others. Secondly, as we've already seen, the lesson of Jesus' parable of the unmerciful servant is that God *will* forgive us just as we forgive others, whether or not we ask him to do so.

This is a sobering teaching. It creates an almost unbearable tension for me, as I don't believe a Christian can lose his salvation. Most importantly, our salvation is not dependent upon any of our works of obedience, including the act of forgiveness. Yet it seems that Jesus suggests God's grace is contingent upon our forgiveness of others. Further, I'm sure that most, if not all, Christians have struggled with grudges and the reluctance to forgive certain people. So what are we to conclude?

This much is clear. We must commit ourselves unwaveringly to forgive others and terminate any grudges that we harbor. The spirit that refuses to forgive others blocks its own forgiveness. So to hold a grudge against someone else is effectively to hold a grudge against oneself. It's ironic that holding a grudge is often seen as selfish, when in reality it's a form of self-harm. The harm it causes to oneself may be interpreted in one of two ways, depending upon whether one is an Arminian or a Calvinist. An Arminian might say that by holding a grudge against someone you place your own spiritual destiny in jeopardy. The Calvinist is more likely to emphasize that in holding a grudge you create a reason to doubt that you are a Christian. Regardless of your theological perspective, it's obviously perilous to hold grudges, and the strong language of Jesus is justified.[5]

The peril in being unforgiving suggests a second principle: *Forgiveness frees the one who forgives.* To forgive someone not only confirms the Christian's salvation, but also has immediate benefits as well for the person who forgives, liberating him from the ugly side effects of unforgiveness. To hold a grudge is to hold yourself in bondage, rather than the person you refuse to forgive. You become enslaved to your own resentment, tortured by your own inner rage, distracted by your own anger, and distressed by your own bitterness. Thus, you only harm yourself by holding a grudge. But to forgive is liberation, a release from self-imposed bondage.[6]

What exactly is a "grudge"? Simply put, to hold a grudge is to damn someone in your heart. It is to wish God's condemnation of a person for something that he's done. Such might take the form of bitter thoughts about a person, imagining scenarios where you harm him or where he suffers in some way. Or it might be manifested in behavior, where you snub the person, act rudely toward him, or say malicious things about him. But as bad as these things are, they are mere symptoms of unforgiveness. A grudge is not just a mental state or pattern of behavior, it is a refusal of grace. But the grudge-holder not only refuses to ex-

---

5.   A further potential harm of grudges pertains to the efficacy of prayer. The psalmist declares, "If I had cherished sin in my heart, the Lord would not have listened" (Ps. 66:18). By holding a grudge, I invite God to ignore my requests.

6.   Johann Christoph Arnold discusses numerous personal accounts illustrating this truth in his poignant book *Why Forgive?* (Farmington, Pa.: Plough, 2000).

tend grace, more than this, he effectively refuses grace on another person's behalf. To do so volunteers someone's damnation. As has been seen, one cannot
refuse to show grace to someone without disqualifying oneself from grace. Thus,
all damning by a mere human being is self-damning. So to hold a grudge is to
experience a bit of hell on earth.

These are the things we ought to tell our souls when we hold something
against someone. But, if your sinful nature is as wily as mine, here's how it re-
plies: "Oh, just bask in this emotional energy for now. Seethe a bit. You'll get
over it later." Or even more insidious, "You can think constructively about how
evil people get their due, as you imagine him getting his due; follow that scenario in your head where you put him in his place. You're imagining a perfectly
just world. And doesn't God love justice?" Have you ever had those conversations with your soul? Just how foolish they are becomes clearer, considering
another reason why grudges produce nothing good. The person whom you begrudge either will or will not know of your grudge. If the person you begrudge
doesn't know of your resentment, then you don't get the revenge you desire and
you fume in solitude. If he does know about your grudge, he'll only think less of
you as a result. Think of how you regard resentful and bitter people, particularly if you're the object of their resentment or bitterness. You probably think
less of them and regard them as weak or pathetic, but we regard gracious and
forgiving people as strong and respectable. Thus, the sum of the matter is that
when you hold a grudge you either suffer in solitude or someone thinks less of
you. Either way you lose.

"Oh, but wait," your sinful nature now retorts, "there's a benefit of grudge-
holding you haven't considered, namely the joy of sharing your resentment
with a friend. Just wait until you tell so-and-so about this, then you can seethe
together!" It's unfortunate that this devilish thinking is often compelling even
to the most resolute Christians. It is, in fact, why the sin of gossip is so pervasive. Just as misery loves company, the same, it seems, is true of bitterness,
resentment, and wrath. We love to share our hatred with others. The problems with this way of thinking should be clear from what's been said already.
If unforgiveness causes internal bondage and self-torture, then to involve
a third party in your grudge is to enslave others with resentment and bitterness and to share one's bondage and torture. This is why gossip is such a serious sin; it makes hatred contagious, and it enslaves our friends and destroys
fellowship.

Moral Judgment and Grace

In addition to the liberation one experiences upon forgiving someone, this act of grace is empowering.[7] To forgive is to throw off the fetters of negative feelings, to free up your energy to be more productive in the kingdom of God, and to sow peace and joy rather than bitterness and wrath. A forgiving spirit is immunized from inner turmoil and disturbance that would otherwise be caused by the spiteful words and actions of those who do intend to hurt you. This is why Jesus says, "Love your enemies and pray for those who persecute you, that you may be sons of your Father in heaven" (Matt. 5:44–45). Loving, then, and praying for those who've hurt you not only proves yourself a child of God but also empowers you to become a more effective servant in God's kingdom. Praying for our enemies—or, if you prefer, those acquaintances that really annoy you—is the occasion for the Holy Spirit to protect you from slipping into a grudge. Think of it as a sort of moral inoculation—and some cases may demand daily booster shots.

An even more effective antidote for grudges is the biblical prescription of *open rebuke*. The parable of the unmerciful servant is, in fact, immediately preceded by this instruction from Jesus on the matter:

> If your brother sins against you, go and show him his fault, just between the two of you. If he listens to you, you have won your brother over. But if he will not listen, take one or two others along, so that "every matter may be established by the testimony of two or three witnesses." If he refuses to listen to them, tell it to the church; and if he refuses to listen even to the church, treat him as you would a pagan or a tax collector. (Matthew 18:15–17)

So the proper response to wrongdoing is not merely passive in nature, a mere avoidance of grudges and gossip. The proper response is the positive action of rebuke. The wisdom in this approach is obvious to anyone who's experienced

---

7. Behavioral psychologist B. F. Skinner—no sympathizer with Christian theology—was fascinated by Jesus' radical doctrine of forgiveness. He writes, "I insist that Jesus, who was apparently the first to discover the power of refusing to punish, must have hit upon the principle by accident. He certainly had none of the experimental evidence which is available to us today, and I can't conceive that it was possible, no matter what the man's genius, to have discovered the principle from casual observation." *Walden Two* (New York: Macmillan, 1948), 261.

the relief of peacefully confronting one's offender, as William Blake sums up so well:

> I was angry with my friend:
> I told my wrath, my wrath did end.
> I was angry with my foe;
> I told it not, my wrath did grow.[8]

Open rebuke not only releases negative emotions that would otherwise fester but also clears the way for genuine reconciliation.

A rebuke, then, presupposes a moral evaluation of another person's actions. Thus, it follows that *forgiveness is consistent with moral judgment.* Consider, the act of forgiveness implies there is a wrong to be forgiven. So the very notion of forgiveness demands, in fact, moral judgment. Some Christians are confused by this point, since Jesus tells us that we ought not to judge, lest we be judged (Matt. 7:1–2). How then, can these two teachings be reconciled?

The answer lies in the distinction between two kinds of judgments: the judgment of condemnation (which is wrong) and the judgment of discernment (which is right). The judgment of condemnation is the judgment of the grudge-holder. It takes the form of personal opposition, wishing harm for the offender. In contrast, the judgment of discernment condemns the sin, not the sinner. It wishes the best for the offender, and for this reason rebukes rather than begrudges, reconciles rather than gossips. All Christians are called to judge, in the sense of discernment. John tells us to "test the spirits to see whether they are from God" (1 John 4:1), and Paul says the saints will one day judge the world and even angels (1 Cor. 6:2–3).

The judgment of discernment involves condemnation of sin and evil with mercy toward persons. But to show mercy is not necessarily to pardon a person from the consequences of actions. Forgiveness is not an admission that the forgiven is not at fault. Rather, it refuses to condemn someone in spite of his moral fault. Nor does your forgiveness free the offender from all condemnation. Its purpose is only to free him from *your* condemnation, which is all God calls us to do. The apostle Paul illustrates this as he closes his final epistle. To Timothy he writes, "Alexander the metalworker did me a great deal of harm. The Lord will repay him for what he has done" (2 Tim. 4:14). Presumably Paul forgave

---

8.   William Blake, "A Poison Tree," in *Poetry and Prose of William Blake,* ed. Geoffrey Keynes (London: Nonesuch Library, 1956), 76.

Alexander for his cruelty, but the text shows that Alexander still needed God's forgiveness.

The principle of forgiveness and consequences translates into more public areas of life as well. Consider, for instance, the Bill Clinton sex scandal several years ago. It was appropriate for U.S. citizens to forgive him for the way he betrayed them—but this doesn't imply that he should have remained in office. Removing him from office would, in fact, have been consistent with the American public's personal forgiveness for Clinton's actions. For doing so might have been the sort of severe mercy that would have, at the time, provided the greatest moral help to the president. Harsh discipline, provided it is just, prompts repentance. But even if someone does repent, this does not exempt him from the consequences of his actions.

I have a friend whose life provides a vivid illustration of this point. After living a life of crime, he finally became a Christian. But after his conversion he was arrested, tried, and convicted for his involvement in an armed robbery and sentenced to five years in prison. His sins had been forgiven, but he still had to serve his time. His repentance and forgiveness before God did not spare him the consequences of his actions, although God's grace enabled him to live joyfully and work productively within the prison. In the same way, God's forgiveness of your sins will not remove their natural consequences, be they physical, psychological, emotional, or relational. When we experience these consequences, however, we should not resent them but view them as God's gracious discipline. As the writer of Hebrews says, such hardship shows that God is treating us as his children, making us better through our suffering. As he explains, "God disciplines us for our good, that we might share in his holiness" (Heb. 12:10). In some cases, of course, God does provide extra healing to spare us the full natural effects of our sin. But this is an unusual grace. Forgiveness for one's sins does not imply exemption from all the natural consequences of those sins.

Another theme to explore is that *forgiveness is unconditional.* All forgiveness is unmerited. No sinner deserves to be forgiven, and no sin deserves atonement. You cannot unmake or make up for a moral wrong, however small. Although one of the more radical claims of the Christian worldview, this seemingly hopeless message is supplemented by the message of grace. Forgiveness is available in spite of our sin and our inability to make up for our moral failures. We are justified in Christ, meaning that we are granted his righteousness in God's eyes while we are still sinners (cf. Rom. 5:8). Such is the wonder of grace, God's unmerited favor toward us. It's a message so profound that even Christians sometimes have difficulty accepting it.

One of the twentieth century's best Christian writers, Flannery O'Connor, communicates the wonder of grace as well as anyone. Her stories feature some characters that are repugnant but who, nonetheless, receive divine favor. A Christian reader was so repulsed by some of O'Conner's characters that she declared, "They don't deserve grace."[9] Yes, God's grace is so profound that even a Christian can be shocked by it. Such a response is just what O'Conner likely intended to evoke in her readers. The point is that none of us "deserve" grace. (This is true by definition of the term.) Because you can't fix your own moral faults or make up for your own sins, you are no more worthy to receive the gift of salvation than any child molester or Ku Klux Klansman. In fact, recovering racists and pedophiles are just the sorts of people to whom the essence of grace is most clear. They have no illusions about their own moral status and standing before God and, as Jesus suggests in Luke 7, they are most thankful for grace. For he who is forgiven much, loves much.

Consider Adolf Hitler and Jeffery Daumer. Might you see either of them in heaven? If this question bothers you, consider—we don't know much about Hitler's last hours, and there's always the possibility that he came to Christ before he died. As for Jeffery Daumer, some say that he did become a Christian before he died in prison. About such people—cannibals and mass murderers—it's tempting to say, "They don't deserve grace." But as you utter those words, God says to you, "You know, that's true about you, too. You don't deserve grace." That's the point. It wouldn't be grace if we deserved it.

The lesson here is that since forgiveness is a form of grace, it must be extended unconditionally. Forgiveness takes initiative and demands nothing in return. It does not wait for confession of sin or repentance on the part of the person to be forgiven. Just as God loved us while we were still sinners, so we should do the same toward others. Forgiveness makes no boasts and compiles no lists. It recognizes that we are all at the mercy of God's grace, and no one can out-forgive him, so we must forgive indefinitely (seventy times seven). Forgiveness does not choose the worthy, for no mere human is worthy. If God had waited for you to become worthy of his forgiveness, he would have waited all eternity. He extended his forgiving grace unconditionally, and you must do the same.

I'm sometimes asked by my students who are married or engaged to be married, "How can I maximize my chances to have a strong marriage?" Invariably,

<hr>

9.   Jill Pelaez Baumgaertner, interview with Ken Myers, in *Mars Hill Audio Journal* 37 (March–April 1999).

my answer is, "Grow in grace." Learn to be more gracious, and try to marry someone who is gracious. The most crucial expression of grace, of course, is personal forgiveness. If you and your spouse don't forgive one another, your mutual resentments will grow and your marriage will fail. And even some who do not divorce become so deeply embittered that all of their other relationships are adversely affected, including their relationship with God.

The divorce rate in the evangelical church is looking more and more like that of the rest of the country. Why? Because Christian couples aren't practicing grace. They do not forgive one another. So to the unmarried I recommend using the criterion of grace when considering marriage. Find someone who really practices grace, who is quick to forgive others who have sinned against him or her. Beware of those who tend to hold grudges. If the person you're dating has difficulty forgiving you, that's a danger sign. If you have difficulty forgiving that person, then perhaps you're not ready for marriage. Grow in grace and the virtue of forgiveness before you make that huge step. Because when you're married, your mutual sins will be compounded. As they say, familiarity breeds contempt. To remain in another person's intimate presence guarantees that you will be sinned against regularly, even as you will sin against that person. If you're not inclined to forgive one another, you're in for trouble. But if both of you are well-practiced at the virtue of forgiveness, you'll know the real joy of marriage.

This brings the topic of forgiveness to a final point: *Forgiveness acts on principle, not feelings.* While pleasant emotions often follow particular good actions, it's essential to remember that one's feelings are never the foundation for the virtue of forgiveness. For rarely do we *want* to forgive someone who has caused harm to us or to someone we love. Plenty of times arise when we're in a generous mood or when we're naturally inclined to be gentle or when we feel carefree and it's easy to be patient. But unlike these virtues, we're rarely "in the mood" to forgive. Unless you're a masochist, your natural response to those who sin against you is to develop vindictive emotions. Thus, the exercise of forgiveness is especially difficult, the most challenging of all virtues. It can *only* be exhibited in contexts in which ill-feelings are natural. Further, the elimination of such feelings as resentment and hatred is itself the *goal* of forgiveness. So until you learn to act on principle rather than feelings, you won't get very far in the practice of forgiveness.[10]

---

10. A dramatic example of forgiving against one's emotional inclinations is related by Holocaust survivor Corrie Ten Boom. After the war she encountered one of the Nazi soldiers who worked in the camp where she was tortured and where some of her relatives were killed. She describes how he held out his hand to

Even more difficult, forgiveness is a process. Usually the act of foreswearing one's vindictiveness doesn't immediately eliminate all negative feelings toward one's offender. Those feelings might go away fairly quickly, but when an offense is especially severe, one might struggle with anger and resentment for a long time. Consequently, you might wonder whether you've really forgiven the person. How do you know when you've forgiven someone? First, being concerned about whether you've really forgiven someone is itself a good sign. If you were maintaining a grudge unrepentantly you probably wouldn't care. That you do *want* to forgive someone is the crucial first step toward forgiving.

Now to answer the question, you know you've forgiven someone when you no longer condemn him for his actions (whether before others or in your private thoughts). Usually getting to this point takes time, but you must at least resolve to work toward this goal. The negative feelings should diminish in time, although it might take a long while. Persistence is the key. Grudges are persistent condemnations, so forgiveness must be equally persistent. To hold a grudge is to continually hold someone in contempt and to remind oneself of this fact. Likewise, forgiveness continually commits the offender to the grace of God.

The practice of forgiveness may require a great deal of resolve to act counter to one's inclinations. In this regard, forgiveness is a form of repentance. To forgive is to repent of the sin of condemnation, which is the sin of the unmerciful servant. To forgive is to refuse to grab your fellow servant by the neck and demand that he pay you the small fraction of debt that your master forgave you. Like all repentance, forgiveness can be a long process, repeated at irregular intervals by a soul that waxes and wanes in earnestness. Such long-term struggles are not themselves to be seen as failures but as a likely scenario, given the strength of the temptation to condemn and the intoxicating effect of bitterness. Make no mistake about it—holding grudges is an addictive habit. Resentment is a moral narcotic that distracts as it destroys. It lures the heart farther and farther away from the cure. So it takes great discipline to put the biblical antidote into practice.

---

shake hers, but "angry, vengeful thoughts boiled through me." Somehow she forced herself to take his hand, and "the most incredible thing happened. From my shoulder along my arm and through my hand a current seemed to pass from me to him, while into my heart sprang a love for this stranger that almost overwhelmed me." Ten Boom notes of her discovery that it wasn't in her to forgive this man; it was God's doing: "When He tells us to love our enemies, He gives, along with the command, the love itself." *The Hiding Place* (New York: Guideposts, 1971), 215.

Conclusion

We all have feet of clay. As the apostle James says, "We all stumble in many ways." To be a Christian is to know that you fall far short of the glory of God. That's why we begged for his mercy in the first place. We didn't come to God asking him to polish us off with the finishing touches on an already decent moral project. None of us approached him saying, "Oh Lord, make me even better than I already am." Nor do we pray, "Dear God, forgive me if I have sinned." No, we pray, "Please, God, have mercy on me, a sinner, who was 'conceived in sin,' who has rebelled against you and deserves nothing but your wrath." The good news is that he does show mercy to us—through Christ. His finished work atones for the sins we were powerless even to *recognize* on our own, much less *cure.* We were granted his righteousness, in spite of our own hatred of righteousness. He makes us holy, although we made ourselves his enemies. And he will preserve us until the end, establishing us more firmly in the faith, in spite of our rebellious tendencies, our selfishness, our petty squabbles, and ridiculous pride. He will continue to show us grace until, in the next world, we'll be like him, made perfect in our humanity, displaying every virtue and grace that is fitting for the child of God. What motivation to forgive those who wrong us!

15

BEING THANKFUL

The Virtue of Gratitude

Few phrases are as pleasant as "Thank you." To be the recipient of any display of gratitude is, in fact, a joy. One writer puts it this way: "Gratitude is a second pleasure, one that prolongs the pleasure that precedes and occasions it, like a joyful echo of the joy we feel, a further happiness for the happiness we have been given."[1] Showing gratitude for a gift is, of course, just, which is one reason why giving thanks is appropriate. But the power of gratitude to spread joy and inspire good will is morally significant as well and perhaps a major reason why Scripture so often commands us to be thankful.

The Essence of Gratitude and How to Nurture It

The previous chapter demonstrated that the virtue of forgiveness is fundamental to the Christian life. The parable of the unmerciful servant is a powerful illustration of the virtue of forgiveness. Although the story's main theme is forgiveness, an equally important lesson pertains to *why* the servant is so unforgiving of his fellow servant. The basic problem with the unmerciful servant is that he is an ingrate. He's not sufficiently thankful for his blessing. While ingratitude is the moral vice that gives rise to his lack of forgiveness, that vice in turn requires an explanation. Immanuel Kant proposed that ingratitude boils down to pride; one refuses to show gratitude "because one is afraid of being thought a dependent on a level below one's patron, something repugnant to genuine self-esteem (pride . . . in one's own person)."[2] An ingrate, such as the unmerciful

---

1. Andre Comte-Sponville, *A Small Treatise on the Great Virtues,* trans. Catherine Temerson (New York: Henry Holt, 1996), 132.
2. Immanuel Kant, *The Metaphysical Principles of Virtue,* trans. James Ellington (Indianapolis: Bobbs-Merrill, 1964), 124.

servant, refuses to humble herself and recognize her dependence. Conversely, such implies that the virtue of humility is a prerequisite for gratitude. Here, then, is the first step in nurturing gratitude: Humble yourself. Recognize your dependence upon, and therefore your indebtedness to, God and other people.

What precisely, though, is gratitude? Essentially, it's a positive response to a benefactor.[3] The grateful person has a desire to reciprocate the gift or kindness that she's been shown. This desire is not restricted to good feelings; it's somehow demonstrated, as by a gesture (a handshake and a smile) or a verbal expression of thankfulness. Like forgiveness, gratitude is fundamentally attitudinal but also is expressed in behavior. Unlike forgiveness, which involves renouncing vindictive feelings, gratitude is primarily positive, a cultivation of joy and good will toward the one who benefits us. A proper expression of thankfulness will depend upon the nature of the gift. Often, all we owe for someone's kind deed is a heartfelt "Thank you." But as Fred Berger observes,

> There are times when a mere "Thank you" or warm handshake will not do, when an adequate showing of gratitude requires putting ourselves out in some way, at least a little. The sort of continual sacrifice and caring involved in a decent upbringing is not reciprocated to parents by a warm handshake at the legal age of independence. While the notion of gratitude to one's parents can easily be overdone, it is clear enough that an adequate showing of gratitude to them cannot be made with mere verbal gestures.[4]

How does one properly show gratitude to those, such as good parents, who have given us so much? It can be presumed that a properly grateful response will translate into our giving to them long-term care and an affection that reflects what we've received. As was observed in the previous chapter, proportionality is essential to the virtue of gratitude. The greater the gift received, the greater the dedication owed in response. While a true act of grace or generosity does not demand repayment in kind (otherwise it's bribery), it does create a debt, and this is "paid" by some sign of thankfulness. So the failure to do so is unjust, not to mention unkind. Because my parents were so generous toward me, the least I can do is take care of them into their old age and see to it that they're

---

3. My account here is fairly standard, but in key respects it blends those of Rene Descartes, *The Passions of the Soul*, trans. Stephen H. Voss (Indianapolis: Hackett, 1989), 123–26; and Fred R. Berger, "Gratitude," *Ethics* 85 (1975): 298–309.
4. Berger, "Gratitude," 303.

comfortable as they live out their days. To do so is, we might say, a minimally decent response. We should, of course, aim to do more than this, emotionally supporting our parents as they cope with the trials of aging, showing respect to our siblings, and diligently parenting our own children. These are all gestures of gratitude and together contribute to a fulfillment of God's commandment to honor one's parents. While the import of this divine command extends beyond gratitude, this virtue is surely a significant dimension of displaying such honor.

The child-parent relationship is the most vital human context for gratitude. But the gratitude we owe God is the primary one from which all other contexts of gratitude are derived. Our parents are our procreators and, it is hoped, our nurturers. But the Lord is our Creator and the sustainer of all, including our parents. Our debt to God, then, could not be more fundamental. He thought us up, wove us together in our mothers' wombs, and has maintained our heartbeats from our early fetal days until now. In short, he owns us and maintains us, so he may justly do with us as he pleases. That God has kept us alive as long as he has is, by itself, an incomparable grace. How grateful, indeed, we should be. Yet he has done so much more.

We must also take stock of our moral debt to God. The more aware a Christian becomes of her sin, the more grateful she should become. This translates to one of the psychological paradoxes of practical theology—because of divine grace, an otherwise depressing fact is transformed into an occasion for joy; we've sinned against a holy God and deserve his wrath. But he shows us mercy, not only pardoning our sin but blessing us immeasurably besides. To sense the gravity of our sin is to increase our appreciation for how good God has been to us. In turn, this motivates us to serve. As the old saying goes, one good turn deserves another. That basic concept is essentially the idea behind the Christian theme that forgiveness motivates good deeds. And the motivational pivot point is, of course, gratitude. We serve out of thankfulness for the grace we've received.

This book earlier emphasized the importance of the doctrine of original sin. Gratitude's being a moral virtue presents another reason why a strong doctrine of sin is so crucial. Grasping the depths of one's sin brings a sense of how much one has been forgiven, which increases one's gratefulness, which in turn motivates service. This point is illustrated in a story I once heard about Abraham Lincoln. It is said that he attended a slave auction and offered bids on a young slave girl. He outbid everyone, and at the end of the auction he was awarded the slave. But when she was presented to Lincoln, he removed her chains and told her she was free to go. She gave him a puzzled look, and he repeated himself, noting that he had bought her so he could set her free. To this the girl replied, "I want to go with you." The girl's gratefulness motivated her to freely serve her generous new friend. Nothing inspires devotion like unmerited favor—grace.

It might seem odd that Scripture directly commands giving thanks. Paul tells us to "give thanks in all circumstances, for this is God's will for you in Christ Jesus" (1 Thess. 5:18; see also Col. 3:15). We are inclined to run past this verse as if it were something less than a serious biblical injunction. When we take it seriously, though, we see that its implications are profound, reminding us of an important fact about gratitude. As is true of all the virtues, gratitude does not come and go independently of our wills. It, too, is a moral skill developed through intentional, sometimes even painful, practice. Paul tells us to practice gratitude by giving thanks.

This practicing of virtue to develop virtue is but one application of a broader truth within biblical psychology, namely that *behavior therapy works.* (Most of the practical advice in this book is premised on this point.) Many biblical commands reveal this, as they tell us to *do* certain things without any reference to feelings or natural inclinations. We are simply commanded to be patient, kind, gentle, self-controlled, generous, joyful, courageous, etc. And how are we expected to become virtuous in these ways? By waiting for God to mysteriously endow us with the desire to be so virtuous? By merely praying for the will to exhibit such virtues? No, this is moral passivity, and Scripture endorses nothing of the sort. Prayer is crucial, of course, but it's not the whole story. God commands us to *perform* particular actions that, when done repeatedly, will form a virtuous character in us. He commands us to "rejoice always," which, we may assume, will lead to the virtue of joy. God tells the Israelites to be courageous by commanding them to go into the land, and by fighting the Canaanites. He tells us to be generous by commanding us to give. And, to return to the present topic, he tells us to be grateful by commanding us to "give thanks in all circumstances." We will become grateful if we do so habitually. That is, by frequently giving thanks, a disposition of gratitude will form in us. Thankfulness will become part of our characters.

Counting Your Blessings

How else can one intentionally develop gratitude? The old method of counting one's blessings is a sound policy. Every time I hear or read about a natural disaster or political unrest in some region of the world, I contrast that situation with my own. I consider how fortunate I am to have been spared that particular difficulty, at least so far. I consider how wealthy I am in so many areas, including

my physical and mental health, the health of my family and friends, the blessings of my house and other possessions, my job, and the hundreds of resources
connected with it. God did not have to give me all these things. He could have
allowed me to be afflicted with physical and psychological maladies in an oppressed society. He would have been perfectly just in doing so. How grateful,
therefore, I should be.

When I was a kid my mother always told me, "You should thank God every
day for your brain." She said this repeatedly and forcefully. (I always found it
strange that she singled out my brain when, to me, sports and tree forts were
more worthy of thankfulness.) I listened to her and tried to thank God for this
and other things when I thought about it. Perhaps this is why to this day I'm so
concerned to be a properly grateful person. It seems that her vigorously cueing
me in to this important activity actually made me more thankful. (Such should
be an encouragement to us parents, as it proves that our repetitious commands,
even just to say, "Thank you," are not ineffectual.) You can actually instill gratitude in a child, because sincere convictions can follow from even mechanical
behaviors. The beauty of this approach is that in refusing to wait for a feeling of
gratitude and deciding to give thanks anyway, a genuine feeling of gratitude
usually comes as a result. If you set your mind to finding things for which to
thank God, you'll discover in the process just how much you *do* have to be thankful for. And this realization will move you emotionally.

One may also grow in gratitude by meditating on the work of Christ and the
specific ways that God has blessed one spiritually. If you're a Christian, it's because God decided to work in your heart and open you up to receiving his
grace. Jesus says that no one comes to the Father unless the Spirit draws him.
We do choose to follow Christ, but only because he chose us first. This is cause
for gratitude that knows no bounds. How do we thank God for not only rescu-
ing us from eternal destruction but also giving us an eternity of unspeakable
joy, especially since he did so while we were still sinners, fist raised defiantly in
his face? It's clear that no measure of gratitude can match such grace, which
only means that our gratitude has room to grow indefinitely. There's literally
more to thank God for than any of us can imagine.

It seems the limits of Christian gratitude are determined only by the weakness of the human imagination. Paul says, "No eye has seen, no ear has heard,
no mind has conceived what God has prepared for those who love him" (1 Cor.
2:9). It's evident that we can't even conceive of the riches that await us in a
paradise that even Paul could not begin to describe. In 2 Corinthians 12 Paul
notes that he was taken up to what he calls the "third heaven" where "he heard

inexpressible things, things that man is not permitted to tell" (v. 4). The heavenly paradise is described to some degree in the books of Ezekiel and John's Revelation, but there we are given all sorts of metaphors and symbols, which can be very confusing. Even Jesus himself stops short of describing heaven, referring to paradise in only the most vague terms. Why all the abstract and vague references? It means that our life to come is too wonderful to be communicated or understood in our present state.

Still, at the risk of underestimating our future glory, we may at least imagine in general terms what awaits us. For starters, consider our sensory experience. Perhaps in paradise we'll be able to see the whole light spectrum, rather than just the narrow range of colors from red to violet we see now. Nor may our vision be limited to a single perspective. Instead we might enjoy the capacity to perceive objects from multiple points of view. Maybe we'll hear sounds from the shortest to the longest wavelengths, rather than the narrow range we hear now. We might hear and comprehend music that transcends the twelve notes and their intervals that we now experience. Perhaps whole new sensory dimensions will open up to us, forms of perception that we cannot now comprehend.

We do know there will be no sin, which means we will rightly understand our place in creation and will no longer struggle with wrong desires, pride, selfishness, anger, and resentment. Nor will we misunderstand one another as we do now. Rather, as Paul says in 1 Corinthians 13:12, "[We] shall know fully, even as [we are] fully known." Therefore, I imagine paradise as a place where we will enjoy faultless communication with one another, involving something like mental telepathy. Where everyone has a healthy self-image, informed by the understanding of who God is and what he has done for us. Where each of us possesses an irrepressible will to serve God and bless other people through the countless productive activities in which we'll be involved. Where the chief of these activities is artistic endeavor of various kinds, as God's people mirror his creativity by making beautiful objects, poems, and songs, the least of which will match or exceed the beauty of Pachebel's Canon or Handel's Hallelujah chorus. And where paradise itself is so vast and detailed in its artistry that it would take a millennium for even a glorified human mind to fully appreciate the aesthetic riches of its smallest garden.

Moral beauty, too, will be revealed by the saints in paradise, as everyone will display the virtues they acquired on earth and had perfected in heaven. We will see just why we had to suffer all that we suffered here. All tragedy will be transformed into triumph, and every instance of pettiness, impatience, greed, obscenity, injustice, cruelty, and every other vice will be redeemed in a universe of moral beauty. The character traits we began to develop in this realm will come to full fruition then, as we behold ultimate patience, justice, gentleness, kindness, generosity, peace, and joy in the multitudes of friends we will have. Here is why Paul says, "Our present sufferings are not worth comparing with the glory that will be revealed in us" (Rom. 8:18). Such everlasting virtues will be more than worth the few fleeting years of suffering it took to begin their formation on this fallen planet. We will see with perfect clarity what we only vaguely comprehend now, that many virtues (e.g., compassion, mercy, courage, perseverance, patience) develop only where there is suffering and evil to overcome.

The lesson in all of this—understanding and nurturing gratitude through an act of the will for present and future blessings—is that *there are no circumstances in which gratitude is inappropriate.* This principle is directly implied by Paul's admonition in 1 Thessalonians 5:18 to "give thanks in all circumstances." Paul was no hypocrite in this matter, as in several of his letters he gives thanks for the church to whom he is writing or for his present circumstances, however difficult his situation.

Grumbling and Spoilage

To appreciate the importance of gratitude is to understand why grumbling is a sin. To grumble is a sign of ungratefulness. Moreover, grumbling implicitly declares that one is not satisfied with what one has been given. It is God who ordained all your days (Ps. 139:16) and in whom you live and move and have your being (Acts 17:28). He is the one who put you in your station in life. So to complain about your lot is to impugn his wisdom and goodness. We read the book of Job and are appalled that he challenges God's wisdom. But we do the same thing when we complain about aspects of our lives that are petty in comparison to Job's problems. How much more appalling are we at times than Job was at his worst? Recall the earlier reference to Kant's point that pride is the root of ingratitude. Another contributing factor is the sheer abundance of divine blessings. That so many of us enjoy relatively decent health, sound minds, and meaningful relationships—particularly in light of our sinfulness—is amazing. All of this is grace, but it's so common and abundant that we've come to expect these gifts. And to expect gifts is to presume grace.

The term for this ugly but familiar pattern is *getting spoiled,* and it reflects another irony in the Christian life: *the very blessings that warrant thankfulness can inhibit the virtue of gratitude.* Not all of our blessings spoil us, of course.

(And it is, most emphatically, *our* fault, not God's, if we're spoiled!) But the more abundantly a person or nation is blessed, the greater the risk that spoiling will occur. Such was certainly the case with Old Testament Israel who, at first, were thankful just for their freedom from Egyptian bondage. But when they had enjoyed a few military victories and began to possess Canaan, they became morally lazy and slowly forgot the Lord who delivered them. They grew accustomed to their success and all they had been given, and eventually took their blessings for granted. Falling into all sorts of idolatry and shameful disobedience, Israel finally refused to honor the God who blessed them. And it all began with the vice of ingratitude.

To the great shame of our culture, we, too, are a thankless people. And we are so in spite of being the wealthiest people the world has ever known. Or could it be *because* we're so wealthy? We take our enormous blessings for granted: our freedom, our national defense, our health care system, our extraordinary means of transportation and communication. Do we marvel at the countless ways God has blessed us? Or have we grown casually accustomed to even his most tangible gifts? Worse yet, are we less apt to acknowledge God's material blessings than we are to complain when something goes awry? Helen Keller once said, "I have often thought it would be a blessing if each human being were stricken blind and deaf for a few days at some time during his early adult life. Darkness would make him more appreciative of sight; silence would teach him the joys of sound."[5] As one who lived her entire adult life in absolute darkness and silence, Keller surely understood how profound the gifts of sight and hearing are.

It's because of the perverse state of human nature that we are so easily spoiled, that the more God blesses us materially, the more difficult it is to remember him. Jesus underscores this tendency when he says, "It is easier for a camel to go through the eye of a needle than for a rich man to enter the kingdom of God" (Matt. 19:24). To be wealthy is to live with the constant temptation to forget one's dependence upon God, to become prideful in one's station in life, as if one can claim sole responsibility for one's own destiny. We are all, in fact, wealthy in many ways. As Christians, we are all spiritually rich. As Americans, we are also materially wealthy, relative to the rest of the world. Some of us are wealthy relative even to this wealthy American culture. In any case, we all have much to be grateful for, and we must be diligent in thanking God for all his mercies and blessings.

---

5.   Helen Keller, "Three Days to See," *Atlantic Monthly,* 1933; reprinted in *The Moral Life,* ed. Louis P. Pojman (Oxford: Oxford University Press, 2004), 491.

Gratitude is pleasant. As we give thanks or happily dwell on our abundance, we experience this "second pleasure" that rides on the tails of our original blessings. It's a wonder we ever refuse ourselves its joy. But, alas, as Spinoza says, "All things excellent are as difficult as they are rare."[6]

---

6.   Benedict de Spinoza, *The Ethics,* in *A Spinoza Reader: The Ethics and Other Works,* ed. Edwin Curley (Princeton: Princeton University Press, 1994), 265.

16

KNOWING WHAT IS BEST

The Virtue of Wisdom

The philosopher Socrates was proclaimed by the oracle at Delphi the wisest man of Athens. Upon hearing of this declaration, Socrates set out to prove it false, thinking there were many wiser than he. He interviewed Athenians with reputations for wisdom and discovered that each reputedly wise man presumed to know more than he actually knew and thus proved himself a fool. Socrates concluded that the oracle's declaration was actually correct, for at least he recognized his own ignorance.

The father of Western philosophy, Socrates embodied the original meaning of "philosopher." Derived from the Greek *philos* (loving) and *sophia* (wisdom), the term literally means "lover of wisdom." Socrates strove for wisdom, prodded his fellow Athenians toward a life of virtue, and declared that goodness comes ultimately from God. This chapter explores what it means to be a philosopher—in this original Socratic sense of the term—and looks into how we may cultivate this important virtue in our own lives.

A Biblical Model of Wisdom

To be wise is to be a person of understanding and good practical sense, perhaps even to be shrewd in a prudent way.[1] Biblical examples of wisdom accord with this general definition, the most outstanding being king Solomon, who is depicted as the wisest person ever to have lived. God gave him "very great in-

---

1. I agree with ethicist Philippa Foot's analysis of the virtue of wisdom: "Wisdom . . . has two parts. In the first place the wise man knows the means to certain good ends; and secondly he knows how much particular ends are worth." From *Virtues and Vices and Other Essays in Moral Philosophy* (Oxford: Clarendon Press, 2002), 5.

sight, and a breadth of understanding as measureless as the sand on the seashore" (1 Kings 4:29). He was a poet who produced three thousand proverbs and over one thousand songs (v. 32), but he was also a scientist, who taught about both plant and animal life (v. 33). Consequently, "men of all nations came to listen to Solomon's wisdom, sent by all the kings of the world, who had heard of his wisdom" (v. 34).

Such versatility of knowledge is remarkable. Today we might say that Solomon excelled in both left brain (analytical) and right brain (imaginative) ability. To achieve much in either area is noteworthy; rare is the person who excels in both. Solomon, too, was a gifted ruler, skilled in applying his wisdom to civil matters. One day he was approached by two prostitutes, each of whom had a baby son. During the night, one of the women had accidentally killed her own son by rolling over on him. She switched her dead son with the other woman's, so that when the latter awoke she thought her own son was dead. But when the second woman examined the dead child, she discovered it was not her own. So the women pleaded their cases before Solomon, each insisting that the living baby was her own. In response to this apparently insoluble dispute,

> The king said, "Bring me a sword." So they brought a sword for the king. He then gave an order: "Cut the living child in two and give half to one and half to the other."
>
> The woman whose son was alive was filled with compassion for her son and said to the king, "Please, my lord, give her the living baby! Don't kill him!"
>
> But the other said, "Neither I nor you shall have him. Cut him in two!"
>
> Then the king gave his ruling: "Give the living baby to the first woman. Do not kill him; she is his mother." (1 Kings 3:24–27)

So Solomon's wisdom involved not only factual comprehension and artistic ability but moral capacities as well. His intelligence encompassed the whole range of human understanding.

How did Solomon become so wise? Part of the answer is found in a humble request he made of the Lord. Overwhelmed by his responsibility as a young new ruler of Israel, Solomon prayed, "Give your servant a discerning heart to govern your people and to distinguish between right and wrong. For who is able to govern this great people of yours?" (1 Kings 3:9). This request pleased God, who replied,

Since you have asked for this and not for long life or wealth for yourself, nor have asked for the death of your enemies but for discernment in administering justice, I will do what you have asked. I will give you a wise and discerning heart, so that there will never have been anyone like you, nor will there ever be. Moreover, I will give you what you have not asked for—both riches and honor—so that in your lifetime you will have no equal among kings. (1 Kings 3:11–13)

It's obvious that Solomon was a unique case. His measure of wisdom was the result of a special divine dispensation. Yet Scripture teaches that wisdom is always God-given: "The LORD gives wisdom, and from his mouth come knowledge and understanding" (Prov. 2:6).[2] As with Solomon, God will grant our requests for wisdom. As James explains, "If any of you lacks wisdom, he should ask God, who gives generously to all without finding fault, and it will be given to him" (James 1:5).[3]

So wisdom is divinely bestowed, but this is not the whole story. Like all moral virtues, growth in wisdom demands effort on the part of each individual. Several passages in Proverbs make this point, as we are commanded to obtain wisdom through careful attention to wise instruction.[4] It is significant, too, that, as Luke records, even Jesus himself "grew in wisdom" (Luke 2:52). Training is required if one is to become wise, and the writer of Hebrews emphasizes training when exhorting Christians to grow in doctrinal maturity. Comparing the elementary truths of the faith to milk, and the more difficult teachings to solid food, he says, "Solid food is for the mature, who by constant use have *trained themselves* to distinguish good from evil" (Heb. 5:14).

Developing such practical moral insight is a long and difficult process, but the payoff is great. Wisdom seems to be in a class by itself. We're told, "Wisdom is supreme; therefore get wisdom. Though it cost all you have, get understanding" (Prov. 4:7). Wisdom is intrinsically valuable, and earthly goods should be subordinated to it. The contrast between this perspective and the prevailing attitude in Western culture, especially the U.S., is striking. The common view is that education is valuable for some further purpose, such as getting a job, which in turn has value because of what it gets us, namely money and material goods.

---

2. See also Ephesians 1:8–9 and Colossians 1:9.
3. See also Psalm 90:12.
4. Proverbs 4:1–2 says, "Listen, my sons, to a father's instruction; pay attention and gain understanding. I give you sound learning, so do not forsake my teaching." See also Proverbs 1:2; 4:5; and 23:23.

It's sad that even Christians succumb to this way of thinking, although it's a blatantly unchristian perspective. If we take seriously the supremacy of wisdom, as the Proverb enjoins us, then we take the opposite perspective, being willing to *sacrifice* material goods and to *give up* our money in order to gain understanding and become more wise. Wisdom should be sought as an end in itself, whether or not it serves to *get* us anything else.

Christians are called to go against the cultural grain, and no calling is more countercultural than pursuing wisdom at the expense of material wealth. Paul tells us, "Do not conform any longer to the pattern of this world, but be transformed by the renewing of your mind" (Rom 12:2). Recognizing the supremacy of wisdom is the first step in this process of mental renewal. A person dedicated to becoming wise will struggle continually against cultural forces that demote wisdom in the list of human priorities.

Loving God with One's Mind

When questioned by a Pharisee, "'Teacher, which is the greatest commandment in the Law?' Jesus replied: 'Love the Lord your God with all your heart and with all your soul and with all your mind'" (Matt. 22:36–37). Christ's response seems to capture both dimensions of the source of wisdom: the Spirit of God and the human diligence by which it comes to us. What, though, does it mean to "love God with all your mind"? First, it means that one contemplates God. One way to do so is to dwell on his attributes and the work of Christ. The psalmist declares, "I think of you through the watches of the night" (Ps. 63:6). And the writer of Hebrews tells us to "fix our eyes on Jesus" (Heb. 12:2). One may also contemplate God indirectly by meditating on creation, as the psalmist does when he says, "The heavens declare the glory of God; the skies proclaim the work of his hands" (Ps. 19:1). Yet another form of divine contemplation is to focus on the law of God. The whole of Psalm 119 is devoted to this idea of loving God by meditating on his precepts and considering his ways.

Loving God with one's mind also involves obedience in one's thoughts when one is not thinking about God himself. So whatever we meditate upon, as the psalmist prays, we should strive to make it "pleasing in [God's] sight" (Ps. 19:14). The good news is that this is not a suffocating restriction; myriad good things are worthy to think about. Paul says, "Whatever is true, whatever is noble, whatever is right, whatever is pure, whatever is lovely, whatever is admirable—if anything is excellent or praiseworthy—think about such things" (Phil. 4:8). Paul's list of adjectives covers too many things to count, from art and astrophysics to trees and bugs to good wine and a human face. All of these things are good and beautiful, each in their own way, and well worth one's time to contemplate and appreciate. This is true of everything in nature and of most things made by human beings, given the proper context.

But the challenge to love God with one's mind goes far beyond a simple consideration of *what* one thinks about. It concerns also, perhaps especially, *how* one goes about his thinking. To gain real wisdom a person must pursue wisdom with diligence. Real understanding and insight come only with persistent effort, as noted earlier. Consider two significant modern examples of such diligence. The first is Marie Curie. Raised in a family that was constantly immersed in literature (her father taught literature), Madam Curie fell in love with chemistry and made clandestine visits to a cousin's laboratory (since in her homeland of Poland women could not attend universities). She eventually went to France and attended the University of Sorbonne. There she discovered how much she lacked in mathematics and physics. But instead of giving up, she dove into her studies, often going days on end without any food. Her commitment led to her groundbreaking discoveries, with her husband Pierre, about radioactivity, leading to radiation treatment for medical problems.

The second example of diligence is Malcolm X. A whoremonger, gambler, and drug dealer from Lansing, Michigan, Malcolm X was thrown into prison for eight years. There seemed to be no hope for him, but in prison he began to study. His efforts at first were frustrating, as he had only an eighth grade education and couldn't read a single page in most books without having to look up the meaning of several words in the dictionary. So he decided to read the dictionary itself, from A–Z. After doing so, he then read everything in his prison library, covering the whole range of disciplines, including history, science, literature, psychology, theology, and philosophy. By the time he was finally released from prison, Malcolm X was a broadly educated and knowledgeable person. From there he went on to be a major player in the civil rights movement, lecturing at Ivy League schools and consorting with international dignitaries.

For both Madam Curie and Malcolm X their defining trait was a diligent pursuit of understanding that overcame severe obstacles. Their hunger for knowledge and persistence in learning enabled each of them to powerfully impact world history. The same can be said of countless other influential persons, whose personal diligence in self-education led them to positions of prominence and influence. Whether one is a Humanist, Muslim, Marxist, Hindu, or devotee of any other worldview, one's impact on human thought and culture is maximized by a relentless commitment to learning. How much more fruitful such learning may be when it's applied by someone with a Christian perspective.

Perhaps one reason the Christian worldview has fallen out of favor over the last few hundred years is because fewer Christians have been so committed to learning. Has our lack of desire for understanding caused this demise? I suspect so, but it's never too late for this desire to be rekindled in the church. In recent years signs point to a sea change being underway, as more Christian scholars in diverse disciplines have risen to prominence. So there's reason to be hopeful.

Characteristics of the Wise

What are the characteristics of a lover of wisdom, the person who seeks understanding above all else? When considering those who are deemed most wise, three primary traits consistently emerge: curiosity, versatility, and critical thinking.

Curiosity is a sincere desire to understand. Philosophy begins in wonder, said Aristotle, recognizing that anyone who asks "Why?" about anything has begun to do philosophy.[5] So it would seem that human beings are naturally philosophical, as we are persistent wonderers and we learn to ask "Why?" almost as soon as we can speak. My four-year-old son illustrates this daily. Asking why is his full-time job. I strive to reward his wonder with explanations when I can provide them, and when I share his ignorance I affirm his wonder and pose a few questions of my own. One of my tasks as a parent is to reward, not squelch, his curiosity. As with all of us, he will only obtain answers if he asks. Those who do not seek do not find. When I was a boy my mother impressed upon me the importance of curiosity and a willingness to admit ignorance. She taught that the phrase "I don't know" is not shameful or a sign of inferiority, but rather an invitation to be taught and a powerful tool for learning. I've since learned that what she advocated was a Socratic posture in the quest for wisdom, recognizing one's ignorance and humbly seeking to be educated. The wisest people I know display this attitude.

Wise people are also *versatile*. They maintain an active interest in diverse subjects. Montaigne writes, "The fine minds are the universal minds, open and

---

5.   Aristotle writes, "For it is owing to their wonder that men both now begin and at first began to philosophize; they wondered originally at the obvious difficulties, then advanced little by little and stated difficulties about the greater matters." From *Metaphysics*, 1.2.982b, trans. W. D. Ross, in *The Basic Works of Aristotle*, ed. Richard McKeon (New York: Random., 1941), 692.

ready for everything; if not well taught, at least teachable."[6] Solomon was such a fine mind, excelling in science, art, and politics. When not naturally interested or competent in a particular area, the wise person does the work to develop that interest or competency. Madame Curie's initial weaknesses at Sorbonne were math and physics. But with diligent study she turned these weak areas into strengths, as we should be prepared to do when it comes to our weak points. As atrophied muscles are improved by working them, our weak cognitive areas are strengthened when we work on them. If we take Solomon as a model for Christian wisdom, then there's no place for shunning a subject because we're "not interested" or "no good" at it. These are not grounds for turning off our minds. We, in fact, gain competency and develop genuine interest in a subject as we practice or study it. "I could never learn to do that" is a self-fulfilling prophecy, while "I'm willing to try that" is a key that opens doors to new worlds. People who have multiple talents not only have native talent but a willingness to try and try again, even though their efforts meet with failure at first. So, as with curiosity, versatility demands humility. One must be prepared to look foolish as one tries new things.

Trying new things reaps benefits whether or not we actually become skilled at what we try. We develop discipline, for instance, by challenging ourselves. Anyone who has attempted to ice skate or learn a new language knows just how much effort such skills demand at first. And we've all known the thrill of success when we make significant progress. But even when we fail, we succeed in building self-control by exerting persistent effort. The very act of trying our hardest builds character. We develop patience and perseverance especially, perhaps, when we fail. So trying something new is always a win-win situation, assuming we give our best effort.

The most obvious benefit of trying new things is the discovery of hidden talent. The treasures of potential skill can only be unearthed by trial and error. You never know the talents you can develop until you give things a try. I'd have never known, for example, that I'd be a good tennis player until I really applied myself. I was a poor player at the start, but practice brought an exponential increase in my skill level. In a similar way, I tried philosophy, which was even more difficult at first. But my curiosity kept me coming back for more. Eventually, I learned that I had a talent for it but only after much effort. We never know where our gifts lie until we truly practice a skill.

---

6.   Michel de Montaigne, *The Complete Essays of Montaigne,* trans. Donald M. Frame (Stanford: Stanford University Press, 1948), 495.

Trying new things, too, has practical theological value. Everything we under-take has the potential to teach us about God, because everything relates directly or indirectly to him. Consider the academic disciplines. History is the study of God's drama, the story he is telling on earth. Anthropology is the study of those players in the drama who are made in God's image. The social sciences, such as psychology and sociology, focus on human behavior and the institutions that we image-bearers construct to organize society and solve problems. The em-pirical sciences of physics, chemistry, and biology study the basic constituents of God's creation. Mathematics and geometry pertain to formal relationships in the mind of God and, when applied, in the cosmos. The fine arts and athlet-ics explore instances of human creativity that mirror divine creativity. And the-ology and philosophy address the nature of God directly, as well as the nature of this world, and the place of humans in it. God is the hub of reality, the center of being and the direct source of everything else that is, so to inquire into literally anything at all is to take yet another look at God. Every area of study is pregnant with divine significance.

A final characteristic of the wise is *critical thinking*. To think critically is to exercise a number of formal intellectual skills that might be summed up gener-ally as discernment or good judgment, the capacity to tell truth from falsehood. At least seven subskills are involved in this trait. First, the critical thinker grasps the meaning of truth claims, being sensitive to nuances and subtle distinctions between ideas. Second, he is skilled at analyzing concepts and understanding their relationships. Third, he carefully assesses beliefs, judging whether or not they are based on good evidence, and is able to tell the difference between valid and invalid reasoning. Fourth, the critical thinker is skilled at identifying pre-suppositions of beliefs, the unspoken assumptions lying behind explicit truth claims. Fifth, the critical thinker sympathetically considers alternative ways of looking at issues, taking seriously the perspectives of others and trying to see things from their point of view. Sixth, the critical thinker strives to anticipate objections to various truth claims and seeks to discover the weak points of par-ticular beliefs, whether held by others or himself. And seventh, when it comes to disputable matters, the critical thinker maintains his convictions provisionally, recognizing that new evidence might come along that undermines or refutes his present beliefs on certain issues.

From a Christian perspective, critical thinking skills are crucial in guarding a person against false doctrine. Paul warns, "See to it that no one takes you cap-tive through hollow and deceptive philosophy which depends on human tradi-tion and the basic principles of this world rather than on Christ" (Col. 2:8).

This does not mean we should shun philosophy altogether, but only that we should not be fooled by *false* philosophy. Rather than instructing us to stay away from philosophy, Paul here implicitly exhorts us to *do* it. Avoiding the deception to which he refers demands training in the critical thinking skills noted above, all of which fall within the philosophical domain.

Peter writes, "Always be prepared to give an answer to everyone who asks you to give the reason for the hope that you have" (1 Peter 3:15). This, too, is an endorsement of critical thinking, specifically the skill of justifying beliefs with good evidence. All of us demand reasons from one another, even in trivial matters. How much more so, then, should we be able to justify our beliefs about what is of supreme importance, about what is most real and most valuable. Even if we cannot persuade others, we have an intellectual duty to provide good reasons for what we believe. Doing so falls in the area of apologetics, a practice in which, if we take Peter seriously, every Christian should be engaged.

So we all have a duty to grow in wisdom. The prospect can be daunting considering the time and effort it demands. So complaints might be raised in light of the challenges of growing in wisdom. Some might say, "I don't have the ability to do such and such, so why even bother?" As noted earlier, this is a self-fulfilling prophecy. If I say I could never learn to do X, then I won't attempt it, so it's certain that I'll never be able to do X. The only reason you can do anything well is because you've practiced it a lot. Everything is hard when you first try it.

For those who've surrendered to the notion that they don't have the ability to think scientifically or artistically, or in whatever way happens to be most difficult for them, a further point is in order regarding the illusion of subject divisions. It's only relatively recently in history that hard divisions have been made between different branches of learning. With the explosion of knowledge, divisions have been made to more easily organize educational institutions, curricula, and society at large. Academic divisions don't necessarily reflect actual, hard divisions between subjects. Physics fades into philosophy, which fades into fields such as psychology, theology, and history. Psychology fades into biology. History crosses all disciplines. Criminal justice involves law and political science, which both fade into ethics. And so it goes with all the disciplines. All learning is interconnected. So devotion to any subject connects one to *all* subject areas.

Time and Effort

Another will protest, "I don't have time to study those other disciplines. It's enough of a challenge to remain competent in my own area." Or "I'm so busy with my work and daily tasks at home that I don't have time to study at all." In response to the latter complaint, I would say that no one is too busy to read at least a little bit each day. That most people watch more than an hour of television a day is proof that people have time to study. It's true that all of us go through hectic periods in which our schedules are packed. But no one is consistently too busy to read. Or, in the case of those who spend much of their time in a particular area of study, we all have some extra time to explore outside our areas of specialty.

Keep in mind that you need not do formal study of all the disciplines to learn about them. You can become more well-rounded by changing your informal approach to issues. If, for example, you hear someone discussing quantum physics, or difference curves in economics, or drive shafts in automobiles, or some other topic about which you're ignorant, don't turn off your attention. Pick up as much as you can and ask questions when possible. You'll be surprised how much you can glean if you simply listen with interest. The problem is that we don't try hard enough. As with all the virtues, growth in wisdom boils down to intentional effort. The ultimate reason we don't love God adequately with our minds is that we're lazy, unwilling to do the work. Again, our culture's preoccupation with television, a sort of junk food for the mind, is a testament to this fact. The whole television culture seduces the mind into being passive when it was created to be active. When I ridded my home of television, my mental outlook changed significantly. My pursuit of wisdom is now more focused, my time better spent, and my mind no longer cluttered by foul and inane content.

Fools and Their Folly

The Bible has a lot to say about fools, particularly in the Wisdom Literature. There we learn that the fool is the antithesis of the wise. The fool is complacent, as opposed to eager to learn (Prov. 1:32), lazy and undisciplined (Prov. 1:7; Eccl. 4:5), lacking in self-control (Prov. 14:16; 29:11), and has poor judgment (Prov. 10:21; Eccl. 10:3). The biblical writers use vivid imagery in depicting foolishness, such as that of a dog devouring its own vomit. In its idols, popular American culture delivers on a regular basis graphic illustrations of folly, whether assaults by professional athletes, the drug abuses of rock musicians, or the latest sexual escapades of film actors. In each of these subcultures, "stars" flaunt their immorality and engage in bizarre behavior calculated to increase their wealth and fame. Some of our most popular cultural icons are simply fools and seem to have committed their lives to enticing others into their folly. Yet the sports, music, and film industries are principal guides for our culture. They shape the thinking of the typical American today as powerfully as any other force.

The wise person will not run and hide from these cultural influences. To do so would, indeed, be futile in America today, pervasive as they are. Rather, the wise will exercise sound judgment and live in a disciplined and self-controlled way, notwithstanding the enticements of our cultural icons. Moreover, they will bring a critical consciousness to bear upon our culture, affirming all that's good about it and rejecting all that's evil. The virtue of wisdom consists largely in the capacity to exercise such discernment in a variety of contexts.

Conclusion

From a biblical standpoint we must cherish wisdom so highly that we'd be willing to sacrifice all that we own to acquire it. Wisdom is literally more valuable than anything else we possess. Like the other virtues, wisdom must be cultivated, requiring work, a devotion of time and energy, and the application of other virtues, including patience, diligence, self-control, and humility. At the same time, wisdom is divinely bestowed. As Solomon recognized and Socrates declared, "Real wisdom is the property of God."[7] Realizing this is the first step toward wisdom and becoming a philosopher in the original sense of the term.

---

7.   Plato, *Apology,* in *The Collected Dialogues of Plato,* eds. Edith Hamilton and Huntington Cairns, trans. Hugh Tredennick (Princeton, N.J.: Princeton University Press, 1961), 9.

17

PRACTICING TRUST

The Virtue of Faith

Mark Twain once penned, "Faith is believing what you know ain't so."[1] Such a view could not be more out of step with the biblical portrait of true faith. Biblical faith is built upon fact, based in real events, and is philosophically reasonable. But faith is not limited to known historical truths or sound logic. It moves beyond reason and into the realms of hope and trust. And, as this chapter will make clear, it's a Christian virtue that demands constant practice.

Biblical Examples of Faith

The Bible gives us strong examples of faith. The story of Abraham and Isaac, for instance, is certainly one of the most dramatic of these. God promised Abraham that he would father a great nation with countless descendants. Moreover, God told Abraham these descendants would come through his son Isaac. How bizarre it must have seemed to Abraham, then, when God commanded him, "Take your son, your only son, Isaac, whom you love, and go to the region of Moriah. Sacrifice him there as a burnt offering on one of the mountains I will tell you about" (Gen. 22:2). These instructions, no doubt, were as perplexing as they were emotionally devastating, making Abraham's response all the more striking. He neither fled, nor protested God's command, nor even questioned the purpose behind it. Instead, he simply set about doing what he was told. The writer of Hebrews says, "Abraham reasoned that God could raise the dead" (Heb. 11:19), which, in a figurative sense, God eventually did in providing a ram at the last moment before Abraham cut his son's throat. But Abraham possessed something more than sound reasoning here, for logic alone cannot compel a man to slay his own son. If anything, it argues against doing so. Why

---

1. Mark Twain, *Following the Equator* (Hartford, Conn.: American, 1897), 132.

would God command the killing of an innocent human being, particularly when it's the one through whom God planned to fulfill his promise? Yet Abraham obeyed. He quietly, unquestioningly took the path of wild devotion.

The prophet Elijah provides another example of intense biblical faith. The sole remaining prophet of the true God at a time when Israel was entrenched in idolatry, Elijah challenged the prophets of Baal to a test. He summoned the people of Israel and all 450 prophets of Baal to Mount Carmel and commenced a sort of competition of the gods. Elijah proposed that two bulls be sacrificed and set upon wood. Then, Elijah announced, "You call on the name of your god and I will call on the name of the LORD. The god who answers by fire—he is God" (1 Kings 18:24). Elijah's method of ascertaining the true God has the look of a scientific experiment. Two theological hypotheses were being tested. If successful, one would be falsified and the other confirmed. But, as in the case of Abraham, proving the true God was not simply a matter of reason. Elijah's life was at stake. If the result did not clearly favor Elijah's God, the prophets of Baal would seize and kill him. So of the three possible outcomes (fire from Baal, fire from the Lord, or no fire at all), two meant death for Elijah. Elijah was confident, of course, that the Lord, not Baal, was God. But he couldn't have known for sure that God would respond with a miracle of fire. This was Elijah's radical act of personal trust—and it paid off. The prophets of Baal beseeched their god for hours, even slashing their own bodies to get his attention. But no fire came. So Elijah repaired the altar of the Lord, arranged the wood upon it, and placed the slaughtered bull upon the wood. Then he boldly flooded the altar with water, as if to rule out any natural explanations of the miracle that was to occur. And he prayed: "Answer me, O LORD, answer me, so these people will know that you, O LORD, are God, and that you are turning their hearts back again" (1 Kings 18:37). At once fire fell from heaven, burning up not only the sacrifice but also the entire altar, along with all the water.

Some less dramatic, but no less instructive, examples of faith appear in the New Testament. During Jesus' ministry he encountered a few people whose faith genuinely amazed him. One of these was the centurion described in the gospel of Matthew. In the town of Capernaum, the centurion approached Jesus, informing him that his servant had been paralyzed. When Jesus indicated his willingness to go heal the servant, the centurion said,

> Lord, I do not deserve to have you come under my roof. But just say the word, and my servant will be healed. For I myself am a man under authority, with soldiers under me. I tell this one, "Go," and he goes; and

that one, "Come," and he comes. I say to my servant, "Do this," and he does it. When Jesus heard this, he was astonished and said to those following him, "I tell you the truth, I have not found anyone in Israel with such great faith." (Matthew 8:8–10)

Just a few chapters later, Jesus encountered a Canaanite woman, whose situation was a bit more desperate. She pled to Jesus for deliverance on behalf of her demon-possessed daughter. Jesus seemed curiously resistant to meet her request. First, he refused to answer her. Then, at last, he responded by declaring, "I was sent only to the lost sheep of Israel" (Matt. 15:24). The woman knelt before him and continued to plead. Again, Jesus resisted, saying, "It is not right to take the children's bread and toss it to their dogs" (v. 26). To this the woman responded, showing both her persistence and cunning, saying, "Even the dogs eat the crumbs that fall from their masters' table" (v. 27). At this Jesus exclaimed, "Woman, you have great faith!" (v. 28). And he immediately granted her request.

What is remarkable about the faith of the centurion and the Canaanite woman is not that they believed Jesus could provide the healing they requested. What made their faith special was that they considered such miracles to be relatively small matters for Jesus. The centurion's comparison of Jesus' authority over disease to his own authority over his soldiers makes this clear, as does his casual observation that Jesus need not even be in his servant's physical presence to heal him. The Canaanite woman's reference to Jesus' miraculous acts as mere "crumbs" communicated a similar conviction that his power extended to much greater things. This further explained her persistence; she would not be put off despite three cool responses.

Defining Biblical Faith

In the preceding section are several powerful biblical illustrations of faith, each biblical figure having a different motivation: One is motivated by obedience to divine command, another by the desire for righteous declaration of divine power, and the others by the hope for divine healing. The one constant is the deep, abiding recognition by the person involved that he or she is not in control of the situation—but God is. As a consequence, each person of faith practices a kind of surrender, the symptoms of which are a confident defiance of the odds and sometimes a persistence without immediate reward. What this shows is that the basic element of faith is trust, and that of a very personal nature. It's not the sort of trust a person practices when climbing a ladder, believing it won't give way. It's more like placing trust in your surgeon when you go under the knife. Such trust requires belief, but it's not limited to this cognitive aspect. Faith is also, and perhaps most importantly, performative. It is something you *do*, that is, faith is displayed through behavior. This is why James says, "Faith without deeds is useless" (James 2:20). Faith is trust put into action.

The writer of Hebrews says, "Faith is being sure of what we hope for and certain of what we do not see" (Heb. 11:1). What we "do not see" is God's sovereign rule of the world. Although the orderly workings of the cosmos are apparent to us (we call them "laws of nature") and demonstrate divine governance of the cosmos, we do not literally see God controlling every detail, down to the atomic level. The Bible assures us, however, that he does just this: "He is before all things, and in him all things hold together" (Col. 1:17); "in him we live and move and have our being" (Acts 17:28). On a more personal level the psalmist declares, "All the days ordained for me were written in your book before one of them came to be" (Ps. 139:16). Faith, then, is an essential recognition of the complete providence of God, an active acknowledgment that he orders all things, that there are no truly random events, not even one arbitrary atom.

Two Vices Opposite Faith

Biblical faith is not irrational. It doesn't contradict the facts. Rather, we have faith on the basis of facts. What distinguishes faith from simple knowledge is that faith moves beyond propositional belief to personal trust. So why should this kind of trust be such a difficult thing? Why do we Christians, who are utterly persuaded of God's power and goodness, so often fail to trust him? To answer this question is to identify the vice directly opposite the virtue of faith. That vice, as philosopher Robert Adams has insightfully noted, is the lust for control. If to exhibit faith in God is to actively affirm his control over one's life, then to lack faith is to assert one's own control over it. Adams writes,

> The supreme threat to our control . . . is God himself. In Christian faith we are invited to trust a person so much greater than ourselves that we cannot understand him very fully. We have to trust his power and goodness in general, without having a blueprint of what he is going to do in detail. This is very disturbing because it entails a loss of control of our own lives.[2]

---

2.   Robert Adams, *The Virtue of Faith and Other Essays in Philosophical Theology* (Oxford: Oxford University Press, 1987), 19–20.

From a Christian standpoint, such lust is basic to our nature. Each of us, at the core of our being, desires fundamental control over our own destiny. Such desire is, in fact, the urge for complete autonomy and reflects a will to be God. For only God has the right (as well as the power) to govern human destinies. What's worse, many of us quietly (or not so quietly) try to govern other persons' lives by manipulating them in various ways. And if we had the chance, perhaps we would even choose to control the entire universe. These impulses, too, are symptoms of our perverse will to be God.[3]

For the agnostic or the atheist, there is nothing unnatural about desiring complete control over one's own destiny. They don't even believe God exists, so to their minds there is no one ultimately to trust but oneself. For the theist, and the Christian in particular, this desire is both logically and morally absurd. The lust for control challenges God's power and goodness. So there's no neutral moral ground here. Either one properly surrenders control to the sovereign God or one seeks control oneself, which is the vice of faithlessness. This vice takes three principal forms. Refusal to trust God regarding one's own life is the vice of *self-reliance*. Failing to trust his governance of others is manifested either as the vice of *manipulation* or *cynicism* (which are the active and passive forms, respectively). The symptoms of faithlessness are many. Anxiety, fear, despair, indecisiveness, regret, and worry are among the most common. Such emotional signposts remind us of our attempt to usurp ultimate control and that we need to reorient our life stance back toward God.[4]

An especially severe and devastating form of faithlessness is cynicism, which is the refusal to hope. The cynic is naturally suspicious of promises and all glad tidings. Where the person of faith trusts, the cynic hesitates and holds back. Where the faithful expects ultimate good, the cynic counts on disappointment.

---

3. Other popular symptoms of the lust for control are occult practices such as palm reading, fortune telling, séances, and channeling. These psychic techniques are spiritual in nature and are, therefore, enticing counterfeits for those who recognize the need to rely on something transcendent. Perhaps this is why these practices are so strongly condemned in Scripture.

4. Some have argued, not without good reason, that faith struggles are essentially struggles with sin. Dietrich Bonhoeffer writes, for instance, "When people complain . . . that they find it hard to believe, it is a sign of deliberate or unconscious disobedience." To the person who struggles to have faith, Bonhoeffer says, the proper response is, "You are disobedient, you are trying to keep some part of your life under your own control. . . . Your difficulty is your sins." *The Cost of Discipleship,* trans. Kaiser Verlag Munchen (New York: Macmillan, 1959), 74, 76.

Where the faithful is joyful, the cynic despairs. But what makes cynicism so insidious is its pretense of maturity and life wisdom. The cynic presents herself as someone who "knows the ropes," who's "been there and done that." She might even say things like "Don't get your hopes up" and "I wouldn't count on it" to those who hope for the best in a situation. The cynic sees such hopes as naïve and foolish. Worst of all, cynicism makes faithlessness contagious, subtly encouraging others to distrust God and to hope only in themselves, if at all.

A few years ago, my brother Robert visited our university to speak to one of our business classes. After spending the day conversing with numerous students and several of my colleagues, he remarked that he was surprised by the lack of cynicism. Having spent a great deal of time with professors from state universities in the past, Robert knows just how cynical our lot can be. Thus, he reacted with puzzlement about his interactions with my colleagues. "I kept expecting the cynicism," he said, "but it never came." As I pondered this, it dawned upon me why this was so. My colleagues are Christians, hence persons of faith, so cynicism would naturally be reduced among us. It's not altogether absent among our faculty, of course, but those who display it are, I think, exceptional. (Nor do I mean to suggest that cynicism is universally present at public colleges!)

And cynicism is a severe symptom of faithlessness not just because of its negative effects but also because it takes so long to develop and thus is a sign of deep-rooted faithlessness. Anxieties and fears can come upon one very quickly, but they can also be quickly exterminated. Not so with cynicism, a vice that grows gradually over many years, as one experiences disappointment after disappointment and eventually suspicion and distrust become one's prevailing emotional stock. This is why cynicism is rare among the young and almost unheard of among children. They simply haven't lived long enough to build such emotional barricades against hope. Perhaps this is why Jesus frequently used children as examples of biblical faith. It is a child's natural disposition to trust, to hope, to have faith that the best scenario will unfold. And for the Christian, who subscribes to a set of beliefs that promises what *seems* too good to be true, such trust is absolutely necessary.

Trials of Faith

Cynicism is the dark result of failing to keep one's faith when challenged. But it's the nature of faith to be tested. The faith of Abraham, Elijah, the centurion and the Canaanite woman was proved only through the challenges they faced. All of the paragons of biblical faith—Moses, David, Isaiah, Jeremiah, Paul, Peter, even Jesus himself—achieved their status as men of faith through the trials they endured. Each of their situations was unique, but that their faith was tested was typical. Trials of faith are as basic to the human condition as faith itself.

The trials of faith come in two basic forms. The most obvious of these is suffering. All the vicissitudes of pain that human beings experience—from poverty and sickness to heartbreak and mental illness—test our faith, tempting us to abandon our trust in God or causing us to wonder whether he really is loving and all-powerful. From a biblical standpoint it's clear that, as has already been noted in other chapters, such trials come to us in order to mature us (James 1:3–4) and refine our faith (1 Peter 1:7), not to destroy our faith and turn us into cynics.

That trials mature and refine us is yet another paradoxical truth about faith and the human condition generally. But all battle-tested Christians will testify to this fact: During periods of intense struggle, crushing disappointment, or excruciating pain, they grew closer to God, and their capacity to trust God was increased rather than quashed. Such wisdom is, of course, existential in nature in that it can only be learned through personal experience. One cannot teach it as one teaches an academic subject. So delicate, in fact, is this profound truth that it's usually inappropriate to remind people of it when they are in the midst of a severe trial. At such times a person needs sympathy, not a theological tutor. Here an ounce of encouragement is worth a ton of lecture.

The other form that trials of faith take, odd as it may seem, is blessing. Our very freedom from suffering, such as good health, wealth, and social esteem, constitute potential snares that can kill faith (even, as noted in a previous chapter, as these things can spoil us). That blessings can result in faithlessness represents a further paradox about the human condition, but is nonetheless evident from human experience. We've all heard stories of how Christians in positions of power, such as televangelists, have succumbed to temptation or lost their faith altogether. This tendency is nowhere better illustrated than in the Old Testament nation of Israel. That nation's faith thrived precisely when they struggled most severely, as they wandered in the wilderness and as they undertook the overwhelming task of taking Canaan. Their trials matured them faithwise, but once they'd taken Canaan—when they'd inherited the land flowing with milk and honey—the faith of the nation began to wane, and eventually the spiritual condition of Israel degenerated into idolatry.

As it was for Israel, so it is for the individual believer. Material blessings can be lures, tempting us away from faith. Why is this the case? How can the very blessings we receive from the hand of God lead us away from him? Two reasons come to mind. First, our material blessings give us a sense of independence. Those who are healthy, wealthy, and powerful naturally sense their needs less keenly, even when it comes to the moral and spiritual needs that their earthly goods and accomplishments do not begin to satisfy. In turn, such pride naturally leads them to exert less moral and spiritual energy. It's a plain and tragic psychological law: You won't work for what you don't think you need. So, as a matter of course, the healthy, wealthy, and powerful tend to lose their faith or at least become less effective stewards in the kingdom of God. This partly explains why Jesus says, "It is easier for a camel to go through the eye of a needle than for a rich man to enter the kingdom of God" (Matt. 19:24).

Prosperity tends to kill faith, too, because it invites us to cling tightly to this world. Otherwise put, material blessings incline us to believe that we've nothing better to hope for. The sick or impoverished know the extent of their need all too well, so they're naturally disposed to hope, to yearn for what might be, to trust God for what he has prepared for them in the future. The prosperous naturally lose this sense of need, and instead obtain more and more incentives to be careful about their earthly goods, even if at the expense of heavenly goods. If faith calls for surrender of all, then the more purchased, the more prestige and comfort acquired, the more called "mine," the more is consequently called to be surrendered to God. As one increases in wealth, then, one's desire to surrender in faith decreases. For most, it seems, consistent surrender of such mass quantities of material blessings proves too great a risk. It becomes a trial of faith more fraught with anxiety than most can endure.

Even in my own life—and I'm far from rich by American standards—I have seen how the slow accumulation of earthly goods can be spiritual quicksand. This is true not only with material possessions but also with human blessings. In the last seven years I've married my wife and we've had three children. They are the four persons I cherish most on this planet. Naturally, I'm inclined to cling to them, to call them "mine" in an ultimate sense. Furthermore, the joy they give me tempts me to love this world more than I should. So the very abundance of goods with which God himself has blessed me tries my faith.

Two fundamental lessons can be drawn from this discussion, which can be cast in the form of general principles. First, *your blessings are your curses, and your curses are your blessings.* When we're blessed, we're tempted (through a sense of independence and an increased love for this world) to lose our faith, which of course would be the ultimate curse. Whereas when we experience the symptoms of the curse of the fall, namely poverty and suffering, we're most inclined to reach out to God, to exhibit the very faith that leads to redemption and long-term blessing. As Thomas Watson puts it, "God makes the saints' mala-dies their medicines."[5]

Second, *your faith will be tried, either by hardship or prosperity.* Since faith is tried by both hardship and prosperity, and everyone experiences one or both over the course of a lifetime, trials of faith are unavoidable. This is not entirely bad news, since by God's grace the testing of faith leads to yet greater faith. The point of our being alive in the first place is to relate to God, so it's not surprising that at every turn we're faced with a decision in matters trivial and momentous, to trust or distrust God, to surrender or seek control, to choose the way of faith or cynicism. There is no neutral ground.

Practicing Our Trust

How does one intentionally grow in faith? How do we practice our trust in God? As with all the virtues explored in this book, the practice of faith involves both cognitive and practical dimensions. On the cognitive side, the first step toward growth in faith is recognition of one's place in the cosmos. When Job questioned God's providence, the Lord rebuked him with a torrent of questions intended to properly humble his servant:

> Where were you when I laid the earth's foundation?
>   Tell me, if you understand.
> Who marked off its dimensions? Surely you know!
>   Who stretched a measuring line across it?
> On what were its footings set,
>   or who laid its cornerstone—
> while the morning stars sang together
>   and all the angels shouted for joy?
> Who shut up the sea behind doors
>   when it burst forth from the womb, . . .
> when I fixed limits for it
>   and set its doors and bars in place,
> when I said, "This far you may come and no farther;
>   here is where your proud waves halt"?
>   —Job 38:4–11

---

5.   Thomas Watson, *All Things for Good* (Edinburgh: Banner of Truth, 1986), 51.

For four chapters running, God declares to Job some of the ways in which God wisely and powerfully governs the universe, illustrating just how unworthy Job is to question God's authority. In the end Job got the point, but it took this extended and terrifying rebuke to get him back into gear faithwise. We would all save ourselves a lot of trouble if we could get this same point.

It's not flattering to say so, but we human beings are puny—infinitesimally small bits of being in a universe that is incomprehensibly big. Each of us dwells in a small corner of a tiny planet within a huge solar system that is one of billions within a galaxy that is, again, but one of billions. From a temporal standpoint the same is true. Even those of us who live into old age occupy only a blip on the timeline of history. Those privileged to accomplish much (by human standards) during their lifetimes are usually forgotten within a generation or two. As Solomon says, "There is no remembrance of men of old, and even those who are yet to come will not be remembered by those who follow" (Eccl. 1:11). Only if you achieve exceedingly great fame will you be remembered at all by later generations. Even then your name will likely be besmirched as well as praised. Furthermore, whatever regard you have by future generations, it will be only your name or a superficial and artificial memory of who you really were, your real essence having passed on into eternity. Considering this perspective, it's no wonder that James says, "What is your life? You are a mist that appears for a little while and then vanishes" (James 4:14).

All of us, it seems, are quite insignificant from a cosmic perspective. And, of course, on top of this we are morally flawed. So we're not only puny, we're bad. Coupled with these humbling facts is the unspeakable wonder that God cares deeply for us. Somehow each of us is an object of very special divine concern. "What is man that you are mindful of him?" (Ps. 8:4) the psalmist asks, because in spite of our smallness, in spite our having made ourselves the enemies of God, he has befriended us and given us direction and purpose. We are puny and bad, but he has given us dignity and worth.

Recognition of these basic facts about us, our place in the cosmos, and our value to God, is where faith is born. Faith is trust in God. To see your own smallness is to see that it's a fool's game to place ultimate trust in yourself. To see God's greatness is to recognize the same thing again, at an even more profound level. You, mere human "mist," living your fleeting life on this speck of a planet, would be a ridiculous fool not to throw all your trust upon the One from whom all meaning, power, and goodness flow.

In addition to gaining the proper perspective on your place in the universe, faith is built by voluntary acts of surrender. First, you must determine where you are aiming to seize control, to grip too tightly what might dissolve in your hands at any moment (e.g., your possessions, the persons you love, your very life). Then, in an act of prayer, you must present these gifts back to God, offering him the full rights to them, which, of course, he already has. Thus, you are simply affirming what is already true. But doing so is spiritual freedom and psychological release.

In surrendering our control of all to God, though, we can be happy that *all* includes not just the things we love. We're commanded to surrender as well the worries that faithlessness causes. As Peter says, "Cast all your anxiety on him because he cares for you" (1 Peter 5:7). We commonly think of faith as demanding energy and being hard, draining work. But it's actually faithlessness that emotionally drains us. No mere mortal can keep all of life's details from going awry so, when we try, we extend ourselves beyond what is healthy.

Our moral condition falls into one of two categories; we are in need of either overhaul or maintenance. Since we're all born into sin, at some point we all need an overhaul of faith, at which time we surrender control of our lives at a fundamental level. This surrender is an active recognition of God's control, which constitutes the sort of trust that is faith. When we have so practiced our trust that our surrendering control is a matter of maintenance rather than overhaul, then our faith becomes less self-conscious, less aware of itself as faith. Such a person displays faith without even realizing it. Consider again the attitude of the centurion. His was a faith that was not self-conscious. It's easy to imagine that he was perplexed by Jesus' response of declaring him a man of great faith. Observers, too, might have been surprised, the centurion's faith being so interwoven into his daily life, so matter of fact, so extraordinarily routine, that it became less obvious to everyone, including the centurion himself. But such constant, moment-by-moment faith is no less virtuous or significant because of its regularity in a person's life. On the contrary, it is all the more remarkable for being so.

18

THE GREATEST OF THESE

The Virtue of Love

To discourse on love is a daunting venture for several reasons. So much of the world's great literature is devoted to love, it's virtually impossible to say anything new on the topic. And even those who are not well educated in the classics are exposed constantly to popular claims and opinions about love. Consequently, everyone nurses various beliefs, however vague or uninformed, about what love is (and is not). So even if one does manage to say something new or interesting about love, one's audience might not be as open to persuasion as when discussing most other virtues.

This chapter does, however, say something new about love. Or at least it will appear to be a new idea because it's been so long overlooked. It's actually an ancient idea. It is herein suggested that love is not only the greatest of the virtues—this is quite obvious to most people—but love is the *sum* of all virtues. Among character traits, love is supreme because it embodies each of the traits that make a morally excellent character.

The Four Loves

Love is an ambiguous term, especially in the English language, where a single word bears the burden of describing a wide range of affections. Classical Greek features a fourfold distinction between familial, friendship, erotic, and divine love. All love is affectionate but the nature of that affection distinguishes each form of love. The most primal kind of love is *storge*, familial love, the natural affection between those most familiar with one another. The love between a parent and child is the classic example of storge, but it can also be extended to affection between animals, such as a dog and her puppies. That is, storge is an instinctive kind of love.

Eros is the most celebrated of loves, the inspiration for much of the world's great art and many of history's most dramatic deeds, both heroic and foolish.

Eros is romantic love, longing for deepest intimacy, both physical and emotional. The sexual union culminates this desire as a manifestation of absolute devotion. The erotic lover is a student of the beloved and is willing to make extreme sacrifices for the beloved's sake. Moreover, eros is famously stubborn, impervious to the will. As classically conceived, eros is not a matter of choice but of fate. Marlowe's well-known poem vividly expresses this idea:

> It lies not in our power to love or hate,
> For will in us is overruled by fate. . . .
> Where both deliberate, the love is slight:
> Who ever loved, that loved not at first sight?[1]

The third kind of love, *philios*, is friendship love. Through participation in a shared project, at work or play, friendships emerge. Philios, one might say, is a happy by-product of some other human involvement. This is very different from erotic love, as perceptively described by C. S. Lewis: "Lovers are always talking to one another about their love; friends hardly ever about their friendship. Lovers are normally face to face, absorbed in each other; friends, side by side, absorbed in some common interest."[2] Lewis rightly adds that by its nature, philios is not exclusively a two-person affair. Friends may come in groups of three, five, or a dozen. As many as can unite in pursuit of a goal can become a community of friends, nor is philios a jealous kind of love.

Familial, erotic, and friendship love are all natural forms of affection, arising without any planning or deliberation on our part. But they are also subject to fading. Friends drift apart, romantic flames are extinguished, and even familial ties are broken. The natural loves are mutable and insufficient by themselves. Nor are they inherently virtuous. Where there is no willful commitment, there can be no moral praise. But one kind of love *is* inherently virtuous, always a matter of will, and lends to the other loves whatever moral goodness is to be found in them. This love is *agape*, divine love. Selfless and unconditional, it always seeks the best for its beloved.

Nowhere is agape better described than by Paul in 1 Corinthians 13:

> If I speak in the tongues of men and of angels, but have not love, I am only a resounding gong or a clanging cymbal. If I have the gift of

---

1. Christopher Marlowe, "Who Ever Loved, That Loved Not at First Sight?" *Complete Plays and Poems* (London: J. M. Dent and Sons, 1976), 404–5.
2. C. S. Lewis, *The Four Loves* (San Diego: Harcourt Brace, 1960), 61.

prophecy and can fathom all mysteries and all knowledge, and if I have a faith that can move mountains, but have not love, I am nothing. If I give all I possess to the poor and surrender my body to the flames, but have not love, I gain nothing.

Love is patient, love is kind. It does not envy, it does not boast, it is not proud. It is not rude, it is not self-seeking, it is not easily angered, it keeps no record of wrongs. Love does not delight in evil but rejoices with the truth. It always protects, always trusts, always hopes, always perseveres. (vv. 1–7)

In short, agape love is infallible—morally perfect and entirely beautiful. There is thus nothing natural about it. Agape is divine. To find such love is to find God. To live such love is to live in God. As John says, "Everyone who loves has been born of God and knows God. Whoever does not love does not know God, because God is love" (1 John 4:7–8).

The Sum of All Virtues

Paul's description of agape in 1 Corinthians is widely regarded as the best definition of agape ever penned. Often overlooked, though, is Paul's defining this love entirely in moral terms. It turns out that agape is fundamentally a *virtue*. Or better, it is the virtue *of* virtues. Consider the elements of Paul's description. Note how each one identifies a moral virtue:

Description	Virtue
Love: is patient (v. 4)	patience
is kind (v. 4)	kindness
does not envy (v. 4)	contentment
does not boast (v. 4)	discretion, humility
is not proud (v. 4)	humility
is not rude (v. 5)	courtesy
is not self-seeking (v. 5)	humility
is not easily angered (v. 5)	temperance, patience
keeps no record of wrongs (v. 5)	forgiveness
does not delight in evil (v. 6)	justice, purity
rejoices with the truth (v. 6)	honesty, wisdom
always protects (v. 7)	courage, kindness

always trusts (v. 7)   faith, generosity
always hopes (v. 7)   hope, faith
always perseveres (v. 7)   perseverance

Paul concludes the chapter by noting that "these three remain: faith, hope and love. But the greatest of these is love" (1 Cor. 13:13). Agape is the greatest virtue because it encapsulates *all* the virtues. So, to define it succinctly, agape is totally virtuous affection. No wonder Paul goes on to declare "love never fails" (v. 8). Such affection is invincible, prepared for every circumstance because it is armed with every moral skill. No wonder it's impossible to cite examples of love without also citing examples of other particular virtues, such as those enumerated by Paul.

To conceive of agape as the sum of all virtues helps us to understand John's declaration that "God is love." Biblical scholars often interpret this phrase as a way of proclaiming that God is perfectly loving, a sort of overstatement to make a point. More cynical types regard the phrase as reductionistic and therefore literally false. But if agape is a totally virtuous affection, then to say God is love is neither reductionistic nor hyperbole. Rather, it is a complete description of God's moral character, because it affirms in a single word that God has each virtue, that he is morally excellent in every way.

To think of God and love in this way also clarifies how, as Paul says, "Love is the fulfillment of the law" (Rom. 13:10). He admonishes us to "let no debt remain outstanding, except the continuing debt to love one another, for he who loves his fellowman has fulfilled the law" (v. 8). This passage is yet another that has baffled theologians for centuries and, as in the case of the 1 John passage, it has sometimes been regarded as a gross simplification, if not a distortion. But if all the virtues are contained in love, then to live in love is to achieve a morally perfect life, which, of course, fulfills all the requirements of the law. Whether expressed in the form of commands—as is found in the Pentateuch and elsewhere in the Old Testament—or as character traits—as found in Proverbs, the beatitudes, and Paul's letters—the import is the same: The child of God must love others unconditionally.

Agape is not only the sum of all virtues but also the affection that runs through them all and unites them. Paul says, "As God's chosen people, holy and dearly loved, clothe yourselves with compassion, kindness, humility, gentleness and patience. . . . And over all these virtues put on love, which binds them all together in perfect unity" (Col. 3:12, 14). It's not enough, then, that we exhibit every virtue (as if that was easy). In practicing these moral skills we must do so with an unconditional affection. Such is the high calling of Christian ethics, an ideal that is unattainable, humanly speaking. But, as Jesus said, all things are possible with God.

It's true that no one but Christ has perfectly lived the agape life. Yet we've all seen instances of divine love displayed, however rare, in the lives of mortals, each testifying to the reality of God and the potential for full and final human redemption. A strong depiction of agape is found in Victor Hugo's classic *Les Miserables*. The story concerns Jean Valjean, who, after serving nineteen years of hard labor, is finally released but destined to be a social outcast. After the Bishop of Digne gives him temporary refuge, the hardened Valjean responds to this kindness by stealing some of the old man's silver. The police eventually apprehend Valjean and bring him back to the bishop to confirm the crime. Facing life on the chain gang, Valjean is amazed to hear the bishop cover for him by lying to the police. The bishop not only refuses to condemn Valjean but also bestows on him both the silver and some valuable candlesticks, saying to him, "My brother, you no longer belong to what is evil but to what is good."[3] In response to this remarkable act of grace, Valjean resolves to live a new life, and the remainder of this epic tale recounts his journey of moral transformation and the impact that his goodness has upon others.

Hugo's story is, indeed, powerful, but even it cannot compare to some of the biblical instances of agape, such as that found in the book of Hosea. There, we find the Lord commanding the prophet, "Go, take to yourself an adulterous wife and children of unfaithfulness" (Hos. 1:2). Hosea obeys by marrying Gomer, who subsequently bears three of his children. But Gomer is unfaithful to her husband, and the Lord says to Hosea, "Go, show your love to your wife again, though she is loved by another and is an adulteress. Love her as the LORD loves the Israelites, though they turn to other gods" (3:1). Again, Hosea obeys and buys "her for fifteen shekels of silver and about a homer and a lethek of barley" (v. 2). Then he says to her, "You are to live with me many days; you must not be a prostitute or be intimate with any man, and I will live with you" (v. 3).

Both Hugo's classic and the experience of Hosea feature dramatic, unconditional love toward vicious people. Neither the bishop nor Hosea was deterred by the moral ugliness of those they blessed. Each story powerfully communicates something of agape, a love that we see full-blown in the work of the savior, Jesus Christ. Paul writes, "God demonstrates his own love for us in this: While

---

3.   Victor Hugo, *Les Miserables,* trans. Norman Denny (New York: Penguin, 1976), 111.

we were still sinners, Christ died for us" (Rom. 5:8). Notice that, as in the case of the Bishop of Digne and the prophet Hosea, a price for retrieval had to be paid in order to purchase redemption. In our case, that price was paid, of course, by Jesus, and with no mere silver or shekels but with his dear life. This is the extreme to which agape is willing to go, even total self-sacrifice. It's significant, too, that in each case a response of gratitude and faithfulness on the part of the beloved is required. Such is the proper response to such extreme love, and doing otherwise is vice to the extreme. To spit in the face of grace is the highest treachery.

Clearly, then, to love people is to show them grace. What, though, does it mean to love God? How are we to understand the commandment to "love the Lord your God with all your heart and with all your soul and with all your mind and with all your strength"? (Mark 12:30). Again, if agape is fully virtuous affection, then our love for God should be understood in essentially moral terms. Yes, to love God is to have a strong affection for him but, most importantly, it is to live virtuously before him. Anyone can have strong feelings toward God, but mere affection in the absence of obedience empties it of any significance. An American citizen may well up with emotion every time he hears the national anthem, but if he cheats on his taxes then is he really in any sense patriotic? In a similar way, a life of virtue is the tangible sign of genuine agape affection for God. We demonstrate our allegiance to him not by having positive emotions but by the life we live. Jesus himself made this very point: "If you love me, you will obey what I command" (John 14:15). Loving God is a moral enterprise. As Kierkegaard once said, "Let a man . . . love God in uprightness of heart."[4] We love God by obeying him, by consistently doing the right thing. In short, the love of God is the life of virtue.

Eros, Agape, and Hatred

In considering strong emotions and their connection with love, one notices the striking difference between agape and eros. While agape is firm and unchanging, romantic love is famously unpredictable and fleeting. Even some of our idioms reflect this: "I'm falling in love"; "She has the love bug." Such phrases show just how far erotic love is from agape love. For one thing, eros is passive, while agape is active. Romantic love hits a person independently of his will. He

---

4. Søren Kierkegaard, *Works of Love: Some Christian Reflections in the Form of Discourses,* trans. Howard Hong and Edna Hong (New York: Harper and Row, 1962), 108.

can only hope he'll find eros with someone; he cannot set out to do it. (Consider the absurdity of this thought: "Hmm, I think that today I shall fall in love.") For the agape lover, on the other hand, there is no mysterious waiting to be nailed by one of Cupid's arrows. Agape is a matter of choice, a conscious decision that is actively manifested. An important indicator that one, in fact, has agape is that it will work against and even overcome strong feelings. Only agape is capable of saying, "I might not like you very much, but doggone it, I *will* love you."

A further difference between the two is that eros is entirely subjective, while agape is a public fact. A person can have romantic passions and a longing to be with his beloved without anyone knowing about it. His erotic feelings may only become public when he says those three words: "I love you." But in the agape sense of love, to utter those words would be the most presumptuous thing in the world. Who would be so boastful as to say, "I have a fully virtuous affection toward you" (which is what "I agape you" means)? How absurd! Since agape is not boastful, the very declaration, in fact, disproves itself! When it comes to agape, the *beloved* knows it best. A more appropriate phrase, then, would be uttered by the beloved: "You love me." Therefore, perhaps instead of reeling off our habitual "I love you" to those most dear to us, we should be asking them, "Do I love you?"

Conceiving of agape as virtuous affection also gives us insight into the notion that hatred is its opposite. It's true that agape is a kind of affection, while hatred is certainly disaffection. But the more fundamental difference between agape and hatred is that they're *moral* opposites. Agape is the embodiment of virtue, while hatred is the embodiment of vice. To love is to show moral excellence toward a person—to be courteous, kind, patient, humble, generous, grateful, forgiving, and so on. To hate is to demonstrate moral vices toward the person—to be rude, unkind, impatient, selfish, greedy, ungrateful, and merciless. So while hatred usually involves an emotion, such as a desire to inflict pain or to feel enjoyment of another person's harm, such feelings are probably incidental. True hatred can be apathetic, void of emotion. So long as you act immorally toward a person, you've succeeded in hating that person. All that is really necessary for hatred is vice.

Vulnerable but Unconquerable

The one who loves is vulnerable. To love is to risk loss and suffering. C. S. Lewis says,

Love anything, and your heart will certainly be wrung and possibly broken. If you want to make sure of keeping it intact, you must give your heart to no one, not even to an animal. Wrap it carefully round with hobbies and little luxuries; avoid all entanglements; lock it up safe in the casket or coffin of your selfishness.[5]

The extent to which a person is willing to make himself vulnerable to all sorts of pain and loss is a reliable measure of his love. As Jesus says, "Greater love has no man than this, that he lay down his life for his friends" (John 15:13). Jesus, of course, practiced what he preached, graciously giving his life for us. The love of God spared not his only begotten Son but delivered him to total humiliation and a cruel death. But the passion of Christ only epitomized his love. The whole character of Jesus, the entire set of virtues that he manifested every day of his earthly life, combined with his deep affection for those he encountered, was love in its essence. The extraordinary depth of his love was, in fact, the doorway to torture for Jesus. Each of his virtues was abused by others: his generosity—he healed ten lepers, and only one thanked him; his patience—he withheld his wrath from Judas, and Judas betrayed him; his self-control—he held his tongue before Pilate and was unjustly condemned; his humility—he humbled himself before the Roman soldiers, and they spat in his face; his forgiveness—he pled for God's mercy toward his crucifiers, and they persisted in their murder.

The love of Jesus did not save him from pain. No, his love *guaranteed* his suffering. In a fallen and hate-filled world, to be Christlike is to solicit the abuse of others, to have one's affectionate virtues trampled underfoot. The spirit of this world hates righteousness and is repulsed by all things holy. Nothing is more holy than love, for this is God's moral essence. To be an imitator of God is to choose the path of Christ and all this entails, including its destiny—the cross. The lover of God and of those bearing his image inherits the kingdom of God, along with all its sorrows. Consider this: Jesus was love incarnate and was called by Isaiah the "man of sorrows." Simply put, true love suffers.[6] Agape is compassionate; it feels the pain of the beloved and shares his grief. Love feels all wounds and mourns with those who mourn.

5. Lewis, *The Four Loves*, 121.
6. See Nicholas Wolterstorff's fascinating discussion of this aspect of divine love in his "Suffering Love," in *Philosophy and the Christian Faith*, ed. Thomas V. Morris (Notre Dame: University of Notre Dame Press, 1988), 196–237.

This does *not* mean, however, that agape is tragic. Rather, the mere earthly loves, storge, philios, and eros—are, by themselves, inherently tragic, sources of frustration and despair. Even these must be completed and perfected by agape. Agape cannot be defeated, is immune from frustration because it is content, makes no demands, and has no self-serving ambition. The agape lover has nothing to lose, because in his perfect humility he has already surrendered self. Boasting and envy are impossible because he is neither possessive nor acquisitive. His affection soars above (though is not removed from) all circumstances. And although sorrow will come, it is the exquisite sorrow of hope, not the worldly sorrow of despair. Real tragedy can occur only when irrevocable loss is a possibility. Agape derives from the eternal and immovable, where no final loss is possible. Agape, then, cannot fail, it always triumphs and, in a universe governed by God, it forever rules.

In a fallen world populated by proud, vicious people, agape is intrusive and peculiar. Where preoccupation with self is the norm, agape can be judged only as foolish. And the unmerited favor bestowed upon us by agape, known as grace, will necessarily appear ridiculous and even offensive. No wonder Jesus, the human embodiment of agape, strikes us as so peculiar. No wonder his grace provoked rage and continues to receive hateful responses from those who know nothing of unconditional love. But agape loves even the hateful and devours them with grace. Agape conquers all.

Conclusion

Agape is the greatest of the virtues because it is the sum of the virtues, perfectly embodying all the traits that make up a morally excellent character. So to strive for moral excellence in any respect is to strive to love in some respect. The apostle John says, "Dear friends, let us love one another, for love comes from God. Everyone who loves has been born of God and knows God. Whoever does not love does not know God, because God is love. . . . No one has ever seen God; but if we love one another, God lives in us and his love is made complete in us" (1 John 4:7–8, 12). If ever there was a litmus test for Christian redemption, agape would be it. If ever there was an impossibly high standard that only the Holy Spirit can aspire to through us, agape is it. May we prove our redemption by living in agape, serving others, acting kindly, being patient, showing mercy, always hoping, always trusting, always persevering.

CONCLUSION

The Life of Virtue

It's hard to be good. So many moral skills must be practiced, and it's not always clear how best to apply them. This book has examined over twenty virtues, but many others could be explored, including fidelity, tolerance, purity, diligence, joy, prudence, hope, obedience, and reverence. At the same time, there is unity among the virtues. While not all virtues reduce to a single moral trait, each one involves or is vitally linked to other virtues. Justice and perseverance call for courage. Courage, sincerity, and modesty demand self-control. Wit, creativity, and peace involve the use of wisdom. Forgiveness and generosity are premised upon gratitude. Most of these virtues, along with patience and kindness, require humility. And love supervenes over all of these traits.

The unity of the virtues is evident in that to be morally excellent in one area naturally enhances one's ability to be virtuous in other areas. One is not likely to encounter someone who is, say, generous but impatient, kind but ungrateful, or sincere but unjust. Virtues beget other virtues, just as vices beget further vices. It has been herein suggested that self-control and humility are two of the more fundamental virtues, moral skills that are prerequisites for nearly every other virtue. These core traits explain why Christian attributes tend to be exemplified in bundles.

It should be emphasized, as in the introduction to this book, that character traits are not the whole story when it comes to Christian ethics. Two other dimensions of moral consideration—duty and utility—are crucial. We all have moral obligations, based on general principles that bind us (e.g., love your neighbor, honor your parents, act justly). And in assessing possible courses of action, consequences must be taken into account (e.g., who will benefit and who will be harmed). We should aim, other things being equal, to maximize happiness for all involved. These further moral considerations supplement virtue ethics

207

and complete a biblical moral framework. Duty, utility, and virtue, one might say, are the three pillars of a balanced Christian ethic, and each are emphasized in Scripture.

While the main theme of this book has been positive, two negative themes have repeatedly emerged: sin and suffering. Most virtues cannot, in fact, be properly understood except in light of these dark facts about the human condition. Some virtues involve mindful *avoidance* of sin, while others require specific *responses to* sin. And the experience of suffering makes possible the highest forms of many virtues (such as courage, forgiveness, generosity, and faith). While the first humans likely led virtuous lives prior to the Fall, the variety of moral traits they could exhibit was much less diverse. Some virtues cannot be displayed in the absence of sin or suffering (e.g., forgiveness, courage, perseverance, and some kinds of justice). The world became much more interesting, from a moral standpoint, once evil entered the picture. So many wonderful character traits feature redemptive responses to sin and suffering that it is tempting to see a pre-fallen human existence as morally truncated. This paradox has led some theologians to describe the first humans' rebellion as the "fortunate fall." Be this as it may, the life of virtue demands careful attention to sin and its consequences. It is true that the light reveals the darkness, but sometimes the reverse is true as well.

What implications, then, are there about heaven in the concept of the "fortunate fall"? If so many virtues are contingent upon evil—whether entirely or just their greater forms—then can we be fully virtuous in the next world, since sin and suffering will be no more? To answer this question, it's necessary to revisit a point briefly made in chapter thirteen. A person is not just a bare soul but an individual uniquely defined by a complex set of attributes, including personality traits and moral characteristics. It can be presumed that we take these attributes with us into heaven or hell when we leave this world. No sense otherwise could be made of the notion that the "me" living on earth today will really be the same "me" that survives death and lives on into the next world. Therefore, we must take our moral formation very seriously indeed. In the afterlife our virtuous (or vicious) characters will be just as real as they are here. Our characters will, in fact, be more well-known, since we will be judged. As Paul says, "We must all appear before the judgment seat of Christ, that each one may receive what is due him for the things done while in the body, whether good or bad" (2 Cor. 5:10).

Jesus Christ will forever be known as "the Lamb, who was slain" (Rev. 5:12) and praised for his courage, perseverance, and generosity. It makes sense to suppose that his people also will be recognized in heaven for their own good traits.

Paul indicates as much when he says, "Train yourself to be godly. For physical training is of some value, but godliness has value for all things, holding promise for both the present life and the life to come" (1 Tim. 4:7–8). In this life we forge the characters we take into the next world. By living virtuously today, we store up for ourselves treasures that are not just external but internal as well. Thus, with every deed we inform our future condition. If this is so, then our earthly life is more than a mere preface to eternity (as some mistakenly conceive it). What we do in this life has significant, long-term consequences. Our deeds here, virtuous or vicious, not only determine what we *receive* at the last judgment but also determine who we will *be* in the next world. This perspective clearly puts a premium on living virtuously.

We can be thankful that we're not called to go it alone in our training for godliness. The Holy Spirit is our helper. He is, in fact, the real source of any moral progress we make. We must exert serious effort to live well, but the power to exert that effort is ultimately divine. These twin truths are summed up by Paul when he says "work out your salvation with fear and trembling, for it is God who works in you to will and to act according to his good purpose" (Phil. 2:12–13). This book can be seen as a meditation on some of the key ways that we Christians should be working out our salvation. But this is just one book. Another book dealing with the second clause of Paul's directive would be just as appropriate. Without the gracious providence of God, we would have no virtue— and we would have no hope.

Let us press on, then, in the life of virtue. Moral growth is sometimes a tedious and painful process, but as the Bible promises, "our present sufferings are not worth comparing with the glory that will be revealed in us" (Rom. 8:18). May we renew our commitment to display all the virtues found in Christ, our moral exemplar. May we resolve to do the training necessary to develop these traits. And may God bless our efforts.

BIBLIOGRAPHY

Adams, Robert. *The Virtue of Faith and Other Essays in Philosophical Theology.* Oxford: Oxford University Press, 1987.

Aristotle. *Introduction to Aristotle.* Edited by Richard McKeon. New York: Modern Library, 1992.

———. *The Basic Works of Aristotle.* Edited by Richard McKeon. New York: Random, 1941.

Arnold, Johann Christoph. *Why Forgive?* Farmington, Pa.: Plough, 2000.

Augustine, Saint. *Confessions.* Translated by R. S. Pine-Coffin. New York: Penguin, 1961.

———. *On Christian Doctrine.* Translated by D. W. Robertson Jr. New York: Macmillan, 1986.

Aurelius, Marcus. *Meditations.* Translated by Maxwell Staniforth. Baltimore: Penguin, 1964.

Barrett, E. Boyd. *Strength of Will and How to Develop It.* New York: Richard R. Smith, 1931.

Baumgaertner, Jill Pelaez. Interview with Ken Myers. *Mars Hill Audio Journal* 37 (1999).

Berger, Fred R. "Gratitude," *Ethics* 85 (1975): 298–309.

Blake, William. *Poetry and Prose of William Blake.* Edited by Geoffrey Keynes. London: Nonesuch Library, 1956.

Bonhoeffer, Diedrich. *The Cost of Discipleship.* Translated by Kaiser Verlag Munchen. New York: Macmillan, 1959.

Bruyere, Jean de la. *Characters.* Translated by Henri Van Laun. New York: Howard Fertig, 1992.

Buss, Sarah. "Appearing Respectful: The Moral Significance of Manners." *Ethics* 109 (1999): 795–826.

Butler, Joseph. *Sermons of Joseph Butler*. Edited by W. E. Gladstone. Oxford: Clarendon Press, 1897.

Chambers, Oswald. *The Psychology of Redemption*. London: Simpkin Marshall, 1947.

Comte-Sponville, Andre. *A Small Treatise on the Great Virtues*. Translated by Catherine Temerson. New York: Henry Holt, 1996.

Descartes, Rene. *The Passions of the Soul*. Translated by Stephen H. Voss. Indianapolis: Hackett, 1989.

———. *The Philosophical Writings of Descartes*. Translated by J. Cottingham, R. Stoothoff and D. Murdoch. Cambridge: Cambridge University Press, 1985.

Dickinson, Emily. *Emily Dickinson: Selected Poems*. New York: Random, 1993.

Dostoevsky, Fyodor. *The Brothers Karamazov*. Translated by Constance Garnett. New York: William Heinemann, 1945.

Edelman, John. "Suffering and the Will of God." *Faith and Philosophy* 10, no. 3 (1993): 383–88.

Edwards, Jonathan. *The Works of Jonathan Edwards*. Vol. 1. Edinburgh: Banner of Truth, 1974.

Eliot, T. S. "The Love Song of J. Alfred Prufrock." In *The Complete Poems and Plays*. New York: Harcourt Brace and World, 1971.

———. "Religion and Literature." In *The Christian Imagination*. Grand Rapids: Baker, 1981.

Elliot, Elisabeth. *Shadow of the Almighty: The Life and Testament of Jim Elliot*. San Francisco: HarperSan Francisco, 1989.

Faulkner, William. *The Sound and the Fury*. New York: Modern Library, 1956.

Foot, Philippa. *Virtues and Vices and Other Essays in Moral Philosophy*. Oxford: Clarendon Press, 2002.

Foster, Richard. *Celebration of Discipline*. New York: Harper, 1978.

Freud, Sigmund. *Jokes and Their Relation to the Unconscious*. Translated by James Strachey. New York: W. W. Norton, 1960.

Hobbes, Thomas. *Leviathan*. New York: Macmillan, 1962.

Hugo, Victor. *Les Miserables*. Translated by Norman Denny. New York: Penguin, 1976.

Hume, David. *Essential Works of David Hume*. Edited by Ralph Cohen. New York: Bantam, 1965.

James, William. *The Principles of Psychology*. Vol. 1. New York: Dover, 1950.

Kant, Immanuel. *Critique of Judgment*. Translated by Werner S. Pluhar. Indianapolis: Hackett, 1987.

———. *Foundations of the Metaphysics of Morals*. Translated by Lewis White Beck. Indianapolis: Bobbs-Merrill, 1959.

———. *Lectures on Ethics.* Translated by Lewis White Beck. New York: Harper, 1963.

———. *Lectures on Ethics.* Translated by Louis Infield. London: Methuen, 1930.

———. *The Metaphysical Principles of Virtue.* Translated by James Ellington. Indianapolis: Bobbs-Merrill, 1964.

———. *Perpetual Peace and Other Essays.* Translated by Ted Humphrey. Indianapolis: Hackett, 1983.

Keller, Helen. "Three Days to See." *Atlantic Monthly,* 1933. Reprinted in *The Moral Life.* Edited by Louis P. Pojman. Oxford: Oxford University Press, 2004.

Kierkegaard, Søren. *Concluding Unscientific Postscript.* Translated by Howard Hong and Edna Hong. Princeton: Princeton University Press, 1992.

———. *Works of Love: Some Christian Reflections in the Form of Discourses.* Translated by Howard Hong and Edna Hong. New York: Harper, 1962.

King, Martin Luther. *Why We Can't Wait.* New York: Harper, 1964.

Kolnai, Aurel. "Forgiveness." *Proceedings of the Aristotelian Society,* (1973–74): 91–106.

Lee, Harper. *To Kill a Mockingbird.* New York: Harper, 1960.

L'Engle, Madeleine. *Walking on Water.* Wheaton, Ill.: Harold Shaw, 1980.

Lewis, C. S. *Mere Christianity.* New York: Macmillan, 1952.

———. *The Four Loves.* San Diego: Harcourt Brace and Co., 1960.

Luther, Martin. *Preface to the Epistle of St. Paul to the Romans.* Translated by Adolf G. H. Kreis. San Diego: Adolf G. H. Kreis, 1937.

Marlowe, Christopher. *Complete Plays and Poems.* London: J. M. Dent and Sons, 1976.

Martin, Judith. *Miss Manners' Guide to Excruciatingly Correct Behavior.* New York: Warner, 1983.

Marx, Karl. *Marx and Engels on Religion.* Amsterdam: Fredonia Books, 2002.

Mele, Alfred. "Real Self-Deception." *Behavioral and Brain Sciences* 20 (1997): 91–102.

Mill, John Stuart. *Mill's Ethical Writings.* New York: Collier, 1965.

Montaigne, Michel de. *The Complete Essays of Montaigne.* Translated by Donald M. Frame. Stanford: Stanford University Press, 1948.

Muggeridge, Malcolm. *Something Beautiful for God.* New York: Harper, 1971.

Murchison, Clint W. *Time,* 16 June 1961.

Murphy, Jeffrie G. "Forgiveness, Reconciliation, and Responding to Evil." In *Ethics for Everyday,* edited by David Benatar. New York: McGraw Hill, 2002.

Murray, Andrew. *Humility.* New Kensington, Pa.: Whitaker, 1982.

Over the Rhine. "All I Need Is Everything." From the album *Good Dog, Bad Dog.* Milwaukee, Wis.: Back Porch Records, 2000.

Pears, David. *Motivated Irrationality.* Oxford: Oxford University Press, 1984.

Peck, John. "Sex in Art: Is There a Place for an Erotic Christian Imagination?" *Cornerstone* 30 (2001): 33–38.

Peterman, James. "Self-Deception and the Problem of Avoidance." *Southern Journal of Philosophy* 21 (1983): 565–73.

Pieper, Josef. *The Four Cardinal Virtues.* Notre Dame: University of Notre Dame Press, 1966.

Plato. *The Collected Dialogues of Plato.* Edited by Edith Hamilton and Huntington Cairns. Princeton: Princeton University Press, 1961.

———. *The Republic.* Translated by Richard W. Sterling and William C. Scott. New York: W. W. Norton, 1985.

Richards, Norvin. "Forgiveness." *Ethics* 99 (1988): 77–93.

Rilke, Rainer Maria. *Duino Elegies.* Translated by J. B. Leishman and Stephen Spender New York: W. W. Norton, 1963.

Rorty, Amelie O. "Self-Deception, *Akrasia,* and Irrationality." *Social Science Information* 19, no. 6 (1980): 905–22.

Ryken, Leland. *The Liberated Imagination.* Wheaton, Ill.: Harold Shaw, 1989.

Sartre, Jean-Paul. *Being and Nothingness.* Translated by Hazel E. Barnes. New York: Washington Square Press, 1966.

Schueler, G. F. "Why IS Modesty a Virtue?" *Ethics* 109 (1999): 835–41.

Seneca, *The Stoic Philosophy of Seneca.* Translated by Moses Hadas. New York: W. W. Norton, 1958.

Shakespeare, William. *The Complete Works of Shakespeare.* New York: Walter J. Black, 1937.

Shalit, Wendy. *A Return to Modesty: Discovering the Lost Virtue.* New York: Simon and Schuster, 1999.

Simon, Robert L. "The Paralysis of Absolutophobia." *The Chronicle of Higher Education,* 27 June 1997, B5–B6.

Skinner, B. F. *Walden Two.* New York: Macmillan, 1948.

Spiegel, James S. *Hypocrisy: Moral Fraud and Other Vices.* Grand Rapids: Baker, 1999.

Spinoza, Benedict de. *A Spinoza Reader: The Ethics and Other Works.* Edited by Edwin Curley. Princeton: Princeton University Press, 1994.

———. *Ethics.* Edited by James Gutmann. New York: Hafner, 1949.

Ten Boom, Corrie. *The Hiding Place.* New York: Guideposts, 1971.

Thomas à Kempis. *Of the Imitation of Christ.* Pittsburgh: Whitaker, 1981.

Tolkien, J. R. R. "On Fairy-Stories." In *The Tolkien Reader.* New York: Ballantine, 1966.

Tolstoy, Leo. *What Is Art?* Indianapolis: Bobbs-Merrill, 1960.

Twain, Mark. *Following the Equator.* Hartford, Conn.: American, 1897.

Watson, Thomas. *All Things for Good.* Edinburgh: Banner of Truth, 1986.

Webb, Stephen H. *The Gifting God: A Trinitarian Ethics of Excess.* New York: Oxford University Press, 1996.

Willard, Dallas. *The Divine Conspiracy: Rediscovering Our Hidden Life in God.* San Francisco: HarperSan Francisco, 1998.

———. *The Spirit of the Disciplines: Understanding How God Changes Lives.* San Francisco: HarperCollins, 1988.

Wolterstorff, Nicholas. *Art in Action.* Grand Rapids: Eerdmans, 1980.

———. "Suffering Love." In *Philosophy and the Christian Faith.* Edited by Thomas V. Morris. Notre Dame: University of Notre Dame Press, 1988.

SCRIPTURE INDEX

SUBJECT INDEX